Cooperation, Conflict, and Consensus in the Organization of American States

COOPERATION, CONFLICT, AND CONSENSUS IN THE ORGANIZATION OF AMERICAN STATES

BY
CAROLYN M. SHAW

3-18-2005
CBC
$ 59.95

COOPERATION, CONFLICT, AND CONSENSUS IN THE ORGANIZATION OF
AMERICAN STATES
© Carolyn M. Shaw, 2004

First published 2004 by
PALGRAVE MACMILLAN™
175 Fifth Avenue, New York, N.Y. 10010 and
Houndmills, Basingstoke, Hampshire, England RG21 6XS
Companies and representatives throughout the world

PALGRAVE MACMILLAN is the global academic imprint of
the Palgrave Macmillan division of St. Martin's Press, LLC and of
Palgrave Macmillan Ltd. Macmillan® is a registered trademark in the
United States, United Kingdom and other countries. Palgrave is a
registered trademark in the European Union and other countries.

ISBN 1–4039–6221–9 hardback

Library of Congress Cataloging-in-Publication Data
Shaw, Carolyn M., 1970–
     Cooperation, conflict, and consensus in the Organization of
  American States / by Carolyn M. Shaw
       p. cm.
     Includes bibliographical references and index.
     ISBN 1–4039–6221–9
      1. Organization of American States. 2. Latin America–Foreign
  relations. 3. United States—Relations—Latin America.
  4. Latin America—Relations—United States. 5. Conflict
  management—Latin America. 6. Security, International—Latin
  America. 7. Pan-Americanism. I. Title.

F1415.S49 2004
341.24′5—dc22   2003065609

A catalogue record for this book is available from the British Library.

Design by Newgen Imaging Systems (P) Ltd., Chennai, India.

First edition: April 2004
10 9 8 7 6 5 4 3 2 1

Printed in the United States of America.

To my Family
David, Adam, and Delaney

CONTENTS

TABLES AND FIGURES

Acknowledgments

It is my pleasure to recognize those friends and colleagues who have greatly assisted me in the completion of this book. My thanks to Henry Dietz at the University of Texas at Austin for his help in conceptualizing this project and offering me constant encouragement. My appreciation to G. Pope Atkins at the University of Texas at Austin and Paul F. Diehl at the University of Illinois at Urbana for their careful reading and apt suggestions for improvements to the text. Stella E. Villagran, reference librarian, and René L. Gutiérrez, technical services librarian, at the Columbus Memorial Library of the OAS in Washington, DC, greatly aided my research efforts. Dexter Boniface, Susan Henney, Manuel Orozco, and Mark Setzler provided useful critiques as well as insights on the case studies and the theoretical framework. David Pervin at Palgrave Macmillan and Brian Whepley provided excellent editorial assistance. My colleagues in the Political Science Department at Wichita State University gave me enthusiastic support in the final stages of the project. My husband, David, stood by me through all of the research and writing, and listened to my endless articulation of ideas and information. My gratitude to all these individuals.

CHAPTER 1

U.S. FOREIGN POLICY AND INSTITUTIONAL RELATIONSHIPS IN THE WESTERN HEMISPHERE

Introduction

A look at U.S. foreign policy in the 1990s revealed a dominant global power in search of a new guiding paradigm for its relations with countries around the world. Once-impossible relationships were being cultivated for the first time with former rivals, including Russia. Relationships that had been taken for granted, and even neglected over the years, were being revived with Latin American neighbors. As the United States has reassessed its national security concerns in the new millennium and evaluated the mechanisms at hand to address them, it has reaffirmed its cooperative relationship with 33 other states in the Western hemisphere through the Organization of American States (OAS).

Although the OAS and its member states have rarely been the primary focus of U.S. foreign policy, the organization has served as a collective security arrangement in the hemisphere for over 50 years. The United States and Latin American states have a long, rich history of cooperation and collective actions carried out in the context of the OAS. The United States has taken advantage of this organization to address security concerns in the region, such as the border disputes between Costa Rica and Nicaragua from 1948 to 1955 and the various regional disturbances instigated by the Castro regime in Cuba in the 1960s. Despite disagreements between members over unilateral U.S. actions and many U.S. policy proposals, the organization has striven to reach consensus before taking actions in the region. This commitment to consensus has led to considerable cooperation among members on issues over the years. This was particularly evident in the 1990s as members rallied to strengthen democracy in the region and to support any regime that faced challenges to its elected government.

The traditional concept of regional security based on geopolitical/ strategic threats has gradually been expanded within the OAS to include a number of concerns that had not previously been considered "security issues." The United States and Latin American states have developed a common agenda of security concerns that includes consideration of human rights, democracy, the environment, government reform, social equality, and a free market environment (Wiarda 1995). The 1990s witnessed strong consensus among members to promote democratic consolidation and economic development through hemispheric cooperation. Many governments, including the Clinton administration in the United States, acknowledged the value of the multilateral approach to resolving transnational problems. The OAS has been revitalized based on the support of members for the priorities and actions of the organization. The organization has been able to respond to the needs of its members in a number of different areas, including security and economic development.

The OAS demonstrated its capacity to act rapidly in response to a security threat to a member state following the terrorist attacks on the United States in September 2001. The Meeting of the Ministers of Foreign Affairs met within days of the attack and issued several resolutions in strong support of the United States. The Inter-American Treaty of Reciprocal Assistance (Rio Treaty) for collective security was invoked and members were called upon to take effective measures to deny terrorists the ability to operate in their territories; to render all assistance to pursue, capture, extradite, and punish anyone found to be connected to the September 11 attacks; and to convoke as soon as possible the Inter-American Committee Against Terrorism (CICTE) to strengthen inter-American cooperation to combat terrorism. Following this call for a meeting of the CICTE, the Committee met in special session in October and November 2001 to identify counterterrorism actions for OAS members to implement. In 2002, the CICTE designed and deployed an antiterrorism database and drafted the Convention Against Terrorism, which was signed by 30 members of the OAS in June. As the United States further redefines its security concerns in the wake of the terrorist attacks, and seeks to root out future terrorist plots, the OAS provides a strong institutionalized framework for working closely with its Latin American neighbors. In order to assess the capacity of the organization to address security concerns in the future, it is critical to understand the dynamic relationships between members within the organization, and the impact of organizational structure and functions on member states. An historical examination of the OAS reveals some surprises about the strength of the organization and its members, and their relations with the United States.

Member State Relations Within the OAS

Since the OAS was founded by Latin American states and the United States in 1948, one of its fundamental tasks has been to promote regional security through pacific settlement procedures and collective security arrangements. The OAS Charter and the Rio Treaty are the two primary instruments that have been used by member states to address conflicts in the region over the past 50 years. The OAS has not always been active or effective in all disputes in the region, but it has adapted to changing international conditions (i.e., the Cold War and the end of the Cold War) and evolving member priorities over the years to emerge as a revitalized regional organization in the new millennium.

Part of the strength of the organization derives from the shared interests of its members. Members have declared that a threat to one is a threat to all and are thus obligated to respond multilaterally to any threats to the peace in order to insure regional stability. In many instances the preferences of Latin American states and the United States are the same, which allows for a unified response to regional conflicts. For example, when Soviet Premier Nikita Khrushchev attempted to install missile bases on Cuban territory, all members of the OAS responded rapidly in opposition to these actions. In this case, the organization acted according to U.S. preferences, but it is important to recognize that these were also the preferences of Latin American members. In other cases, however, relations among members within the OAS have been strained, and disputes over proposals have been contentious. These disputes include not only differences of opinion between the United States and Latin American states, but also between Latin American members themselves. For example, at the Meeting of Foreign Ministers (1962) that banned the participation of Cuba in the OAS, Mexico opposed such actions while the United States and other Latin American states strongly advocated such a resolution. The Dominican case (1965) also saw considerable disagreement between Latin American states, with Colombia, Haiti, and Paraguay openly supporting U.S. intervention, while Mexico, Chile, and Uraguay denounced U.S. actions on the island.

Despite the different preferences of member states on some of the issues taken up by the OAS, many of the final decisions made within the organization have been consensual (i.e., supported by all members).

Consensus is highly valued by member states. They believe that decisions adopted consensually carry more weight than those with only the requisite two-thirds vote. In addition, regional solidarity, which strengthens regional stability, is maintained if compromises can be reached rather than passing disputed proposals by a majority vote. Because members prefer to act consensually, the decisionmaking process within the organization involves bargaining among members to reach mutually acceptable agreements on issues where members have divergent preferences. For example, when the Foreign Ministers met to consider subversive acts carried out by Fidel Castro's regime in 1960, the United States wanted to condemn Cuban actions and other members did not. The compromise reached was a condemnation of Sino-Soviet attempts to subvert the legitimate governments of the Western hemisphere without specific mention of Cuba.

As member states engage in decisionmaking and negotiate compromises to accommodate their different preferences, the United States, as the most powerful member of the OAS, is often able to use its extensive resources and influence to gain support from other members for the proposals that it favors. This is particularly true in cases where the United States has a strong interest (i.e., concerning security issues). The United States has considerably more military, financial, and personnel resources at its disposal than other member states, giving it hegemonic dominance in the region. It has often used these resources in the past, both unilaterally and multilaterally, to safeguard its interests in the hemisphere. For example, when the U.S. government feared that a coup in the Dominican Republic in 1965 might result in "another Cuba" (i.e., a communist government taking power in the Dominican Republic), the United States sent in marines to reestablish order in the country. It is unlikely that any other OAS member would have had the resources to act so swiftly, or the audacity to intervene in a member state's affairs in such a way. U.S. hegemony in the region has given it a unique place within the OAS and in its relations with other member states.

Surprisingly, however, not all OAS decisions are consistent with the preferences of the United States despite its overwhelming dominance in the hemisphere. There are some cases in which the United States has been unable to gain support for its proposals. Latin American members have, on a few occasions, rejected proposals made by the United States, even on security matters in which the United States has had strong preferences and exerted considerable influence. For example, in 1978 during the Nicaraguan revolution, the United States tried to persuade the Meeting of Foreign Ministers that a U.S.-led peacekeeping force was necessary to restore stability to the region. The Foreign Ministers refused to consider such an option and chose instead to encourage the Nicaraguan people to oust dictator President Anastasio Somoza and hold elections to establish a representative democracy. Although the cases in which members reject U.S. preferences outright are not numerous, they are rather striking anomalies within an organization that largely acts consensually and frequently in the U.S. interest.[1]

This study seeks to determine what conditions, beyond relative state power and common interests, affect the level of influence the United States is able to bring to bear within the OAS. Robert Keohane and Lisa Martin once noted, "the difference between realism and liberal institutionalism does not lie in whether institutions are independent or dependent variables, it lies in contrasting understandings of why institutions are created and *how they exert their effects*" (1995, 48, emphasis added). This study uses the unexpected decisionmaking outcomes within the OAS, when the United States does not dominate the organization, to try to answer the second part of this question. I seek to specify what institutional conditions allow an international organization (IO) to affect a hegemonic member state.

Empirical and Theoretical Implications

The ability of Latin American members of the OAS to resist U.S. hegemonic influence is intriguing not only because it is counterintuitive, but also because neither realism nor institutionalism, the two dominant theories in international relations (IR), can adequately explain how such independent action occurs. Although realism's focus on relative power relations among states explains many of the policy outcomes of the OAS, it cannot explain why the United States would fail to dominate the organization when it chose to exert its influence. The puzzling outcomes are directly contradictory to predictions that realism makes concerning the behavior of international organizations (IOs) and the capabilities of a hegemonic power. Realism posits that given the conditions in the international system (anarchy, no world government, lack of trust, concerns about relative power) that the most powerful state will dominate IOs in which it is a member. In addition, realism assumes that states are the primary actors in the international system and that IOs play only a marginal role in international relations (Morgenthau 1948, Waltz 1979, Grieco 1988).

John Mearsheimer (1994) argues that IOs are created and controlled by the most powerful state(s) and are only effective in the international system if they are being used as a tool by a powerful state. If he were to consider the anomalous cases in which U.S. preferences are not adopted by the OAS, Mearsheimer might conclude that the United States had little interest in those particular cases and thus did not choose to exert its influence. It might also reflect cases in which the United States did not view the OAS as an optimal tool to pursue its interests, and thus chose to take unilateral actions instead. Neither of these conditions apply, however, to the cases in this book in which the United States failed to dominate the organization. In each of the cases, the United States had a strong interest and preferred to act multilaterally, but failed to gain support within the OAS for its proposals. The perception by realists of IOs as mere tools used by their most powerful members is oversimplified and mistaken. Realism's focus on power-based relations among states explains many of the policy outcomes in the OAS, but factors other than power are also influential in the OAS.

Institutionalism offers a second perspective on IOs, focusing on the issue of cooperation among states in the international system and the roles played by IOs in facilitating cooperation.[2] One line of inquiry within institutionalism addresses the challenge of creating IOs in an environment of distrust and potentially hostile relations among states. The focus is on how states overcome distrust and begin to engage in cooperation through the creation of an IO. Because members of the OAS have been engaged in cooperative policymaking for 50 years, this focus on the initial creation of an IO is not directly relevant to addressing the research puzzle presented here.

A second body of institutionalist literature examines the rules and procedures established within organizations that facilitate cooperation. In the case of the OAS, the anarchy of the international system is somewhat abated by a formal equality among member states, pacific settlement procedures, and a collective security arrangement protecting the hemisphere from external and internal aggression. One of the key conditions for an IO to be able to promote cooperation is that the states involved share some common interests. This is indeed the case within the OAS. Latin American states and the United States have a number of security interests in common that resulted in the founding of the OAS and its continued existence.

Several problems that institutions must address to promote cooperation are finding an equilibrium point when several exist, and enforcing agreements in an anarchic international system. Institutionalism explains how IOs are able to alter the bargaining calculations of states by reducing uncertainty and promoting iterative relationships. They can promote transparency, extend the shadow of the future to promote iterative relationships, shift focus to absolute gains instead of relative gains, and provide sanctions to punish unacceptable behaviors. Stein (1983) elaborates on how international regimes can promote coordination and collaboration within an anarchic system even when states have divergent interests and preferences by helping them achieve more efficient outcomes than would otherwise occur. The policy debates within the OAS, however, are not about achieving efficient outcomes. When the United States and Latin American members disagree about policy proposals, there are certain structural, procedural, and normative conditions that influence the outcome of the debate that are not accounted for in these discussions of the benefits of institutions.

All of the functions of IOs described by institutionalists are seen in the workings of the OAS, and members do work cooperatively in many policy arenas, including regional security. The level of analysis in institutionalism, however, remains focused on states acting in the international system and within the context of IOs. Institutionalism does not view IOs as separate entities capable of affecting member states beyond simply providing a forum for interstate interactions, or rules for interaction. A focus on the issue of common interests between the United States and Latin American states to explain the use of institutions to promote cooperation fails to address the processes that occur when there is disagreement between member states. Institutionalism does not address the actual internal functioning of an organization that produces different results. Without focusing on the structure and institutions of the OAS itself, institutionalism cannot explain what conditions lead to enhanced or reduced U.S. influence in the organization. Neither realism nor institutionalism are suited to addressing the puzzle at this level of analysis.

Constructivist theory offers a different perspective on the level of analysis problem. The constructivist approach explores knowledge dynamics, communications, and identities in international society (Hasenclever et al. 1997, chapter 1), and thus contrasts with realism and institutionalism, which focus on power relations and shared interests between member states. Constructivism provides a distinct view of IOs in IR. It credits IOs and regimes with a stronger impact on states than realism allows. Regimes reflect the interests of their creators, but also develop an autonomy after creation that allows them to impact states in unanticipated and uncontrollable ways. Some theorists go so far as to claim that organizations do not merely frustrate attempts at their manipulation by powerful states, but that they can actually manipulate states themselves through the establishment of norms and rules and their enforcement through a variety of sanctions and diplomatic coercion (Wendt 1992a).

Based on the arguments made by constructivist theory that highlight the ability of IOs to affect their members, this book focuses on the internal dynamics of the organization to determine what potential impacts such factors have on member states. The theory of organizational sociology provides three different perspectives for examining the internal processes of organizations (Scott 1998). The rational system approach views an organization as a formalized structure oriented to the pursuit of specific goals. The focus is on productivity and efficiency achieved through formal institutions, procedures, and goals. The natural system approach views organizations as a collectivity of people with common interests, who are focused on the survival of the organization. Studies in this perspective focus on the interaction between the formal structure of the organization and the individual participants in it. The open system approach focuses on the interaction of the organization with the external environment, as opposed to the rational and natural system approaches in which the environment is largely ignored in favor of internal dynamics (i.e., a closed system).

The organizational sociology approaches are used to construct an analytical framework for an *international* organization. The framework consists of a synthesis of the three different approaches to organizational sociology. It is not intended to be a new theory of organization. It is, rather, an extension of organizational sociology into the international context that complements realism and institutionalism. The framework takes the study of IOs beyond the generalizations made by realism and institutionalism about IOs. It opens the "black box" and identifies organizational factors to explain IO behaviors that are not adequately accounted for by the current dominant theories of IR. The analytical framework highlights four different organizational perspectives: structural, procedural/normative, internal relational, and environmental. Structural and procedural/normative perspectives are similar to the rational system approach in which formal institutions are the main explanatory variables for organizational outputs (i.e., decisions). The internal relational perspective is based on the natural system approach, and focuses on the internal dynamics between members within the organization to explain organizational behavior. The environmental perspective is derived from the open system approach in which factors external to the organization impact its functioning and decisionmaking. The environmental perspective is most closely related to realism and its focus on the international system as a determinant for state actions.

This work tries to address several of the shortcomings in the study of U.S.–Latin American relations within the institutional context of the OAS. It offers explanations for the unexpected outcomes when the United States is less influential, cases that are not adequately explained by realism and institutionalism. By looking at organizations from a different level of analysis and adapting theories of organizational sociology to the international context, this research provides new insights into IR theory and the organizational variables that affect IO decisionmaking. In addition to understanding the factors that influence U.S. dominance, a greater understanding of organizational decisionmaking allows for an assessment of the viability of the OAS in the future as it continues to address a wide range of issues affecting the Western hemisphere.

This research also provides several empirical contributions. First, since much of the research on the OAS has been policy-oriented and frequently focused on a single case study, the extended historical analysis of 31 cases over a 50-year period allows for a much more comprehensive comparison of cases than has been possible previously. In addition, the analytical framework helps to organize the cases in a meaningful fashion that facilitates contrasts and comparisons among cases. Second, this study provides a good test case for advancing constructivist arguments by providing empirical test cases for the impact of regional principles on organizational decisionmaking. Finding an answer to the puzzling question concerning an IO's ability to limit the influence of its hegemonic member can provide evidence to support the arguments of constructivists concerning the constraining abilities of IOs on states in the international system. Finally, the discussion of consensus among member states and hegemonic influence within the OAS corrects a number of general misperceptions about U.S.–Latin American relations. Many of the cases emphasize that rather than the United States dominating the organization, members frequently act in unison, with common interests and goals in mind. The United States does not always need to exert its hegemonic influence to achieve its goals in the region. Additionally, the cases illustrate that Latin America is not a single unit. Different states in the region have different preferences that can lead to disagreement among Latin American members, not just to confrontations with the United States. These divergent Latin American perspectives are often overlooked.

Implications for U.S. Policy and OAS-Member Relations

By specifying the conditions under which an IO can affect the level of influence a member state is able to exert, this research can determine whether these cases where U.S. dominance has been resisted have been epiphenomenal or not. If these conditions are not epiphenomenal, then there are several policy implications to be considered.

The specification of the organizational conditions that can limit U.S. influence within the OAS will provide empirical evidence that institutions can affect member states, even powerful ones. If the conditions that limit hegemonic influence are manipulable, then one might expect other members to take advantage of such conditions in order to resist hegemonic pressure on occasion. Recognition of this ability may make powerful states more cautious in their participation in IOs. They could be reluctant to engage in policymaking within IOs if they are not assured of dominance. Although a hegemon may recognize that there are certain benefits to acting multilaterally (efficiency, uniformity of policies, shared implementation costs, etc.), it may pursue less efficient and/or less effective unilateral actions, if it is uncertain that its interests will be served within an IO. Such a choice for unilateral action could have repercussions for an IO by depriving it of many of the resources (diplomatic, financial, etc.) provided by a powerful member.

Although this research focuses on security issues and the institutional conditions that limit hegemonic influence in the security arena, there may be overlap in other policy areas. Given the increasing use of IOs on global policy issues, including finance and the environment, evidence of the ability of IOs to limit hegemonic dominance would give IOs a boost as legitimate and influential actors in the international system. Although many IOs attempt to portray an image of impartiality, when a powerful state such as the United States is a member, that image may not be upheld unless there is evidence that the organization does not simply serve the hegemon's interests. There is a trade-off involved in this scenario, however. The boost to an IO's legitimacy as an independent actor might not be worth the loss in resources provided by a hegemonic member should it choose to not to pursue its interests within the context of the IO.

There are also some policy implications concerning the capacity of the OAS to function effectively and successfully. Given that members place a strong value on consensus, the organization has developed mechanisms to promote conciliation and compromise when there are divergent preferences among members. This ability has resulted in members, including the United States, remaining active within the organizational framework at many levels. This engagement strengthens the organization and enhances its reputation, promoting its ability to pursue regional goals multilaterally. There is a downside to the ability of the OAS to achieve compromise among members, however. Compromises can lead to vague and imprecise resolutions and declarations. When such resolutions are applied to a particular dispute, they may result in less successful operations because they can be interpreted in a number of ways. For example, when the pro-democracy resolutions concerning the "self coup" by President Alberto Fujimori in Peru (1992) were loosely interpreted, sanctions were lifted before genuine democratic government was restored.

Overview

In order to explore how an IO has been able to affect its most powerful member, this research focuses specifically on the OAS. The power imbalance between the United States and other member states provides an ideal model to examine the dynamic relations between members and the potential to curb hegemonic domination in an IO. The 26 cases from 1948 to 1989 and five additional cases following the end of the Cold War illustrate a full range of outcomes in organizational decision-making, including U.S. Dominance, Latin American Unity, Compromise, and Consensus. In the case of the Dominican Republic (1965), the United States actively intervened without permission from the OAS, then proceeded to gain OAS approval post hoc for an Inter-American Peacekeeping Force (IAPF) despite considerable protest from some members. In Cuba (1964), the United States also dominated decisionmaking in the OAS by expanding the sanctions imposed against the regime of Fidel Castro. The Caribbean (1959) and Cuba (1960) represent cases of compromise. In the Cuban case (1960), the United States and Latin American members reached a compromise on the final wording of a resolution issued by the Seventh Meeting of Foreign Ministers that condemned international communist intervention in the hemisphere. Members also reached a compromise agreement on democracy and regional instability in the Caribbean case (1959). The case of the Dominican Republic–Venezuela (1960) illustrates Latin American unity and a policy outcome that rejected U.S. preferences. The United States eventually chose to support the Latin American states once its proposal to sponsor Dominican elections was vetoed by the membership. Nicaragua (1978) also represents a case where Latin American members refused to accept a U.S. policy initiative. Latin American members flatly rejected the U.S. proposal for a peacekeeping force to be sent in to promote reconciliation. An example of a consensual outcome can been seen in the case of Panama (1959) when members were unified to help remove a small invading force from the Panamanian beaches.

The examination of membership dynamics within the OAS begins with a theoretical analysis in chapter 2, where an analytical framework is laid out for exploring U.S.–Latin American relations within the context of the OAS. Chapter 2 evaluates both realist and institutionalist literature as they apply to the study of IOs. Theoretical analysis of the OAS using these two approaches suggests that neither approach is able to fully explain the unexpected policy outcomes of the OAS when the United States fails to gain support for its proposals within the organization. Four different perspectives adapted from organizational sociology allow for additional insights into the dynamics of member relations within the OAS. These perspectives identify four factors with the potential to affect U.S. influence within the OAS: necessary resources, strength of regional principles, consensus among members, and perceived level of threat to regional stability. In cases where Latin American members have successfully resisted U.S. pressure in the OAS, each of these factors has affected organizational decisionmaking.

Chapter 3 provides a historical examination of the Inter-American System. It traces relations between the United States and Latin American states back to the Pan American movement of the early 1800s through the creation of the OAS in 1948. The evolution of the regional principles that are embodied in the OAS is evident in numerous regional conferences and Congresses held throughout the 1800s and early 1900s. These norms include respect of state sovereignty and territorial integrity, peaceful settlement of disputes, nonintervention in the domestic affairs of other states, consultation in the event of a crisis, and representative democracy.

Chapter 4 explores the changes in conflict resolution efforts by the OAS from 1948 to 1989 and emphasizes the changes over time in the types of cases that were addressed and the mechanisms used to resolve them. Twenty-six cases are examined by looking at the impact of resources, regional principles, consensus, and threat level on the decisionmaking process. The cases represent each instance in which the Rio Treaty or the OAS Charter was invoked in order to achieve pacific settlement of a dispute. Both the Rio Treaty and the OAS Charter have provisions for OAS members to convene and take collective security measures when security is threatened. These measures may include diplomatic and economic sanctions, or may even involve military action. Some of the cases handled by the OAS required only brief involvement of the organization, such as in Panama in 1959 when a small invasion force of less than 100 men landed on the beach and refused to surrender. A diplomatic delegation was able to persuade the invaders to surrender.

Other cases involved extensive OAS action, such as the creation of the 10,000 man Inter-American Peace Force (IAPF) that restored order in the Dominican Republic in 1965 following a coup. In each case, members had security concerns and wanted to preserve regional stability through multilateral action by the OAS.

In order to trace the impact of institutional factors on U.S. influence, chapters 5 and 6 examine eight different cases in depth based on different policy outcomes. Chapter 5 looks at the Dominican Republic (1965) and Cuba (1964) in which the United States dominated the OAS, and the cases of the Dominican Republic–Venezuela (1960) and Nicaragua (1978) when Latin American unity thwarted U.S. policy preferences. These four cases reveal the two extremes in policy outcomes in the OAS when member states were not in agreement concerning what actions should be taken to resolve regional conflict. These extreme outcomes are less common than those that are either consensual or based on compromise. Chapter 6 looks at four additional cases where members were in full agreement on the actions to be taken (Costa Rica–Nicaragua, 1955; Panama, 1959), and where members reached a compromise (Caribbean, 1959; Cuba, 1960). An examination of structural, normative, internal relational, and environmental factors reveals the decisionmaking process and member dynamics in the OAS.

Chapter 7 explores the changes and continuities in the OAS following the end of the Cold War. It defines an expanded concept of regional security that includes the defense of democracy. Chapter 7 also describes the new mechanisms that have been put in place to strengthen democratic governance in the region, including the Unit for the Promotion of Democracy, Resolution 1080, and the Democratic Charter. The chapter examines five cases of multilateral action taken to restore democracy, which reveal both the consensus among members supporting the norm of representative democracy, and the challenges that members face in upholding that norm. The institutional factors that affect levels of U.S. influence within the organization also help to explain U.S. incentives to take multilateral actions in the hemisphere to address threats to democracy. A discussion of narco-trafficking, with a focus on Colombia, illustrates the limits of consensus among members and their desire to pursue multilateral solutions to regional threats.

Chapter 8 draws conclusions about the decisionmaking processes in the OAS and its ability to resist U.S. hegemonic pressure. It assesses the findings from and the value of the analytical framework, and summarizes the empirical findings. It concludes with an appraisal of the organization's ability to address the security concerns of its members in the future.

CHAPTER 2

DEVELOPING THEORIES OF
INTERNATIONAL ORGANIZATIONS

Introduction

In order to assess the capacity of the OAS to serve the collective security needs of its members, it is important to gain a greater understanding of the dynamics of the organization itself. By tracing out the factors that affect U.S. influence and by gaining a greater understanding of the decisionmaking process, the ability of the organization to address future concerns can also be assessed. Theories of international relations offer some insights into the relations among states in the international system, but do not focus much on how those relationships are affected by interactions in the context of an IO such as the OAS. Not only do member states influence actions taken by the organization, but the organization itself also affects member states through its structure and principles. The United States does not always exercise dominant control of the organization. The organization at times rejects U.S. dominance and pursues alternative policies to U.S. proposals. Organizational factors affect how much influence the United States is able to exert over member states within the institutional context. A theoretical examination of the decisionmaking dynamics of the OAS provides insights into member relations within the organization, and its capacity to resolve conflicts in the region. This chapter introduces an analytical framework to evaluate U.S. influence within the OAS. The first section reviews the relevant literature on IOs that contributes to this project. The second section presents a framework derived from organizational sociology and advances specific hypotheses concerning member influence within the OAS. The concluding section discusses the usefulness of this framework as it applies to the study of international organizational dynamics and decisionmaking.

The framework derived from organizational sociology provides scholars of IOs with new insights concerning the significant variables that influence organizational decisionmaking. The framework as it is laid out is not intended to be a new theory of organization. It is, instead, an extension of organizational sociology into the international context that complements realism and institutionalism. The framework takes the study of IOs beyond the generalizations made by realism and institutionalism about IOs. It identifies organizational variables to explain IO behaviors that are not adequately accounted for by the current dominant theories in IR. This research examines the constituent parts that make up the OAS in order to explain member interactions and organizational decisions. An understanding of how the OAS is constituted is essential to explaining how an IO behaves and what causes particular outcomes. By providing a more complete understanding of the structures, procedures, and member interactions within the OAS, this research offers a better explanation of how certain IO behaviors are possible and why. Not only does the use of this framework expand the study of IOs in the field of IR, but it also contributes to the field of organizational sociology from which the framework is derived. By applying the key characteristics of social organizations to the context of an IO, this study helps to determine whether these sociological theories have more generalizable applications than have previously been considered.

Studies of International Organizations

In order to address the question of what conditions facilitate or mitigate the influence of the United States within the OAS, this study draws on several bodies of literature, which are presented here. The discussion begins with an examination of realism and institutionalism. These literatures shape the research question, presenting a puzzle concerning the impact of an IO on states in the international system. Next, hegemonic stability theory is discussed, which further problematizes the role of a hegemon within an international regime. The third section reviews the constructivist approach to regime theory, which explores the issue of normative influences on states. Finally, theories of organizational sociology are adapted to present a framework that facilitates the examination of factors affecting member influence and organizational decisionmaking, and the exploration of the case studies in chapters 5 and 6. [3]

The debate about the impact of institutions on states has been raised in a series of articles in *International Security* (1994, 1995). In these articles, John Mearsheimer summarizes the debate by stating:

> [It] is about whether institutions can have an independent effect on state behavior, or whether instead institutional outcomes reflect great power

interests, and are essentially tools that great powers employ for their own selfish purposes. (1995, 82–83)

Mearsheimer argues strongly against the ability of institutions to affect state behavior. He begins by summarizing the assumptions of realism about the international system and the effects these conditions have on the behavior of states. He lays out five conditions in the international system: anarchy (no central authority), the existence of offensive military capabilities, uncertainty, the survival motive of states, and the strategic thinking of states. These conditions lead states to fear each other. States must guard their own survival in this self-help system (Waltz 1979). Furthermore, states seek to maximize their relative power positions. Mearsheimer argues that based on these conditions and behavior patterns, cooperation is inhibited by relative gains concerns and concerns about cheating. He does not believe that institutions successfully overcome these problems. He is critical of "liberal institutionalists" for not addressing the issue of relative gains, which he maintains is critically important even if the problem of cheating is solved by institutional arrangements. Grieco (1988) also emphasizes that while states are not exclusively focused on relative gains, they are concerned about them. Advocates of collective security, such as Charles Kupchan, are criticized for not explaining *how* states overcome their fears in order to trust each other and accept three new "anti-realist" norms (renouncing the use of military force to alter the status quo, thinking in terms of the broader international interest, and trusting each other) (Mearsheimer 1994, 28–30). Mearsheimer (1995, 82) argues instead that institutions largely mirror the distribution of power in the system and are used by powerful states to maintain or increase their share of world power. For example, the North Atlantic Treaty Organization (NATO) was constructed to deter Soviet aggression in Europe. The United States and its allies formed this alliance based on balance of power logic, and the United States used the organization to its advantage in balancing the Soviet threat. Mearsheimer contends that, based on the argument that organizations reflect the distribution of power in the system, institutions themselves are not very influential. They are not able to get states to think beyond short-term power calculations and thus do not have significant independent effects on state behavior.

If Mearsheimer were to consider the role of the United States within the OAS, he would likely emphasize that the OAS frequently adopts policy proposals presented by the United States that reflect U.S. preferences. In order to explain those anomalous cases in which U.S. preferences are not adopted, he might conclude that the United States had little interest in those particular cases and thus did not choose to exert its influence within the organization. Additionally, the anomalies might reflect cases in which the United States did not view the OAS as an optimal tool to pursue its interests, and thus chose to take unilateral actions instead. Based on power relations between states, realists would predict that when addressing security issues, the most powerful state is likely to dominate organizational decisionmaking and to determine organizational actions based on its own national preferences (see table 2.1).

Realists and institutionalists have similar views of the international system, but their beliefs diverge concerning the impact of institutions on state behavior. Institutionalists accept the idea that states are rational egoists operating in an anarchic international system. They also acknowledge that power plays an important role in interstate relations. Nevertheless, they argue that institutions make a significant difference *in conjunction with* power realities (Keohane and Martin 1995, 42, emphasis added). Keohane and Martin further note that the need for institutions does not mean that they operate without respect to power and interests. They have an "interactive" effect that varies according to interests and power, but impacts state behavior just the same (see also Martin 1992). When considering the power relations within the OAS, institutionalists would acknowledge that the OAS pursues numerous policy proposals that reflect U.S. interests. They would also note, however, that in many of these cases the policies also reflect the preferences of Latin American members. Institutions are created and maintained based on common interests among their members. This facilitates cooperation and mutually beneficial relationships. For example, the OAS was founded in 1948 as a collective security organization for the Western hemisphere. States in the region wanted to establish an organization through which security threats to the hemisphere could be addressed multilaterally. In addition, the organization has served for over fifty years as a regional forum on a wide range of issues of common interest to its members.

Institutionalists might describe "U.S. dominance" of the OAS as "U.S. leadership" in the pursuit of common interests within the region. On those occasions when the OAS does not adopt a U.S. policy proposal, it is because U.S. and Latin American interests do not coincide and cooperation is more difficult. For example, in the case of the Guatemalan coup in 1954, members were not in agreement concerning the communist nature of the threat in Guatemala and thus failed to take effective collective action. In a number of cases where there are disagreements among members, compromises are seen rather than policies reflecting solely U.S. or Latin American preferences. This was

Table 2.1   Theories and hypotheses

Variables	Hypotheses
Realism/neo-realism	
Relative state power	When addressing security issues, the most powerful state is likely to dominate organizational decisionmaking and to determine organizational actions based on its own national preferences
Liberal institutionalism	
Shared interests	• If the U.S. has shared interests with other members in the OAS, it will work multilaterally through the organization to accomplish common goals
	• If the U.S. does not have shared interests with other members of the OAS, it will not work within the context of the organization to accomplish its goals
Perspective one: structural	
1. Resources needed	The more resources that are needed to support the Meeting of Consultation and carry out the resolutions of the Organ of Consultation, the more influence the U.S. has on those resolutions
Perspective two: internal relational	
2. Degree of consensus	The greater the disagreement among Latin American members, the greater the influence the U.S. has in the council/meeting of Foreign ministers
Perspective three: normative	
3. Regional principles	Any proposal or unilateral action by the U.S. (or other member state) that does not clearly uphold the principles of the organization will have less support than a proposal that is based on principled action, and will face strong opposition in the Council/Meeting of Foreign Ministers
Perspective four: environmental	
4. Type of conflict/threat of regional instability	The greater the risk of regional instability that is perceived by member states, the greater influence the U.S. has within the organization

the case in the early 1960s when dealing with Cuban-sponsored uprisings in the region. Institutionalists would predict that if the United States has shared interests with other members in the OAS, it will work multilaterally through the organization to accomplish common goals.

However, if the United States does not have shared interests with other member states, it will not work within the context of the organization to accomplish its goals (see table 2.1). Based on these predictions, the United States does not need to exercise hegemony within the OAS because the member states come together with common interests to promote cooperation. When interests do not coincide, the United States can use its strength as a hegemon to act unilaterally if it chooses.

Although Mearsheimer is skeptical that institutionalism can lead to a "genuine peace or a world where states do not compete for power" (1994, 9), institutionalists do not make such broad claims. Rather, as Keohane and Martin note in their response to Mearsheimer, "... institutions sometimes matter, and that it is a worthy task of social science to discover how, and under what conditions this is the case" (1995, 40). One of the conditions that institutionalists believe is significant for cooperation to occur is for states to have significant common interests. Institutions can provide information, reduce transaction costs, make commitments more credible, establish focal points for coordination, and facilitate reciprocity (Keohane and Martin 1995, 42). The impact of institutions on state behavior when states share common interests can be seen when addressing two different problems: concerns with cheating and problems with coordinating actions around a cooperative outcome. Institutions can help reassure states that cheating is not occurring, largely through facilitating transparency. For example, in negotiating an arms reduction agreement, both parties have a common interest to reduce their stockpiles of weapons, but fear to do so unilaterally. An institution can engage in regular inspections of both parties to ensure compliance. The institution would make any violations known and could facilitate further dialogue to remedy the situation and reduce tensions between the competing states. Institutions are also able to coordinate cooperation when dealing with distributional issues. When multiple equilibria exist, institutions can help states reach cooperative agreements.

Mearsheimer implies that cooperative ties are easy to forge if states desire them, but are not when states have diverging interests. Keohane and Martin point out that institutions can promote cooperation even under such difficult circumstances, however. For example, Britain had a difficult time convincing European Union (EU) states to impose an embargo on Argentina during the Falklands conflict (1982) in support of Britain. The EU as an institution, however, enabled cooperation by reducing fears of cheating in the form of taking advantage of the situation to profit from trade with Argentina while others observed the embargo. In this case, Britain used the EU to help uphold sanctions even though not all members desired or actively sought them. Keohane and Martin further add, "the difference between realism and liberal institutionalism does not lie in whether institutions are independent or dependent variables, it lies in contrasting understandings of why institutions are created and *how they exert their effects*" (1995, 48, emphasis added).

This research puts the debate about the impact of IOs on states into concrete terms by examining the relationship of the United States with other member states in the OAS. Realism and institutionalism explain many of the interactions among states within the context of the OAS, but they are unable to explain the puzzling cases when the United States, by far the most powerful member of the OAS, does not successfully manipulate the organization to serve its national interests. Realism focuses on power relations in order to explain the dominance of one state over another, or of one state over an IO. Realists would predict dominance of the OAS, disinterest, or unilateral actions on the part of the United States when pursuing its interests in Latin America. There are instances, however, when the United States had a keen interest in the outcome of an issue under discussion within the OAS and had a desire to act multilaterally, but did not succeed in dominating the organization. For example, in the case of the Nicaraguan Revolution in 1978–79 when the United States wanted to send in peacekeeping troops, the OAS Meeting of Foreign Ministers refused to take such action. The organization was considered a valuable forum for the United States in terms of pursuing its interests multilaterally since its unilateral efforts had not been successful. The OAS, however, was not as easily manipulable as one might have expected.

Institutionalists focus on the issue of common interests between the United States and Latin American states to explain the creation and use of the OAS to promote cooperation, but fail to adequately explain the processes that occur when there is disagreement between member states and the United States decides to pursue multilateral action. Institutionalism explores the bargaining dynamics between states within the institutional context but does not address the actual internal functioning of organizations. For example, Axelrod and Keohane (1986) emphasize how international institutions can affect such factors as the shadow of the future, the sanctioning problem, and the payoff structure to promote cooperation between states in an anarchic system. When considering the OAS, which has been functioning for over 50 years, members are well aware of the values of cooperation achieved through the institution. An examination of the benefits of sanctioning and lengthening the shadow of the future in iterative relations does not get at the puzzle of certain policy outcomes based on the unequal distribution of power in the region.

Studies of international regimes are linked to the institutionalist discussion in terms of highlighting the contributions regimes make to promoting cooperation. Stein (1983) elaborates on how international regimes can promote coordination and collaboration within an anarchic system even when states have divergent interests and preferences by helping them achieve more efficient outcomes than would otherwise occur. Although applicable in describing how the OAS serves as a regional forum, this literature does not directly address the question of state influence within the OAS. The policy debates within the OAS are not primarily about achieving efficient outcomes. When the United States and Latin American members disagree about policy proposals, there are certain structural, procedural, and normative conditions that influence the outcome of the debate that are not accounted for in these discussions of the benefits of institutions and international regimes. Neither realism nor institutionalism examines what organizational or environmental conditions might affect the level of influence that a member state has within the OAS.

Hegemonic stability theory, stemming from realist theory, offers some additional insights into member relations within the OAS based on relative balances of power, but is still limited in its ability to fully explain organizational decisionmaking.[4] Regimes are established and maintained by actors who hold a preponderance of power. The focus of hegemonic stability theory is on the effectiveness of regimes and is closely linked to Mancur Olson's theory of collective action (1965). Free rider problems result in the need for a dominant actor to establish a regime in order for states to cooperate. The hegemon imposes its norms on the system and all institutions conform to the hegemon's preferences. When power becomes more equally distributed among members, these regimes decline. It may be that hegemons are essential in the creation of some regimes and successfully maintain their regimes by setting norms of behavior in the system. This emphasis on the centrality of a hegemon to a regime, however, does not provide an adequate explanation for the relationship between the United States and other Latin American states within the context of the OAS. Despite its overwhelming power, the United States does not dictate all policies of the OAS, nor establish all operational and normative principles of the organization. As critics of hegemonic stability theory point out, the claim that regimes are neither created nor maintained without a hegemon is not tenable (Snidal 1985). Chapter 3 discusses the origins of the principles of the Inter-American System, providing evidence that the United States was not the prime shaper of the principles that currently structure inter-American relations within the OAS. Many of the principles that are in the OAS Charter derive from Pan American agreements reached between Latin American states in the previous century prior to regular U.S. involvement in the region. Principles such as nonaggression and the peaceful settlement of disputes among members were included in the Treaty of Confederation signed in Lima in 1847. The Treaty of Union and Defensive Alliance signed in 1864 called for the collective protection of the region against recolonialization. Latin American states continued to pursue the codification of these norms at the First International Conference of American States (1889) when the United States began to take a greater interest in such multilateral, regional discussions. Even when the United States was reluctant to accept such principles as nonintervention, Latin American states continued to place it on the diplomatic agenda despite U.S. objections. Thus, the anomalies of when the organization does not act as a tool of the United States remain to be explained. Variables other than power and interests must be used to explain the different outcomes within the OAS when the United States achieves its goals and when its preferences are not accommodated. There are two additional bodies of literature that will help to answer this question of the relationship between the OAS and its most powerful member.

The first body of literature is the constructivist approach to regimes, which emphasizes the importance of rules and norms within organizations and the international system. The constructivist approach explores knowledge dynamics, communications, and identities in international society (Hasenclever et al. 1997), and thus contrasts with realism and institutionalism, which focus on power relations and shared interests between member states. Constructivism credits IOs and regimes with a stronger impact on states than realism allows. Regimes reflect the interests of their creators, but also develop an autonomy after creation that allows them to impact states in unanticipated and uncontrollable ways. Some theorists go so far as to claim that organizations do not merely frustrate attempts at their manipulation by powerful states, but that they can actually manipulate states themselves through the establishment of norms and rules and their enforcement through a variety of sanctions and diplomatic coercion (Wendt 1992b).

Martha Finnemore (1996) elaborates on this idea of organizational manipulation, arguing that IOs play an even more fundamental role by shaping the actual interests of states. Realism and institutionalism both treat interests as given. They do not question how interests are formed. Finnemore argues that the norms established by IOs influence preference formation within states. Thus, according to constructivists, states are not so much rationalistic as they are sociological in their reasoning, shaping their interests based on the norms in international society (Finnemore 1996, 29). For example, although political scientists tend to think of war as a Hobbesian state of nature, war is actually highly regulated by rules that have changed over time, such as the Geneva Convention. Finnemore argues that states have actually been taught by groups such as the International Committee of the Red Cross that such rules of war are in their best interest.

Constructivists assert that states follow a "logic of appropriateness" instead of an instrumental logic of rationality. Rather than asking a means-end question, "How do I get what I want?" states ask, "What kind of situation is this? What am I supposed to do now?" (Finnemore 1996, 29). Finnemore offers an example of the emergence of state bureaucracies to coordinate scientific developments in essentially science-less states. She contends that the international organization, the United Nations Education, Scientific, and Cultural Organization, taught states that a science bureaucracy was a necessary component of "the modern state," resulting in a worldwide creation of a state scientific bureaucracy (Finnemore 1996, 4). The logic of appropriateness provides the opportunity for IOs to influence the preferences of states by shaping the context in which states are making decisions. Finnemore (1996, 35) further notes that IOs are not "neutral" forums. Organizations often produce unintended results. The ideas that are input are not necessarily going to be identical to the output of the organization. Thus, even when a strong state such as the United States pressures the OAS, the filtering process that occurs within the organization may not yield the desired results for the United States. Proposals for action made by member states are rarely voted on in their original format. Frequently proposals that are made to the governing Council are sent to a committee for investigation and recommendation. Within the committee, member states can submit proposed revisions to the original text, resulting in a significantly altered text in some cases. Furthermore, once the Council votes on a matter, the implementation is in the hands of the secretary general or other organizational actors, which may result in a further "shaping" of the resolution in ways uncontrolled by the United States (or other member states).

The constructivist approach supports the argument made here that neither power nor shared interests adequately explain the member relations or their influence within the OAS. The organization itself, as a body of norms and procedures, has an impact on relations between member states and on the multilateral decisions that they make. Constructivism predicts some degree of autonomous function within organizations, rather than viewing their actions in terms of manipulations by the most powerful member states. Although this research does not go so far as to claim the OAS is an autonomous or even purposive actor, it does view the organization as an entity that produces unexpected and unintended results separate from the desires of its creators/members.

The constructivist approach provides a normative perspective for examining organizational decisionmaking. Although some norms exist independent of IOs, the latter frequently include institutionalized principles as part of their formal structure. These principles are commonly established as part of their charters, through multilateral treaties or declarations, or in other joint agreements. In some cases adherence to these established principles is weak, but in others the norm is so well established that violation would likely bring condemnation or other punitive measures against the violator. An examination of the OAS in a constructivist/normative context reveals the types of regional principles that are embodied in the organization, and the impact of these norms based on the degree to which they are supported by member states. Chapter 3 traces the evolution of norms in the Inter-American System, and chapters 4 and 5 examine the way these norms serve to limit the influence and behavior of states within the OAS.

The second body of literature that contributes strongly to the theoretical framework comes from the field of organizational sociology. Although there are a number of studies that go below the international level of analysis to examine such factors as bureaucratic politics (Halperin 1974; Haass 1999), complex organizations (Thompson 1967; Perrow 1979), and individual bargaining behavior (Cyert and March 1992) to explain organizational behavior, these studies are largely focused on domestic institutions such as corporations or the government bureaucracy, not on international institutions such as the OAS. These "domestic organizational" perspectives are particularly difficult to adapt to the context of IOs because of the added level of analysis when examining IOs, which includes not only individuals and agencies but also numerous states. Studying the individual ambassadors and the politics of their corresponding foreign ministries does not fully get at explanations of how they interact within the larger context of an IO.

Representatives to the OAS are essentially part of organizations *within* a larger organization (the OAS). In order to focus this research on institutional factors within an *international* organization, this project adapts three perspectives from organizational sociology to construct an analytical framework suited to the study of an international organization. Although organizational sociology does not examine organizations at the international level, it does provide a useful categorization of different aspects of organizations that can apply to domestic or international organizations. Organizational sociology approaches examine structural/functional, relational, and environmental factors to explain organizational decisionmaking. This project adopts these categories and applies them to the context of the OAS.

The three approaches to organizational sociology focus on different aspects of an organization and provide different insights into organizational functions and decisionmaking. The first approach is a rational system perspective in which an organization is defined as a formalized structure oriented to the pursuit of specific goals (Scott 1998). The focus is on productivity and efficiency achieved through formal institutions, procedures, and goals. Individual participants in the organization and the impact of the environment are considered irrelevant. It is the role or position that participants fill that is significant, not their individual characteristics. This approach has been characterized as "organizations without people" (Scott 1998).

The key explanatory variable in the rational system perspective is organizational structure. The fundamental argument is that outputs are shaped by organizational inputs. Productivity and quality of production can be improved if the optimal structures and procedures are implemented within the organization. For example, when a status structure among workers emerges within the workplace, tensions are generated among individuals who entered the workplace with the assumption of being equals. Status battles are reduced when status in the workplace is prestructured before any individuals are placed in roles within it. Formal structuring results in individuals spending less time asserting power and less resistance to leadership efforts by work leaders. When applied to the international organizational context, this perspective implies that organizational outcomes (i.e., OAS decisions and actions) are largely influenced by the structure within the organization. Thus, this perspective points to structural answers to the puzzle concerning U.S. influence within the OAS.

The second organizational sociology approach is the natural system perspective, which emerged as a response to the rational system perspective.

Organizations are viewed as a collectivity of people with common interests, who are focused on the survival of the organization above all other goals. Studies in this perspective focus on the "informal structure" of organizations, which include the interaction between the internal structure of the organization and the individual participants in it. This approach has been called "People without organizations" (Scott 1998).

Contrary to the rational system perspective in which individuals are merely employees fulfilling specified tasks, the natural system perspective focuses on people's unique qualities and their impact on the organization. Interactive dynamics are the key variable to explaining variations in output. For example, if employees are not inspired by their supervisor to perform well, they may not produce at their maximum capacity regardless of the specific procedures they are following or the structure of the organization. Furthermore, the continued existence of the organization is not taken as a given. Employees, in order to assure their own indispensability, place a high priority on the continued survival of the organization itself, even if this means subverting the explicit goals of the organization. In the context of the OAS, this perspective suggests that a greater understanding of membership dynamics can provide insight into state influence within the organization. It also suggests that threats to the organization and its members should be evaluated as well.

The third organizational sociology approach that has developed most recently is an open system perspective.[5] This perspective focuses on the interaction of the organization with the external environment, as opposed to the rational and natural system approaches in which the environment is largely ignored in favor of internal structure and dynamics (i.e., a closed system). In an open system, there is a close connection between the condition of the environment and the characteristics of the systems within it (Scott 1998). The environment is a force in its own right, a source of resources and constraints that profoundly shape the structure and functioning of the organization. Subunits monitor the relevant environment for opportunities and threats, to formulate strategic responses and adjust organizational structure accordingly (Scott 1998). Open systems stress the complexity and variability of the components in organizations and the loose connections between them. Attention is shifted from structure to process. The emphasis is on the problems involved with organizing in a dynamic system. Open systems models stress the reciprocal ties that bind the organization with those elements that surround and penetrate it. The environment is perceived as the source of order rather than a hostile force. Organizations are not closed, self-contained, self-sufficient entities—they are vitally linked to other systems. The organization is composed of shifting coalitions that are adaptive and flexible in response to internal organizational and external environmental changes.

This third approach comes closest to stressing variables utilized in the IR literature. The focus in open systems is both internal (on the organization itself) and external (on environmental influences). In the international context, this duality is similar to noting the impact of the international system on states within it. Realists and institutionalists contend that state priorities and decisions are shaped by the international system. States that are best able to adjust to changes in the system thrive, while the less flexible ones may not. When considering the case of the OAS, the open system perspective implies that the environmental context in which decisions are being made shapes the behavior of the organization. Thus, the international context should also be kept in mind when trying to explain U.S. influence in the OAS.

This open systems approach is also useful in that it helps address the fact that international studies focus on states as actors, whereas the sociological approaches assume actors are individuals. In the international arena, individuals may function within an organization, but these individuals also represent the interests of their respective states. This adds an additional level of analysis to the examination of IOs. If the OAS is viewed as a closed system (i.e., if the focus is solely on the internal dynamics of the organization) then the impact of the shared and divergent interests of its member states are not easily accounted for. If the OAS is viewed as an open system, then it is easier to understand the impact of states on the organization and to discern the organization's response to states' influences in a context broader than the single state representative within the organization. This aspect of open system perspective allows a more complete evaluation of the variables influencing the actions of IOs.

Taken individually, none of the sociological perspectives nor the normative perspective offers a complete picture of the OAS. By combining them to examine OAS decisionmaking, however, one is able to determine more precisely the conditions necessary for the United States to have influence within the organization. Each of these approaches suggests that certain factors are important to consider when explaining the decisionmaking process within the OAS. The normative perspective focuses on the impact of regional principles on member influence. The rational system approach raises questions about what structural features of the OAS impact U.S. influence. The natural system approach focuses on internal membership dynamics and organizational maintenance (i.e., survival). The open system approach raises questions concerning the impact of the environment on the organization and its ability to react and adapt to environmental changes. Overall, theories of organizational sociology allow for greater insight into the functioning of the OAS itself to answer questions that theories of IO and IR are unable to answer. These sociological theories do not replace realist or institutionalist explanations of IR, but a synthesis of all three combined with a normative perspective does offer greater insights into the puzzle of the impact of IOs by focusing on the organization itself.

Deriving a Framework for Analysis

This section outlines the framework to be applied to the OAS cases of peaceful settlement of disputes in order to analyze U.S. influence within the organization. Four different perspectives on the OAS are derived from the three approaches to organizational sociology and the constructivist approach discussed earlier. By analyzing the structure, internal relations, and principles of the OAS, and the external environment, this framework establishes a synthesis of the organizational factors that affect U.S. influence within the organization (see table 2.1).

Structure
According to the rational system approach, the formal structure of an organization is deliberately designed to achieve a specific set of goals. Two apparent goals shaped the structure of the OAS when it was created: (1) the desire to achieve hemispheric security through collective action, and (2) the desire to prohibit external intervention in the domestic politics of member states. The implicit purpose of the second goal was to reduce the level of intervention by the United States in Latin American politics. The inter-American principles of equality among states, nonintervention, collective security, and pacific settlement of disputes that shaped these two goals of the OAS are all reflected in the formal rules of the organization: (1) all member votes are equal; (2) the chairmanship of the Council is rotated among members; (3) all members are represented in the Council and Meetings of Foreign Ministers; and (4) the Rio Treaty and Charter embody the elements of collective security, nonintervention, and pacific settlement.[6] Thus, the formal structure of the organization does not provide any inherent structural advantages to the United States to influence the organization.[7] The United States does not have the privilege of an overriding veto as it

does in the UN Security Council. The United States can use its power in only a limited way in the OAS, as long as it works within the established framework. There is, however, one circumstance that may allow the United States (or any other member with the necessary resources) to influence the organization's actions despite structural limitations: the need for diplomatic and military expertise, and financial and military resources.

Although the formal structure of the OAS appears to limit the ability of the United States to use its overwhelming power to influence the organization's decisionmaking directly, the United States does have a decided advantage when it comes to actual implementation of Council decisions. Resources are related to structure in that they are a part of the financial obligations of the organization. The cost of actions taken under the Rio Treaty and Charter for pacific settlement are not budgeted items in the OAS. These costs must be covered by voluntary member contributions. Some actions are costly in monetary and military terms, and others require a significant number of personnel and degree of expertise. Any actions that the Organ of Consultation (Council or Foreign Ministers) debates must include considerations about the coverage of costs. Thus, if the Council is considering actions that are quite costly in terms of finances or personnel, it needs U.S. support in order to be able to fully implement its resolutions. Even if *all* Latin American states were willing to contribute significantly to the actions determined by the Organ of Consultation, which is unlikely given the variety of interests and preferences within the organization, the United States still has considerably more resources to contribute. Equality can only go so far in terms of finances. Thus, the United States is able to get around the structural equality established in the formal institutions in order to influence the organization. This leads to hypothesis number one:

> 1. The more resources that are needed to support the Meeting of Consultation and carry out the resolutions of the Organ of Consultation, the more influence the United States has on those resolutions.

Internal Relations

The previous section focused on the formal structure of the OAS, which is shaped by the regional goals of hemispheric security and reduced internal intervention. The organization, however, has been only partly successful in achieving these goals, primarily because factors other than formal institutions have an impact on organizational decisionmaking and actions. Just as natural system advocates in sociology have emphasized the importance of the people within an organization, this section emphasizes the importance of internal dynamics among member states within the OAS—the "informal" structures.

Informal structures, including the interactions between actors based on their personal relations and characteristics, are in contrast to formal structures discussed earlier, which are associated with the patterns of behavior that exist regardless of the characteristics of actors. The natural system approach in sociology suggests that the informal structures in an organization are not simply idiosyncratic beliefs and behaviors, but are structured and orderly. Participants within a formal organization generate informal behavior patterns shaped by such factors as status and power systems, communication networks, and working arrangements (Scott 1998). Sociologists further add that there are positive aspects to this informal structure, including increasing ease of communication, facilitating trust, and correcting for the inadequacies of the formal system (Scott 1998).

This section extends natural system analysis to focus on the dynamics between member states in the OAS, rather than relations between individuals within an organizational environment. Representatives of member states are more than bodies filling Council positions as the formal institutional perspective might suggest. They have ideas, expectations, and agendas as well as differing values and abilities that derive from their own national interests (Scott 1998). These shape the interactions among member states within the context of the OAS.[8]

The variable to be considered concerning internal relations is the level of consensus within the organization. There are two different aspects to consider when examining consensus within the OAS. One aspect involves the degree of consensus among only the Latin American member states. The second involves the level of agreement between the United States and Latin American members. In many cases, no disagreement exists among members as to what actions should be taken to address regional conflict. When there is disagreement between Latin American members and the United States, however, there are two different outcomes to controversial U.S. proposals based on the level of consensus among Latin American members. If Latin American states are unified in opposition to a U.S. proposal, the United States is unlikely to get its proposal passed. If Latin American states are divided and unable to present an alternative proposal for action, the United States has the opportunity to provide strong leadership and gain support for its own proposal. Members seem to prefer a U.S. plan of action to no plan. Latin American members place a high value on consensual, multilateral action. When an event in the region occurs contrary to the principles of the organization, OAS members feel compelled to respond in order to maintain the integrity of the organization. Even if it means accepting a less than ideal U.S. proposal, Latin American members would rather act on such a proposal than fail to respond at all. This gives the United States considerable leverage when there is disagreement among Latin American members. The formal equality of members that restricts U.S. influence through formal structures is only useful if Latin Americans can achieve unity to resist U.S. pressures through a vote of the majority. This leads to the next hypothesis:

> 2. The greater the disagreement among Latin American members, the greater influence the United States has.

Principles

A number of principles are important to the member states of the OAS. These principles have been developed and strengthened over time, and are embodied in the OAS Charter and Rio Treaty as well as numerous other treaties among member states. Not only do these principles represent the strong beliefs in pacific settlement of disputes in the region, they also oppose intervention in the domestic affairs of member states. These principles were first established with the intention of limiting the risk of warfare in the hemisphere by constraining states' aggressive behaviors toward their neighbors. When all the states in the region chose to adopt these principles as they were laid out in the OAS Charter, the Pact of Bogotá, and the Rio Treaty, hemispheric security was increased. Any state violating these principles not only risked sanctioning by other members, but also bore the stigma of a violator. As constructive theorists argue, norms create a sense of obligation for states. They must comply with agreed-upon rules and norms even when they have incentives to break them and the capacity to do so (Franck 1990). Rules are not easily broken; to do so risks pulling at the entire fabric of the international community, not just the single violation of rules (Hasenclever et al. 1997).

Because no predetermined set of responses to handle disputes exists, all issues of conflict resolution are open for discussion and debate within the established structure of the organization. Each action taken by the organization will be crafted by members attempting to uphold their states' particular interests on the issue. The options open to the Organ of Consultation according to the Rio Treaty and the OAS Charter include (but are not limited to): issuing a series of resolutions calling for peaceful settlement; providing for negotiation, mediation, and arbitration; breaking diplomatic ties; and imposing economic sanctions including arms and munitions. Resolutions can be expanded if necessary, or revised based on updated reports coming from investigating committees. The options considered by members are shaped by the organization's normative principles.

The impact of norms not only limits certain state behavior, but can also promote other actions (i.e., multilateral actions taken through the OAS). When the OAS acts in concert, its actions have considerably more moral authority than any single member acting alone, even if that member is the United States. Although hegemonic stability theorists might argue that the leading state establishes the norms in its region, and changes them as necessary to serve its own interests, such control of norms has not been possible for the United States in Latin America. The norms underlying the Inter-American System date back to the late 1890s and the Pan American movement. They were established before the United States even became an active participant in the system. Latin Americans have strongly resisted any U.S. pressure to alter these historic principles in any way. (The closest they have come to altering the region's fundamental principles was in 1954 when they agreed to define international communism as a threat to the hemisphere because of its extracontinental origins.) Thus, principles play a significant role in inter-American relations. As the most powerful state in the region, the United States is one of the few members of the organization that can take effective unilateral action when its national interests and/or security is threatened. The United States can (and does) act unilaterally when its preferred actions do not coincide with OAS principles. It does, however, risk condemnation from the OAS for such action.[9]

When the Organ of Consultation is considering how to respond to a disturbance in the region, it must keep the organization's guiding principles in mind. Proposals that are put forth in the OAS are carefully phrased to uphold the principles of the Inter-American System. These principles thus constrain the actions of all members. Although many different actions can be framed so as to support these principles, there are certain actions that are not acceptable to members that they will resist strongly. This leads to the next hypothesis:

> 3. Any proposal or unilateral action by the United States (or other member state) that does not clearly uphold the principles of the

organization will have less support than a proposal that is based on principled action, and will face strong opposition in the Council/ Meeting of Foreign Ministers.

The Environment

Rather than perceiving the OAS as operating in a vacuum in which only organizational variables affect its actions, it is important to recognize that the organization affects and is affected by its external environment, the international system. The international system is a complex environment to describe, with innumerable variables and relations. Two factors have been chosen to represent the impact of the international environment on the organization. The type of conflict being handled by the organization and the perceived level of threat to regional stability both reflect certain characteristics of the environment that impact the organization's decisionmaking in dispute settlement.

The perceived level of threat to regional stability directly influences the organization's decision to initiate pacific settlement procedures. Because one of the principal functions of the organization is to provide collective security for the hemisphere, any dispute that threatens peace in the region can be brought before the organization. This includes both internal and international conflicts. All members have a vested interest in maintaining the stability of the region and restoring peace when a dispute occurs. Not only is there pressure for the OAS to resolve a conflict because it threatens member states, but it must also handle the dispute because it potentially threatens the survival of the organization itself. If the OAS does not adequately address the issue, it may risk becoming obsolete (i.e., no longer of use to its members).[10]

The type of dispute is also important in assessing the level of threat. Latin America does not have many significant ethnic conflicts like those experienced in a number of African countries. Most disputes are ideological and/or territorial. In terms of escalation and threat level, certain conflicts lead to greater regional instability than others and thus a higher level of threat. For example, territorial disputes are less threatening than ideological disputes on issues of democracy versus dictatorship and on international communism. Historically, the latter two risked drawing many more members into a conflict either directly or indirectly than a territorial dispute did. In addition, disputes over communism inherently risked the involvement of the (former) Eastern bloc nations and/or the (former) Soviet Union. Thus, disputes that involve ideological threats are much more likely to cause regional instability. Furthermore, with the emergence of the Cold War and U.S. preoccupation with communist movements in Latin America, the United States made a strong effort in the OAS to define communism as a threat to the hemisphere, an extracontinental intervention of the Soviet Union.[11]

The perceived level of threat to the region also has implications for the types of actions to be considered by the Organ of Consultation to address a conflict. Clearly if many members of the OAS feel that their security is threatened, they will be willing to take significant actions to restore peace to the region, including taking military action. When the perceived level of threat is not high, however, a number of diplomatic options are available to the Council and Foreign Ministers to address regional disputes.[12] Indeed, Latin Americans have historically preferred to take diplomatic steps before resorting to military measures. This appears to be a principled preference as well as a practical one. When members have few military resources to contribute to ending a dispute, they rely on diplomacy instead. Many skilled Latin American diplomats have contributed to strengthening peace in the region over the years. The United States, not facing similar constraints, has frequently resorted to military maneuvers to achieve its objectives in Latin America. Given the military power of the United States, Latin American countries have also resisted military action recognizing that this would result in U.S. leadership of the force.

When there is a perceived major security threat to the region, and given that the United States considers the Western hemisphere to be its own "backyard," the United States has taken a strong interest in addressing such security threats. The United States has often been willing to provide resources and leadership in many peaceful settlement operations. Its strong participation has relieved the burden on other members to provide the resources and leadership when it was necessary to enforce strong resolutions.

Just as the study of open systems in organizational sociology struggles to specify all of the complex interactions between a bureaucratic organization and the environment, the relationship between the environment and IOs is also quite complex. It is this perspective to which realism is most applicable because it is a system-level approach. Realism focuses on states and not organizations, but some of the assumptions may apply in this context. For example, when considering environmental influences, power relations seem significant in predicting levels of influence in the OAS. Formal equality among members does not fully counter the imbalance of power. In cases of threatened regional stability,

Latin Americans look to the United States for leadership. This leads to the final hypothesis:

4. The greater the risk of regional instability that is perceived by member states, the greater influence the United States has within the organization.

Applying the Analytical Framework

The framework developed here will be used to further examine member relations and influence within the OAS. The framework is a synthesis of three different perspectives, combining structure, relations, and the environment with a normative perspective to offer greater insights into member relations within IOs. The framework builds on the explanations offered by realism and institutionalism, but goes below the international level of analysis to explore organizational dynamics and decisionmaking.

Realism, with its focus on power politics, accurately describes many of the interactions between member states in the OAS, but not all of them. The fact that the most powerful state, the United States, has not gotten its way in several cases over the years indicates that additional factors beyond political power must be at work. In addition, a number of actions taken by the OAS have been based on consensual decisionmaking where there is little evidence of power politics involved. A more extensive framework that includes power as well as other factors is necessary to explain member relations and organizational decisionmaking.

Although institutionalist arguments accurately describe some aspects of member relations in the OAS, they do not paint a complete picture. Institutionalist explanations for cooperation between states in IOs are based on shared interests, predicting cooperative multilateral action when interests coincide, and unilateral action when they do not. Looking specifically at cases in the Western hemisphere, one can identify a number of cases where this institutionalist explanation accurately describes regional relations. In some instances, U.S. and Latin American interests have coincided, resulting in multilateral action taken through the OAS. One example is when Cuba was sanctioned by the Twelfth Meeting of Foreign Ministers in 1967 for repeatedly intervening in Venezuelan politics and trying to overthrow the government. There are other instances where U.S. and Latin American interests have not coincided, such as in the Falklands/Malvinas War (1982) between the United Kingdom and Argentina. In this case the United States had little interest in acting multilaterally within the OAS because it would be unable to achieve organizational support for Britain, a long-time U.S. ally.

Even though institutionalism explains these cases of cooperation or noncooperation well based on common interests, there are other cases that are not as easily explained. A number of cases exist where U.S. and Latin American interests have diverged and yet the United States has still chosen to address the regional issue within the context of the OAS rather than unilaterally. The cases addressing Cuban intervention in the region (1960, 1962, 1964) provide a good example of this desire to work through the OAS even though members were divided on what actions to take. These cases indicate that the institution was relevant to and utilized by member states to deal with regional problems. Despite conflicting views on how to handle Cuba, members were able to reach compromise agreements in order to take effective multilateral action. The United States as well as other members recognized the value of acting in unison. The resolutions issued by the Foreign Ministers sent a clear message to the Castro regime and had greater authority than any declarations made by one or a few states in the region. In addition, by emphatically addressing the problem, rather than ignoring it or taking indecisive measures, the organization was strengthened as an effective regional actor. By focusing particularly on the cases in which states have differing interests and yet remain multilaterally engaged, the analytical framework examines decisionmaking in the OAS seeking more complete explanations than those offered by institutionalism.

The analytical framework serves as a means for examining the cases in which the Rio Treaty, OAS Charter, Resolution 1080, or the Democratic Charter have been invoked for pacific settlement in the last half century.[13] It facilitates the discovery of similarities and contrasts among the cases, and helps to organize them in a meaningful fashion. Each of the perspectives (structural, relational, normative, and environmental) emphasizes a different set of variables as the key to understanding U.S. influence within the OAS. Each provides insights that have not been previously examined in the IO context and that complement existing international theories. For example, hypothesis 1 builds on the realist argument. By having significant resources, the United States does have an influential advantage within the OAS. An examination of member resources in the context of organizational structure, however, suggests there are limits placed on hegemonic power. Because of the procedural rules giving every state an equal vote on resolutions, and the fully inclusive membership of all states in the Council and Meeting of Foreign Ministers, the United States cannot simply dominate the organization because of its hegemonic status. U.S. influence is reduced, despite its power, when significant resources are not needed to carry out the resolutions of the Organ of Consultation.

Hypothesis 2 similarly expands on institutionalist theory, which predicts cooperation when there are common interests between states. The second hypothesis, however, makes a further distinction, recognizing that disagreement among Latin American states and disagreements between the United States and Latin American states can have two different consequences in terms of organizational decisionmaking and U.S. dominance. Latin American states have divergent interests from each other as well as the United States from time to time. When these disagreements divide members, it reduces the ability of Latin American states to unite against unpopular U.S. proposals and use their majority of votes to defeat them. This perspective also emphasizes a point that is often overlooked when examining Latin America, that is that this region is not homogenous. Members have a wide variety of interests that they pursue within the context of the OAS. Member relations are far more complex than a simple division of the United States versus the rest.

Hypothesis 3 is based on the constructivist literature that norms do affect state behavior and that the United States will have less influence if it tries to take action that violates regional principles. Examining this proposition in the context of a number of case studies illustrates the impact of regional norms on decisionmaking within the OAS. Although the United States can and does act outside the OAS, when it pursues multilateral action its arguments supporting that action are strengthened when they are based on regional principles and weakened when they are not.

Hypothesis 4 is closely linked with hypothesis 1, and is one that realists would likely agree with. However, this proposition is not based on relative power per se to explain dominance within the OAS. It is based on an external factor, the perceived level of threat to the region. U.S. power does not necessarily give it hegemonic dominance unless external conditions are right. Because the types of threats the OAS addresses vary from case to case, there are many instances when Latin American members may not require or desire U.S. assistance. When threat levels are low, U.S. influence will likely be reduced.

Together the structural, relational, normative, and environmental perspectives impart a better understanding of the way IOs function. When applied to the case studies that follow, the analytical framework provides new insights into member influence within the OAS and its decisionmaking processes.

CHAPTER 3

COOPERATION: HISTORIC HEMISPHERIC RELATIONS AND THE FORMATION OF THE OAS

Introduction

Before examining the specific cases of conflict resolution handled by the OAS between 1948 and 1989, and the interventions in defense of democracy in the 1990s, it is important to explore the historical relations between the United States and Latin American states that preceded the founding of the OAS. These relations reveal that U.S. policies toward Latin American countries have alternated among benign neglect, multilateralism, and active unilateral intervention for over one hundred years. U.S. dominance in the region has often led to policies that Latin American states have been obliged to accept despite their contrary preferences, resulting in hostility and resentment toward the United States on many occasions. For example, during the first quarter of the twentieth century, under Presidents Theodore Roosevelt, William Howard Taft, and Woodrow Wilson, U.S. troops actively intervened on many occasions in Central American and Caribbean states to enforce order and security in the region and to increase American economic dominance in the area. There have also been times of cooperation and productive relations, however, when inter-American ties have drawn the Americas together. For example, the Good Neighbor Policy of President Franklin D. Roosevelt promoted cooperative, less imperial policies and led to improved Latin American relations. At the Seventh International Conference of American States (1933), a mood of cooperation and goodwill replaced the suspicion, resentment, and rancor that had been displayed at the previous conference held in 1928 (Atkins 1997, 287). New principles and agreements were adopted on which diplomats had not been able to gain consensus prior to the Seventh Conference.

It took four decades of discussion and work to achieve this new level of consensus however. At the First International Conference of American States in 1889, the United States and Latin American states came together with different goals in mind and achieved only very limited agreements. At this conference the United States first became active in the Pan American movement that had been underway since 1826. The First Conference and the ones that followed,[14] however, provided a forum in which a variety of inter-American activities could be developed and coordinated. They also provided an opportunity for states to reach agreements on common hemispheric values and principles. This forum and discussion was beneficial to states in the hemisphere in helping build new relations between them. The OAS, which evolved out of the Inter-American System, was unable to resolve all the tensions that existed between the United States and Latin American states. Neither was it able to balance the asymmetry of power. It did, however, establish a framework in which the states could discuss their differences on a somewhat more equal footing.

The framework, which established the formal equality of member states, was not arrived at quickly or easily, nor were many of the other principles that the OAS now upholds. The principles of state sovereignty, nonintervention, territorial integrity, pacific settlement of disputes, representative democracy, and respect for human rights evolved for over a century before they were incorporated into the treaties and documents that are a fundamental part of the current Inter-American System. This evolutionary process was not a well-defined plan with clear goals in mind; rather, it was a less purposive process. There were periods of significant progress when members reached consensus concerning the emerging principles and structures of the Inter-American System. There were also periods with little progress, when members discussed but could not agree on important issues. Even when members were unable to reach consensus, however, the system continued to evolve as members considered new and/or controversial ideas that were being proposed. These inactive periods were also important, however, because until new ideas were articulated in the public forum, they would stand no chance of being accepted as international norms. Thus, even though there was little agreement on the ideas during these periods, there was much discussion that would eventually lead to consensus.

The process of norm development in the Inter-American System provides a good illustration of constructivist arguments on the evolution of international norms. Finnemore and Sikkink (1998) discuss the evolution of norms as a three-stage process. In the first stage, Emergence, organizations can serve as platforms for norm entrepreneurs to advocate new principles for state behavior. The inter-American conferences held after 1889 are an example of how an organization can serve in this manner. Although Latin American states had negotiated agreements on a number of principles to promote peace and security, the United States was not a part of this normative consensus. Most of these agreements took the form of bilateral treaties and included the principles of nonintervention, territorial integrity, arbitration of disputes, and renunciation of war. Latin American states thus had a common framework of principles even before the United States began actively participating in the Inter-American System.

The second stage of norm evolution, Norm Cascades, is an active process in which norm supporters induce other states to become norm followers through socialization. This may be accomplished using praise and/or ridicule, as well as through diplomatic and economic sanctions and incentives. States comply with norms due to pressure to conform and to enhance their international legitimacy (Finnemore and Sikkink 1998). Following the establishment of the Pan American Union in 1910, certain statesmen would work within the inter-American conferences to persuade the United States to adopt those principles commonly adopted by many Latin American states. As discussed later, the United States finally came on board through a process of pressure, persuasion, and calculation of interests.

The third stage of norm evolution, Internalization, is not an inevitable end point. In this stage norms are internalized, institutionalized, and strengthened through iterated behavior and habit. Some norms may never reach this stage. It is difficult to identify when this stage has occurred, although one indicator is when there are no longer debates about certain norms, they are taken as a given. In the case of the regional norms in the Western hemisphere, the norms of democracy, nonaggression, and peaceful settlement of disputes have arguably reached this stage.

The inter-American conferences held over the past century have provided the opportunity for participants to advance new principles, trying to persuade other states that adoption of these norms would benefit the entire region. In her discussion on the evolutionary model of norms, Ann Florini (1996) points to the importance of "coherence" in the spread of norms. New norms are more likely to spread if they fit coherently with existing norms and existing norms are strengthened when they are logically linked. For example, the renunciation of war and the principle of nonaggression are closely linked to the principle of peaceful settlement. If a dispute occurs and war has been renounced except in self-defense, then it logically follows that a state would accept alternative peaceful methods to resolve disputes including arbitration, mediation, negotiation, and adjudication. When Latin American diplomats began to discuss new ideas such as consultation on foreign policy issues, regional solidarity, and collective security, these principles fit well with existing norms of nonaggression and peaceful settlement. All these principles promote a more peaceful and secure region. By consulting with other states during a security crisis and pledging to collectively come to the defense of others if they are attacked, states could prevent or deter aggression.

The impact of Latin American and U.S. acceptance and adoption of these new norms was significant, especially in the creation of processes to resolve conflicts in the region. This chapter traces how these norms and member solidarity developed prior to and during the formation of the OAS. The impact of inter-American principles is examined further in chapters 4–6, where case studies indicate that in order for an organization to affect or resist pressure from a powerful member, norms must be in place and accepted by all, and there must be unity of purpose among the other members.

This chapter provides historical background about the OAS and its antecedents, and places U.S.–Latin American relations on the issues of peace and security in context. In the first section I look at the Inter-American System leading up to the formation of the OAS. The evolution of the Inter-American System can be seen by examining the conferences that were held, the treaties and principles that were adopted, and the creation and reform of its governing bodies and agencies. This section reveals the ebb and flow of ideas as the principles of the Inter-American System developed. It also portrays the struggle between the Latin American states and the United States over the handling of "political" issues by the Inter-American System that gave rise to the creation of a juridically based, multipurpose organization (i.e., the OAS). The evolution and developing consensus around the norms of nonintervention, nonaggression, and peaceful settlement of disputes are evident in the four phases of inter-American development. The second section examines the Rio Treaty (1947), the OAS Charter (1948), and the American Treaty on Pacific Settlement (Pact of Bogotá 1948). These documents form the foundation upon which hemispheric security, cooperation, and pacific settlement have been based. The evolution and development of consensus around the norms of pacific settlement and nonintervention are evident in the four phases of inter-American development. The second section also describes the way that the evolving principles of the Inter-American System are formally incorporated into these documents and the new organizational structures that were created. A greater understanding of these historical relations and the evolution of regional norms for peaceful settlement of disputes in the hemisphere provide a foundation for understanding more recent relationships and regional efforts at conflict resolution.

The Inter-American System

As the Inter-American System developed, it passed through four phases prior to 1948.[15] The priorities and issues of the Inter-American System as well as the relations between the United States and Latin American states have differed in each of these periods. The first phase began in the 1820s and lasted until 1889. It was exclusively a Latin American movement. The second phase, which was characterized by U.S. dominance, lasted from 1889 to 1923. The third phase from 1923 to 1933 was a brief transition period during which Latin American nations reasserted themselves. The fourth phase from 1933 to 1948 was a cooperative, unifying period in which the foundations for the creation of the OAS were laid, beginning with the cooperative policies of the new administration of President Franklin D. Roosevelt and concluding with the formal signing of the OAS Charter.

First Phase

During the first phase of development of the Inter-American System, the Spanish–American movement, led by Simón Bolívar, was focused on establishing a confederation of Hispanic–American states to protect against European (primarily Spanish) aggression. The United States under the Jackson administration pursued an isolationist policy during this time that prevented the realization of a system that included all of the Western hemisphere. The Latin American states of Colombia, Chile, Peru, Argentina, Mexico, and Central America, however, did sign a series of treaties with each other in the 1820s. These states convened the Congress of Panama in 1826 to establish common principles for security and peace among the nations of America. They pledged to unite to protect their independence and prosperity, and to promote greater harmony between their citizens. They adopted four treaties providing for broad multilateral cooperation in defense and other matters. The most important treaty was the "Permanent Alliance, League and Confederation of the Republics of Colombia, Central America, Peru and the United States of Mexico." This treaty established an "alliance [between participants] in times of peace and war," and affirmed an "inviolable friendship and close union between all contracting parties" (Glinkin 1990, 25). The introduction of the principles of collective security and regional solidarity thus date back to the earliest years of the Pan American movement.

Despite the apparent positive beginning with the conference in 1826, the Panama Congress was considered a failure because only one participating state, Colombia, ratified the treaties and the states did not follow through with a planned meeting to be held in Mexico the next year (Whitaker 1954, 43). Some attribute this failure to the lack of dynamic economic connections between the countries that would have helped the process of unification (Glinkin 1990, 26). A second meeting of these states was not held until 1847 in Lima. Although the participating states established the principles of nonaggression and peaceful settlement of disputes among members in the Treaty of Confederation, none of the participants ratified the Treaty, rendering the second meeting a limited success. The United States still chose not to be involved in these diplomatic conferences and in fact was on poor terms with Latin American states as it engaged in a war with Mexico. The states met a third time in Santiago (1856) and signed the Continental Treaty which included a number of "nonpolitical" provisions concerning contracts, shipping, and postal service (Whitaker 1954, 56). A fourth conference was held in Lima in 1864. It concluded with the signing of four treaties, including a Treaty of Union and Defensive Alliance, which set an anti-European tone to protect the region against recolonialization. Each of these Congresses was an effort to promote regional security since the latter two came at a time when concern about Spanish reconquest was greatest.[16]

These early Pan American meetings inspired over fifty bilateral treaties on peaceful settlement of disputes and promoted solidarity among Latin Americans. However, no permanent governing bodies existed at the time to oversee the operation of these treaties, although some were proposed. Cooperation among states was limited to bilateral efforts and the agreements reached at the Congresses. Yet the principles of nonintervention, territorial integrity, arbitration, solidarity, and renunciation of war became fundamental ones in many treaties during this time. Throughout this period, the United States watched the growing number of interactions and agreements, but did not actively participate. The main focus of U.S. policy in Latin America was on fostering trade and avoiding political commitments. The "political" focus (i.e., security concerns) of these early Congresses did not appeal to U.S. administrations. There were mixed opinions among Latin American participants concerning U.S. participation in these conferences. Bolívar did not want to include the United States, preferring to maintain an exclusively Latin American focus (as opposed to a truly "Pan American" one). Other states, including Mexico and Central America, did extend an invitation to the United States to participate, hoping to induce the United States to undertake specific obligations of support beyond the vague statements for hemispheric defense made in the Monroe Doctrine (Glinkin 1990, 36).

Second Phase
The anti-American sentiment expressed early on changed in the latter half of the nineteenth century to a more inclusive hemispheric view of inter-American solidarity. Latin American states were willing to accept U.S. leadership in order to achieve political effectiveness (Whitaker 1954, 62). The second phase of development of the Inter-American System began with the First International Conference of American States held in Washington in 1889. At this conference, the focus of the Inter-American System shifted away from security matters toward economic concerns. Unlike the first phase in which the United States remained uninvolved, the United States took the lead in bringing Latin American states together to discuss how to keep peace among themselves, to avoid European intervention, and most importantly, to promote trade. United States Secretary of State James Blaine promoted this new Pan Americanism, arguing that the people of the Western hemisphere had a "special relationship" with one another. He was also concerned, however, that current Latin American conflicts would invite European intervention and thus threaten the Monroe Doctrine (Mecham 1961, 50). The Monroe Doctrine originated with President James Monroe in 1823. It warned European powers, specifically Russia, France, and Spain, that any attempt to control the newly independent Latin American states would be considered a threat to U.S. peace and safety. Throughout the 1800s, the declaration did not play a large role in U.S. policy. However, with the rise of the United States to Great Power status at the end of the nineteenth century, it became the "cornerstone" of U.S. foreign policy (Atkins 1997, 341). Secretary of State Blaine believed active U.S. participation in the hemisphere could prevent European intervention. The growth of the industrial and agricultural sectors in the United States also provided an incentive for the government to actively seek greater markets in Latin America as well.

During the 1889 conference, the United States largely confined discussions to the subjects of economics, education, and scientific and social relations, all of which afforded the best prospects for friendly agreement. The U.S. Congress suggested to the president that the agenda include setting up an American customs union, introducing a single silver currency, establishing a single set of customs duties, and adopting an arbitration plan for the solution of disputes and conflicts (Glinkin 1990, 53). Some of the "political" questions avoided during the conference included concerns with juridical equality, territorial integrity, national independence, international obligations, and rights of American states (Mecham 1961, 49). Security was not a primary concern for the United States because it had already assumed responsibility for the security of the hemisphere from external attacks under the Monroe Doctrine. The United States offered assurances to Latin American states that it would participate as an equal with them at the conference, not as a counselor to them. This assurance helped secure Latin American participation despite disappointment that certain "political" issues would not be on the agenda.

There were tangible achievements at this first conference. The first was the creation of the Commercial Bureau for the International Union of American Republics. This Bureau was limited to collecting and publishing commercial, economic, and other information (Glinkin 1990, 55). The second achievement was the adoption of an arbitration convention for settling disputes, which paved the way for the elaborate inter-American peace system of today. The conference was more successful than its predecessors in terms of achieving greater participation. All Latin American states took part (whereas only four had attended the conference in 1826 and seven had participated in 1864). Although Latin American states raised some political issues at the first conference, and at the next three conferences (1901, 1906, 1910), there were no unanimous agreements on any principle other than arbitration. Latin American states were able to reach agreement on a resolution concerning alien rights at both the first and second conferences, but the United States refused to sign it.[17] This weakened the resolution considerably since Latin American states were seeking to establish an international principle to be observed by all states. Despite such disappointments, U.S. leadership during this early period was virtually unchallenged (Mecham 1961, 58). The United States continued to exercise extreme caution in approving the agenda for the Fourth Conference (1910), sanctioning only two "political" topics concerning the pecuniary-claims treaty and the reorganization of the International Bureau of American Republics (discussed later).

When World War I began, Latin American states were forced to address war issues on an ad hoc basis because the United States, prior to the war, had largely prevented discussion of security issues such as neutrality. No multilateral efforts to take concerted action were successful, but many states voiced support for "regional solidarity," thus reinforcing the ideal of Latin American unity. The United States briefly supported a Pan American Pact that provided a guarantee of territorial integrity and political independence under a republican form of government (Whitaker 1954, 123). By 1916, however, Wilson shifted his support to a universal rather than regional forum. He devoted his energies to the establishment of the League of Nations. When the League of Nations formed after the war, 15 out of 20 Latin American states became charter members and the other five states eventually joined as well. There was only sporadic attendance, however, because of the extensive focus on European problems within the League. When the United States chose not to join, many Latin American states viewed this as a betrayal of their ideal of pacific settlement of disputes through an IO.

The U.S. refusal to join the League, for a number of reasons unrelated to Latin American relations, was symbolic of its lack of solidarity with Latin American states. Throughout this period, the United States took the lead in the Inter-American System without much support or protest from Latin American states. Latin Americans, however, remained distrustful of the United States, especially after President Theodore Roosevelt established protectorates over Cuba (1898–1902) and Panama (1903), and intervened in the Dominican Republic (1905) to force it to pay its international debts. U.S. marines occupied Nicaragua from 1912 to 1913, and Haiti in 1915. In a survey in 1924, only six of 20 Latin American states were free from U.S. interference in the form of official direction of financial policy or the presence of armed forces (Whitaker 1954, 128).

Although U.S.–Latin American relations were not friendly and there was little agreement on common principles during this period, the Inter-American System did succeed in creating an administrative organ to carry out the work of the Conferences. At the First Conference, the first permanent secretariat was established. This body served as a modest administrative agency, collecting and distributing commercial information. It was located in Washington, D.C., under the supervision of the U.S. Department of State. At the Second Conference in 1901, the secretariat was transformed into the International Bureau of American Republics. Its functions were expanded slightly, no longer limiting it to a commercial role. The International Commission of Jurists was formed at the Third Conference (1906) to draft codes on international law and states' rights. At the Fourth Conference (1910), the International Bureau became the Pan American Union (PAU). The PAU expanded upon the activities of the International Bureau and developed a more complex administrative structure (see Ball 1969, chapter 1; and Kelchner 1930). It was specifically prohibited, however, from dealing with "political" matters (i.e., peace and security issues). The U.S. Secretary of State became chairman of the Pan American Board, and the United States refused to consider making the chairmanship an elected position. The United States thus maintained its control over the administration of the Inter-American System as well as over Conference agendas. To many Latin American governments, however, the value of this new Pan Americanism found in the Inter-American System was too high to be abandoned because of U.S. dominance (Mecham 1961, 73).

Although the first four conferences did not produce many results in terms of agreement on new principles, they did lay the foundation for greater achievements in the future. Adoption of international principles guiding the behavior of all states could not proceed quickly, but each discussion that was held brought states closer to consensus on a number of principles, including nonintervention, sovereignty, nonaggression, and pacific settlement of disputes.

Third Phase

A third phase in inter-American relations began with the Fifth Inter-American Conference in 1923. At that conference, Latin American states became more assertive and brought more political topics to the agenda. These topics included: (1) the organization of the PAU; (2) consideration of the work by the Commission of Jurists; (3) consideration of a closer association; (4) consideration of wider application of the principle of judicial and arbitral settlement of disputes; (5) reduction and limitation of armaments; (6) consideration of questions arising out of an encroachment by a non-American power on the rights of an American state; and (7) consideration of the rights of aliens resident within an American State (Mecham 1961, 95). Latin American states were no longer willing to confine their discussions to topics on which unanimous agreement was assured. This willingness to tackle difficult questions and struggle toward consensus helped to introduce for discussion many of the principles on which the OAS stands today.

Latin American states expressed concern with many of the U.S. political and economic policies and mounted an attack on the U.S. view of Pan Americanism, which resisted multilateral security arrangements.

The United States chose to take a "hands off" approach rather than directly confronting Latin American states on controversial issues. The United States was not particularly interested in transforming the organization as many Latin Americans were. Latin American states were interested in reducing U.S. preponderance within the PAU, in expanding the role of the PAU, and in promoting conflict resolution through multilateral instruments. The United States did its best to delay and weaken the proposals that were put forward along these lines. For example, when the Uruguayan proposal for an "American League of Nations" based on the Monroe Doctrine was put forward, the U.S. representative stated that the Monroe Doctrine would remain a unilateral policy. The United States was not interested in cooperating to form an international or regional League of Nations at this time. It was equally uncooperative on the issue of arbitration, believing that existing peace instruments were adequate.

Eventually, however, some reforms were passed. They included revisions to the Pan American Board. All states were allowed to have a designated representative, not just their ambassador to the United States, sit on the Board. This allowed all states to be represented whether they were on good diplomatic terms with the United States or not.[18] The chair and vice-chair became elected positions weakening U.S. control over the Board. Four standing committees were created to assist the PAU in handling issues of economic and commercial relations, international labor, public health, and intellectual cooperation. This expansion addressed the Latin American concern that the PAU was simply a bureaucracy for a commercial organization rather than the secretariat for an international, multipurpose organization. Thus began the gradual expansion of the organization into many different areas of regional concern. The Treaty to Avoid or Prevent Conflicts between the American States (Gondra Pact 1922) was the most important of several efforts by American states to establish an inter-American regime for dealing with interstate conflicts. The Pact provided guidelines for submitting to a commission of inquiry all controversies not settled through diplomatic channels and not submitted to arbitration in accordance with existing treaties. A commission of five members would investigate the dispute over the period of a year, during which time the disputants would agree not to make war preparations. After the investigation, the commission would report its findings in hopes of helping the parties reach a negotiated settlement (Mecham 1961, 98). This Pact helped codify in a multilateral agreement the norm of peaceful settlement that had previously been embodied mostly in bilateral treaties.

When the Sixth Inter-American Conference met in 1928, relations were more contentious than ever between Latin American countries and the United States. U.S. policies were criticized, particularly its armed interventions in the Caribbean (Glinkin 1990, 79). This lack of solidarity within the Inter-American System stemmed from the Roosevelt Corollary (1904) to the Monroe Doctrine, which had led to regular U.S. intervention in Latin America for security purposes. The Roosevelt Corollary was added to the Monroe Doctrine by President Theodore Roosevelt, stating that "chronic wrongdoing" within Latin American states might result in the United States exercising an international police power. Following in Roosevelt's footsteps, President Taft intervened in Nicaragua and Honduras to restore order and stability to the Canal Zone. Latin American states highly resented these acts of intervention. The United States, however, simply refused to accept the principle of nonintervention. This principle, which held that "no state has the right to intervene in the internal or external affairs of another," was of crucial importance to Latin American states. It was a corollary to the principle of juridical equality of sovereign states on which inter-American relations were based. Latin American states recognized, however, that a resolution on nonintervention without the concurrence of the United States would be meaningless. Thus the topic was postponed until the Seventh Conference.

Latin American states were not as willing to accept U.S. intransigence on the issue of reforming the Governing Board of the PAU. In order to further limit U.S. power on the Board, Latin Americans voted to restrict the Board from having "functions of a political character." The Latin American members wanted the Inter-American System to address political issues of concern to them, including issues of security, but they did not want the PAU to have control over these issues. Control was to remain in the hands of the state representatives to the international conferences at which these topics were discussed. By using their majority power, Latin American states could hypothetically control political issues in this forum, but in reality, the United States maintained a strong influence over many of the smaller member states and thus still blocked political issues from the agenda. U.S. resistance to adopting resolutions concerning nonintervention and the juridical equality of states prevented further progress toward establishing these as international principles.

Fourth Phase
During the fourth phase of development, from 1933 to 1948, relations between the United States and Latin Americans gradually improved beginning with the Good Neighbor Policy of President Franklin D. Roosevelt. At the Seventh Inter-American Conference held in Montevideo in 1933, the United States reversed its long-held position and declared that it was

open to discuss any topic of general interest to the hemisphere. This reversal was the culmination of a number of changes in U.S. policy that were initiated shortly after the Sixth Conference. The hostility evident at the Sixth Conference provided a clear indication that the tensions between the United States and Latin America could not be resolved except by reorienting U.S. policy. The Coolidge administration had recognized that U.S. acceptance of the principle of nonintervention would be necessary for further institutional cooperation with Latin American states. President Calvin Coolidge had sent diplomats to Mexico and Nicaragua to resolve tensions over prior U.S. imperial policies. President Herbert Hoover took even more significant steps toward reconciling the United States with Latin America by repudiating the Roosevelt Corollary to the Monroe Doctrine, withdrawing marines from Nicaragua and Haiti, and notifying American investors in Latin America that they must exhaust local remedies before appealing for diplomatic protection. President Roosevelt continued this trend toward more cooperative, less imperial relations with Latin America with his Good Neighbor Policy. He stated that the essential qualities of a good neighbor included mutual understanding and a sympathetic appreciation of the others' point of view. In this way he hoped to build a system in which confidence, friendship, and goodwill were the cornerstones (Mecham 1961, 114).

Roosevelt's willingness to expand the discussions at the Seventh Conference led to significant progress on adopting many of the principles that Latin Americans had advocated for years. The Convention on the Rights and Duties of States was drafted at the conference. It included provisions on the juridical equality of states, nonintervention, peaceful settlement, nonrecognition of territorial conquest, and subjection of foreigners to local legal jurisdiction. All the principles that Latin American states had come to embrace and had pressed the United States to accept were adopted. A number of procedures were defined as instruments of pacific settlement, including arbitration, conciliation, mediation, and negotiation. Although pacific settlement was not linked to mutual security in the 1930s, by the 1950s it became intertwined with the concept of hemispheric security. States recognized that a dispute in one country or between members destabilized and weakened the system as a whole. Members took an active interest in the disputes in the hemisphere, encouraging the belligerent parties to pursue peaceful settlement of their disputes in order to maintain regional stability. As long as mechanisms for settlement were engaged and escalation was not an immediate concern, members did not need to risk intervention in order to protect their own interests. Thus, peaceful settlement and mutual security became closely linked (and still upheld the principle of nonintervention).

Another component of pacific settlement, the principle of consultation, was formally integrated into the Inter-American System at the Eighth Conference (1938). Most of the provisions for the resolution on consultative procedures had been drawn up at the Inter-American Conference for the Maintenance of Peace held in 1936. At the conference, it had been established that any act that disturbed the peace of an American state affected each and every state and justified the initiation of consultation between American states. At the Eighth Conference in Lima, the means to achieve consultation, which had been left unspecified in 1936, were laid out. The machinery to implement the procedure of consultation was to be handled by a Meeting of Foreign Ministers. The Latin American states did not want to entrust such an important political task to the Governing Board of the PAU at this time, still fearing U.S. dominance of the Board. Thus, the Foreign Ministers were to handle any requests for consultation concerning threats to the peace.[19]

As the Inter-American System matured and developed regulations specifying the actions of the Governing Board and Meetings of Foreign Ministers, the number of new agencies and functions in several areas within the Inter-American System were increasing rapidly. For the most part, there was little regulation or coordination of these agencies and they operated separately from the authority of the Governing Board. Some of the issue-areas included technical exchanges in health and scientific fields, as well as cultural programs.

During World War II, a common enemy united most of the hemisphere.[20] Unlike the ad hoc declarations that had been issued during World War I, World War II led to the development of mutual security mechanisms that had never been a part of the system before. The Treaty of Chapultepec (1945) included provisions for *enforcement* of the principles of nonintervention and pacific settlement for the first time. Acts of aggression were to be met with multilateral sanctions. Activities and conferences on topics other than juridical and commercial topics began to increase, thus signaling the increased political focus (i.e., security focus) of the emerging organization.

With the cooperation between the United States and Latin American states on issues ranging from trade to mutual security, the Inter-American System of the 1940s no longer resembled the U.S.-dominated system of the 1890s, nor the Latin American movement of Simón Bolívar initiated in the 1820s. During the 50 years following the First International Conference of American States (1889), the Inter-American System underwent considerable change. Although the first four conferences were initiated and dominated by the United States, Latin American determination and assertiveness were slowly able to transform relations within the Inter-American System. Latin American states and the United States gradually developed more cooperative relations and were able to interact on more equal footing. The United States recognized that further progress in building inter-American relations would require the end of Caribbean imperialism. With the start of the Good Neighbor Policy, stronger ties were made between the United States and Latin America. Once greater cooperation was established, many of the norms that had been evolving in the past decades were formally incorporated as principles of the Inter-American System.

The initial focus of the Inter-American System in the early 1800s was on regional disputes and threats that shaped the principles of nonintervention and pacific settlement of disputes. The disengaged United States displayed little interest in the Pan American movement during this time. The development of the norm of peaceful settlement stemmed from the bilateral negotiations between Latin American states in this early era and continued to develop throughout the next century. The emergence of the principle of regional solidarity/unity was also evident in this early era.

During the period of U.S. dominance from 1889 to 1923, few advances were made in establishing regional principles concerning security issues. Latin American states reasserted themselves at the Fifth Conference in 1923 and brought the principles of nonintervention, arbitration, and consultation to the agenda again. Latin American states pursued the multilateral codification of these principles despite U.S. reluctance and resistance. The impacts of World Wars I and II on the hemisphere expanded the focus of the Inter-American System to address not just regional threats, but extracontinental threats as well. The United States became a more cooperative partner and formal instruments for handling mutual security and consultation emerged after World War II. The United States finally accepted the long-standing regional norms of nonintervention and the juridical equality of states. Beginning with the signing of the Rio Treaty in 1947, and followed by the drafting of the OAS Charter and the Pact of Bogotá in 1948, the Inter-American System underwent a significant transformation. The next section will follow these developments in the Inter-American System and their implications for pacific settlement, hemispheric security, and interstate relations.

The Formation of a Security Regime—The Rio Treaty

The Inter-American Treaty of Reciprocal Assistance, better known as the Rio Treaty, was drafted at the Inter-American Conference on

Maintenance of Continental Peace and Security in Rio de Janeiro in 1947. It was adopted by all 20 Latin American states and the United States and was designed to provide a permanent treaty for "mutual security" after the temporary Act of Chapultepec was dissolved at the end of World War II. The Act of Chapultepec had been drawn up to protect both the territorial integrity and political independence of American states against aggression (regional and extrahemispheric). For the first time, the Act specifically provided for enforcement, stipulating that acts of aggression were to be met by sanctions ranging from the recall of chiefs of diplomatic missions to the use of armed force (Atkins 1997, 12). Following the end of World War II, American states met and drafted the Rio Treaty. The purpose of the Rio Treaty was twofold: (1) to deal effectively with armed attacks and threats of aggression against member states; and (2) to assure peace in the region through improved pacific settlement procedures. The treaty incorporated many of the principles embodied in previous inter-American treaties and declarations including formal condemnation of war or the use of force against other sovereign states, support of nonintervention, and continental solidarity.

On the issue of armed attacks or threats of aggression, the Rio Treaty establishes in Article 3 that an attack on one is considered an attack on all and that all members should undertake to assist the one under attack. Thus, a collective security regime was established. Article 6 states that the Organ of Consultation shall meet immediately "if the inviolability or the integrity of the territory, or the sovereignty, or the political independence of any American state should be affected by an aggression which is not an armed attack, or by an extra-continental or intra-continental conflict, or by any other fact or situation that might endanger the peace of the Americas." This article provides for the defense of the hemisphere from both external and internal threats. Additional acts of aggression are defined in Article 9 as "unprovoked armed attacks by a State against the territory, the people, or the land, sea or air forces of another state; or invasion, by the armed forces of a State, of the territory of an American state, through the trespassing of boundaries demarcated in accordance with a treaty, judicial decision or arbitral award." When any such act of aggression or attack occurs, the Meeting of Foreign Ministers is designated to serve as the Organ of Consultation, with the Governing Board of the PAU to act provisionally until the Foreign Ministers can meet (Articles 11 and 12). After the founding of the OAS the next year, the Council of the OAS was given the responsibility of serving as provisional organ instead of the Governing Board.

In terms of promoting pacific settlement of disputes in the region, the Rio Treaty gives authority to the Meeting of Consultation to "call upon the contending States to suspend hostilities and restore matters to the status quo ante bellum [and to take] all other necessary measures to reestablish or maintain inter-American peace and security for the solution of the conflict by peaceful means" (Article 7). The measures that the Meeting of Consultation has available to it include: recall of chiefs of diplomatic missions, breaking of diplomatic relations, breaking of consular relations, partial or complete interruption of economic relations, of rail, sea, air, postal, telegraphic, telephonic communications, and use of armed force (Article 8). Because the signatory states desired to "consolidat[e] and strengthen their relations of friendship and good neighborliness" (preamble), they promoted consensual action under the Treaty in two ways. First, they determined that decisions must be carried by a two-thirds vote (excluding those states that are directly involved in the dispute). Second, they established that sanction measures are binding on all member states, with the exception that no state will be required to use armed force without its consent. Unlike the UN Security Council, the United States was not given veto power. All states were committed to carrying out the decisions made by a two-third majority of the member states whether they supported the action or not (with the exception of engaging in military action). An example of the application of sanctions can be seen in the case of the Dominican Republic, handled by the Sixth Meeting of Foreign Ministers in 1960. Dominican dictator Rafael Trujillo was accused of intervention in the sovereign domestic affairs of Venezuela. The Organ of Consultation voted to impose sanctions. Member states were to cut diplomatic ties and to interrupt economic relations with the Dominican Republic, ending trade and arms shipments (other applications of the Rio Treaty are discussed in chapters 4–6).

The Charter of the OAS and the Pact of Bogotá

The OAS was created in 1948 at the Ninth Inter-American Conference of American States held in Bogotá.[21] Its creation signaled a new era in inter-American relations in which states in the Western hemisphere came together to "achieve an order of peace and justice, to promote their solidarity, to strengthen their collaboration, and to defend their sovereignty, their territorial integrity, and their independence" (Article 1, OAS Charter).[22] Just as the Rio Treaty included many of the principles concerning pacific settlement that had evolved within the Inter-American

System over the years, the OAS Charter embodied these same principles in a more summary form. Chapter IV of the Charter outlined a number of procedures to promote pacific settlement of disputes, including: negotiation, good offices, mediation, investigation and conciliation, judicial settlement, and arbitration. Chapter V of the Charter reaffirmed the principle of collective security, stating that an attack on one is considered an attack on all. In addition to these principles concerning peace and security, however, the Charter also affirmed that:

1) social justice and social security are bases of lasting peace; 2) economic cooperation is essential to the common welfare and prosperity for the peoples of the continent; 3) spiritual unity of the continent is based on respect for the cultural values of the American countries and requires their close cooperation for the high purposes of civilization; 4) American states proclaim the fundamental rights of the individual without distinction as to race, nationality, creed, or sex; and 5) the education of peoples should be directed toward justice, freedom and peace. (Article 5)

Despite the affirmation of these principles in the Charter, there was some debate at the Ninth Conference on whether to incorporate chapters on economic, social, and cultural cooperation in the Charter. Panama and Mexico argued strongly to include them. In the end, three brief chapters were adopted (Chapters VI–VIII).

It was particularly important to Latin American states that the Charter also include provisions for the juridical equality of states as well as delineating their fundamental rights and duties. These are included in Chapter III of the Charter, which specifically guaranteed states' political and territorial sovereignty. This chapter also promoted peace in the hemisphere by reminding states that they had duties as well as rights: "The right of each State to protect itself and to live its own life does not authorize it to commit unjust acts against another state" (Article 11).

In order for the OAS to uphold the principles listed earlier, and to carry out its stated purposes, the Charter established a number of Organs to oversee peaceful settlement and security, as well as economic, educational, and cultural functions. The Inter-American Conference was established as the supreme organ of the OAS, convening every five years to determine the general actions and policies of the organization. Chapter XI established that the Meeting of Foreign Ministers would convene to consider any problem of an urgent nature and of common interest to the American states, and to serve as the Organ of Consultation. Although the Charter did not include the Rio Treaty in its entirety, it did coordinate the two instruments by including provisions such as the one concerning the Organ of Consultation. The Council was responsible for the proper discharge by the PAU (the secretariat) of the duties assigned to it by the Conference and the Meeting of Foreign Ministers. There was some debate in Bogotá concerning the amount of political power the Council should have. In the end, Latin American states prevailed and limited the scope of political powers the Council possessed. It simply provided oversight of the activities of other organs within the organization. The one provision that gave the Council some political power was the specification that the Council would serve as the provisional organ prior to the Meeting of Foreign Ministers as necessary. Three additional councils were established to oversee more technical duties: the Inter-American Economic and Social Council, the Inter-American Council of Jurists, and the Inter-American Cultural Council. The PAU was designated as the general secretariat of the OAS, headed by the secretary general who was elected for a ten-year term.[23]

The Ninth Inter-American Conference also adopted the American Treaty on Pacific Settlement (Pact of Bogotá). Unlike the Charter and the Rio Treaty, the Pact was rarely used or referred to by member states. The Pact of Bogotá integrated a number of treaties in an effort to consolidate pacific settlement procedures in the hemisphere. A variety of peaceful settlement techniques were included in the Pact: adjudication, arbitration, conciliation, diplomacy, good offices, investigation, and mediation. Once a state ratified the Pact, all previous treaties on pacific settlement were no longer binding. Those states that did not ratify it were still bound by the previous treaties that they had signed. During the Conference, there were disputes about whether states should be obligated to submit disputes for settlement or whether submission should be voluntary. There was also debate about the scope of the disputes that required submission. Delegates eventually decided that all disputes of all sizes must be resolved by peaceful procedure and that they would not be withdrawn until settlement was reached. Only 14 of 21 states ratified the Pact and seven of those did so with reservations. Thus, it has not been as encompassing or effective as the Charter or Rio Treaty have been.

The Rio Treaty and OAS Charter created a new regional security regime unlike any other that existed at the time. The OAS was not merely a collective security arrangement, although the Rio Treaty and certain OAS Charter provisions established the defensive military nature of the organization. Provisions in the Charter also established economic, cultural, and social development functions for the OAS. The internal structure was also unlike that of other organizations. In an effort to counter U.S. dominance in the organization, member states were given an equal vote in the governing Council. Unlike the permanent members in the UN Security Council, no OAS member had veto power. Policies were to be made by majority rule, preferably by consensus. All the values that had evolved into regional principles helped shape the OAS, which would be the new forum for inter-American relations. The Charter and the Rio Treaty codified the regional norms that had evolved over the past century and serve as the most comprehensive, multilateral documents to date.

Summary

The creation of the OAS did not fundamentally alter relations between the United States and Latin America, although it did institutionalize them in many respects. The periodic episodes of antagonism and cooperation seen prior to the founding of the OAS are seen after its creation (and are discussed in chapter 4). The creation of the OAS gave Latin Americans a forum outside of the United Nations in which they could lodge formal complaints against U.S. policies that they considered to be contrary to international law. Latin American states hoped that the OAS would serve to protect state sovereignty from both U.S. and extra hemispheric intervention efforts. Whereas prior to 1948, relations had been shaped by bilateral agreements and other treaties to which not all Latin American states were parties, the OAS Charter and the Rio Treaty united all of Latin America and the United States under uniform rules and mechanisms. The principles that had evolved over a 100-year period beginning with the Pan American movement were included in these documents, further codifying the norms of state sovereignty, nonintervention, peaceful settlement of disputes, territorial integrity, consultation, and representative democracy. Ironically, although Latin Americans were more unified than they had been before, the consolidation of previous agreements also resulted in a single organization that the United States could attempt to use to pursue its policies in Latin America.

CHAPTER 4

THE OAS AND CONFLICT RESOLUTION 1948–89

Introduction

Chapter 3 presented the events leading up to and shaping the formation of the OAS in Bogotá in 1948. This chapter builds upon that historical foundation and examines how the organization has used the formal mechanisms of peaceful settlement and collective security to resolve disputes in the hemisphere. Between 1948 and 1989, the OAS addressed 26 cases of dispute settlement among member states. These disputes took place within the context of the Cold War, with tensions between Latin American military dictatorships and democracies. The conflict resolution efforts varied over time in terms of the level of consensus reached among member states about what principles to invoke, measures to adopt, the extent of the threat posed to the region, and which instruments to apply.

The first section of this chapter lays out the general sequence of events that occur when a dispute arises. The next section briefly discusses the relevant literature on the OAS. I then define my research design in the third section, and discuss the implications of each variable for member relations within the organization. The fourth section examines the first decade of conflict resolution efforts by the OAS. This section depicts a relatively consensual period in which the OAS Council handled consultations under the Rio Treaty. The fifth section explores the changes to the OAS in the 1960s with an examination of the issues raised in the organization concerning the communist revolution in Cuba. The cases during this time indicate a shift in procedure in handling threats related to international communism. The sixth section takes a look at the changes in the organization throughout the 1970s as the OAS went through a period of decline. Although the 50-year period is discussed in three different sections, there are no specific characteristics that make these time periods distinct "eras." Each decade reveals gradual shifts in the types of conflicts that arose and the means used to address them. The three sections help to highlight these changes. The final section applies the hypotheses derived in chapter 2 to the cases collectively to determine which factors most clearly affect U.S. influence within the organization.

The OAS as an Organ for Pacific Settlement

Although the principle of pacific settlement predated the principle of mutual security by nearly three decades, by the end of World War II the two were inextricably intertwined and became common elements of a single system of hemispheric peace and security (Atkins 1997, 93). Prior to World War II, peaceful settlement had emphasized juridical–legal–diplomatic settlement of inter-American disputes. Mutual security, formally introduced in 1936, involved political–military defense against extrahemispheric threats. In the post–World War II era, however, the mutual security and pacific settlement procedures were applied simultaneously to a large number of cases (Atkins 1997, 344). Thus, when disputes arose among members, they were treated as security issues with an emphasis on peaceful settlement. The Charter and the Rio Treaty established coordinated provisions for handling conflicts in the region that upheld the principles of nonintervention and sovereignty valued by members. This section traces the provisions and the standard procedures that were invoked when a dispute arose among members.

When a dispute occurs between or among members, four general options are available (see figure 4.1). The Charter may be invoked; the Rio Treaty may be invoked; the Inter-American Peace Committee (IAPC) may be asked to investigate;[24] or no request may be made of the OAS. Once the Charter or Rio Treaty is invoked, the Council meets to determine whether the request is justified and votes whether to convene the Organ of Consultation. The Council has two choices if it decides to convoke the Organ of Consultation: (1) to choose to establish itself as the provisional Organ while calling for a Meeting of Ministers of Foreign Affairs; or (2) to call for an immediate Meeting of Ministers of Foreign Affairs to serve as the Organ of Consultation.

In practice, once the Organ is convened, the most common action taken is to form an investigating committee. This committee travels to the countries involved and then reports back to the Organ. After hearing the committee's report, the Organ considers resolutions proposed by

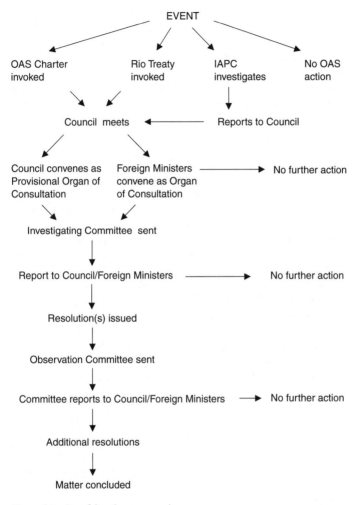

Figure 4.1 Peaceful settlement procedures

various members and then votes on them. Under the Charter and Rio Treaty, the Organ of Consultation (or Provisional Organ) has the authority to impose a variety of sanctions, including recalling diplomatic personnel, breaking diplomatic relations, interrupting economic relations, and using armed force. At this point, the Organ may decide to take no further action, assuming that its resolutions address the problem at hand. If the dispute is unlikely to be resolved by issuing resolutions alone, the Organ may choose to send an observation committee to the scene to report on further incidents and on compliance with the Organ's resolutions. In difficult cases, a small military contingent may be put in place to ensure compliance and report on technical military matters. Additional resolutions may be declared based on further developments in the situation. At any point in this process, the conflict may be resolved and/or the organization may choose not to take any further action.[25]

Contributing Literature

One body of literature that contributes to this research, but that was not discussed in chapter 2, is the literature on the OAS itself. The OAS literature provides an empirical rather than a theoretical context for this research and is used throughout the rest of the book. These works provide a wealth of information about the organization and its numerous functions and activities over the years. Some studies are historical, examining and evaluating the organization's successes and failures (Mecham 1961; Ball 1969; Atkins 1997). Others delve into organizational structure, examining charter principles and decisionmaking processes (Gosselin and Thérien 1997, Tascan 1998). Still others are more policy-oriented, studying the organization in its post–Cold War context and making recommendations for reforms based on changing international norms and emphasizing its new potential (Vaky and Muñoz 1993; OAS Annual Report 1995; Villagran de Leon 1992a,b). Other policy studies review past relations between member states and make predictions for the future (Pastor 1992). Each of these aspects sheds light on the working of the OAS, and its relations with the United States. Most of this literature, however, is descriptive and policy-oriented, lacking deeper theoretical analysis. By combining this empirical work with the theories of organizational sociology discussed in chapter 2, this research establishes a framework to test what institutional conditions affect state influence within the OAS.

The empirical literature on the OAS is combined with a number of single case studies and historical summaries to analyze the functioning of the organization in a more theoretical fashion. Previous studies of the OAS provide details on the different aspects of the OAS that have the potential to impact member states. Studies of the evolution of the organization that emphasize the development of regional principles stress the importance of normative factors within the organization. The literature on the OAS Charter and the legal/juridical aspects of the organization emphasize the potential of structural and procedural variables to impact decisionmaking. The policy literature focuses on the dynamic relations among member states, and suggests that relational factors also ought to be included in an analysis of OAS decisionmaking. Each of these bodies of literature provides a different empirical focus that is incorporated in the analytical framework.

Research Design

This chapter examines 26 cases handled by the OAS under the Rio Treaty and Charter from 1948 to 1989, beginning shortly after the OAS was founded, and ending at the same time as the Cold War drew to a close. Following the end of the Cold War, regional priorities, security concerns, and member relations changed considerably and additional considerations beyond the Cold War analytical framework are necessary to examine these most recent cases. In the 1990s, several new mechanisms were established to address threats to democracy in the region. Cases of conflict resolution following the Cold War are addressed separately in chapter 7 based on the organizational changes, and because the Rio Treaty was not invoked from 1989 (when the United States invaded Panama) to September 2001 (following the terrorist attacks on the United States).

The 26 cases examined in this chapter reveal varying levels of threat to the region over a 50-year period. The greatest perceived threats were seen in the 1960s, with lower-level threats seen in the 1950s and in the 1970s and 1980s. The cases also indicate a gradual shift in the level of consensus within the organization, in the organ convened to address the conflict, and in the types of conflicts addressed. Shifts in policy preferences are evident in the level of consensus members are able to achieve when issuing resolutions to resolve regional disputes. The greatest consensus among member states is seen during the 1950s, following the creation of the OAS, with a gradual decline seen over the next several decades. Changes in the organizational environment can be seen in the different way that cases are handled by the Organ of Consultation over time. Whereas the Council handled all of the earliest cases, by the 1970s the Foreign Ministers had become the primary organ for addressing conflict resolution. Finally, changes in the international and regional environment are reflected in the types of cases handled by the organization including struggles between democratic and nondemocratic governments, and efforts at communist subversion. An exploration of these cases provides a comparison and contrast of the four organizational variables presented in chapter 2 that influence interstate relations within the OAS. The historical examination also reveals changing trends in conflict resolution efforts in the region.

Threat Level

The first characteristic of the cases to be evaluated is the level of threat to regional stability. This variable is difficult to measure since it is the *perception* of threat on which member states base their actions. It is important to be able to characterize the level of threat to the region that arises from a dispute because it influences not only the level of interest of member states in the dispute, but also the type of responses to be considered by the OAS. Disputes that pose a considerable threat to members are much more likely to provoke a military response, whereas ones that do not immediately threaten the security of members are more likely to inspire diplomatic efforts. In addition to considering the threat to individual members' security, there is also consideration of how threatening a conflict is to regional stability. If there is a risk of the conflict escalating to include other member states, the threat to regional stability is higher. The perceived level of threat to the region has an indirect impact on the United States as it considers what proposals to present to the Council or Foreign Ministers. As noted in chapter 3, the United States has historically resorted to military options when responding to crises in Latin America. Latin American states have long expressed a preference for diplomacy over military force. This creates the potential for disagreement within the organization whenever a dispute arises, particularly one that is only mid-level, and not a high threat to the region.

Threats are classified as high, mid, or low based on the number of countries involved and the potential for escalation. Individual member states might base their evaluations on such factors as the degree of militarization and public explanations for the conflict. For example, a dispute that the combatants claim is territorial would not be viewed as threatening to a non-border state. However, rather than trying to measure individual assessments and then aggregate them, threats are assessed based on a region-wide perspective such as would be taken in the Council or a Meeting of Foreign Ministers. Such factors as militarization and justifications for the conflict as well as threats of use of military force all fall under assessments of the potential for escalation. Disputes that are considered a high level of threat to the region are those that include widespread violence (based on military and civilian casualties) and/or the risk of affecting all member states. Violence is considered widespread when engagement by the military forces with other armed forces, or civilian riots or other violent confrontations result in over 1,000 casualties. A nuclear threat in the region is one event that places all members at risk (i.e., the Cuban missile crisis, 1962). Members would be at risk environmentally if a nuclear weapon(s) were to be detonated. Such a threat would also risk initiating a military arms race between competing armed forces and would undermine the regional nuclear-free zone established in the Tlatelolco Treaty.

Based on the criteria of widespread violence and impact on all member states, only two Latin American conflicts fall into this category (both Cuban 1962 cases). A few conflicts have had a high number of casualties but have not necessarily been conflicts that risk affecting all members. For example, the Soccer War between El Salvador and Honduras resulted in over 1,000 dead and at least 6,000 wounded, but did not risk escalating to include other member states. The dispute was over immigration issues between the two states that did not involve other Latin American states.

A mid-level threat is one in which two or more members are involved and in which members believe regional stability is threatened, but without the widespread violence or the risk to all members seen in cases with a high level of threat. Conflicts can generate regional instability in a number of ways. For example, in 1948, the ideological tensions arising from the border clashes between rebels in Nicaragua and the Costa Rican military produced a "situation [that was] abnormal and dangerous to inter-American peace . . . [causing] an atmosphere of mutual distrust, constant anxiety, and open hostility [in Central America and the Caribbean]" (Inter-American Treaty of Reciprocal Assistance Applications vol. 1, 1948). Regional stability can be threatened either by political/ideological circumstances (as in the example given here) or by the direct or indirect support of the disputants by other member states. Thus, if Latin American states are divided over an issue, such as the democracy versus dictatorship cases throughout the 1950s, there is considerable potential for member states to become involved indirectly in supporting the disputants. Conflicts can affect regional stability by generating floods of refugees, instigating domestic uprisings, and disrupting trade.

A conflict considered a low-level threat is one where there is little risk of escalation or regional instability and/or only a single member is involved (i.e., a civil war). The case of Honduras–Nicaragua (1957) is a good example. The two states were involved in limited military engagements in a disputed border region. The OAS brokered a cease-fire and troop withdrawal plan and the case was submitted to the International

Court of Justice. No other states were threatened by the border clashes, nor did they feel an ideological affinity to support either Nicaragua or Honduras in this dispute. Thus, the threat level was low.

The two examples given here also indicate that the type of dispute is important in assessing the level of threat. Latin America has not had many significant ethnic conflicts on the scale of those in Africa. Most disputes are ideological and/or territorial. In terms of escalation and threat level, certain conflicts can lead to greater regional instability than others and thus a higher level of threat. For example, territorial disputes are less threatening than ideological disputes on issues such as democracy versus dictatorship and international communism. The latter two risk drawing many more members into a conflict either directly or indirectly than a territorial dispute does. When members feel that a certain ideology threatens their regime then they are compelled to support a neighbor who shares their ideology and is engaged in a dispute. For example, in the 1950s, President José Figueres of Costa Rica engaged in rhetorical challenges to the dictator of Nicaragua, Anastasio Somoza, in an effort to promote democracy and socioeconomic reform in the region. Figueres' aggressive campaigns aroused the bitter opposition of several dictatorial leaders in addition to Somoza, including Pérez Jiménez of Venezuela and Rafael Trujillo of the Dominican Republic (Mecham 1961, 403). When a military conflict broke out along the Nicaraguan/Costa Rican border in 1955, the dispute was considered a threat to regional stability because of the risk of more states becoming involved. Territorial disputes do not invoke the same kind of sympathy among member states. Disputes that involve ideological threats are much more likely to cause regional instability by involving more members than a territorial dispute would.

Consensus

The second factor to be considered in comparing cases and examining changes over time is the level of consensus among members. There are two different aspects to consider when examining consensus within the OAS. One aspect involves the degree of consensus among only the Latin American member states. The second involves the level of agreement between the United States and Latin American members. In many cases, there is no disagreement among members as to what actions should be taken to address regional conflict. Two different outcomes to controversial U.S. proposals are possible, however, based on the level of consensus among Latin American members. If Latin American states are unified in opposition to a U.S. proposal, the United States is unlikely to get its proposal passed. If Latin American states are divided and unable to present a proposal for action, the United States has the opportunity to provide strong leadership and gain support for its own proposal. Members seem to prefer a U.S. plan of action to no plan. For example, when a countercoup occurred in the Dominican Republic in 1965, the Council did not take any action until the United States unilaterally intervened and then proposed a multilateral peace force. Although some members strongly opposed U.S. actions, their inability to propose appropriate alternative measures resulted in the creation of an OAS-approved peace force dominated by the United States. Although Latin American states did not favor a U.S.-dominated force, their failure to approve the multilateral force would have weakened the organization and given it even less control over the situation than their sanctioning of the U.S. force. By acting on U.S. plans when there are no other alternatives, the organization maintains at least nominal multilateral control over U.S. actions.

Consensus also impacts the ability of the organization to issue strong, clear resolutions. Member states value consensus within the organization and prefer to act in a unified manner whenever possible. In order to satisfy all members, and thus act consensually, the wording of resolutions sometimes becomes weak and ambiguous. Because the level of consensus among Latin American members can directly impact the ability of the United States to influence OAS responses to conflicts, it is important to have a sense of the level of agreement among member states in each dispute case. By looking at the degree of consensus between Latin American members and the United States, one is able to pinpoint which cases might be of the most interest to evaluate in terms of examining U.S. influence within the organization (i.e., cases in which there is considerable disagreement/low consensus between the United States and Latin American members).

Consensus is classified as "high" when there is general agreement on the actions to be taken by the organization (i.e., unanimity). This means that Latin American states are in agreement with each other and that the United States is also in agreement with Latin American members. When some Latin American members are in disagreement, and/or the United States is in mild disagreement with proposed actions, there is mid-level consensus.[26] Mild disagreement generally occurs in cases when members have shared goals, but prefer differing means to pursue them. For example, when the Foreign Ministers imposed sanctions on the Dominican Republic (1960) for intervention in Venezuela, Brazil opposed coercive measures in favor of moral sanctions and persuasion to preserve inter-American unity. Members most frequently express their dissenting opinions through the inclusion of Statements (or Reservations) attached to the end of resolutions with which they are not in full agreement. These statements allow members to express divergent views while still upholding consensus by voting in favor of a resolution. Thus, if there are between one and five statements expressing points of disagreement with the text of a resolution, I consider the degree of consensus to be mid-level. An example of mid-level consensus can be seen in the Fifth Meeting of Foreign Ministers in 1959 that met to seek solutions to Caribbean tensions and the extensive revolutionary activity in the region. Most members, including the United States, favored a strict nonintervention stance while also condemning unnamed dictatorships in the region. The Foreign Ministers adopted the Declaration of Santiago, which supported representative democracy, and created the Inter-American Commission on Human Rights (IACHR). Although Uruguay and Argentina voted in favor of the Declaration and the creation of the Commission, they both issued Reservations. Uruguay had constitutional reservations concerning the Commission. Argentina was concerned about the structure and power to be invested in such an international agency.

Finally, an acrimonious debate among Latin Americans, or between the United States and Latin American states, results in a "low" level of consensus. Evidence of strong disagreement among members can include abstentions or votes in opposition to a proposal in addition to statements or reservations made by members. Within the OAS, where much value is placed on consensus, an abstention or opposition vote is a strong statement. In addition, when there is strong debate within the organization, there are likely to be public statements made concerning state preferences and defending the governmental positions of members. There are two main distinctions between mid- and low-levels of consensus based on the kind of disagreements among members, and the number of divergent opinions. In mid-level cases, the debate is over the *means* used to pursue a common goal, and five or fewer members express their disagreement. In cases with a low level of consensus, members disagree about the *goals* and actions being pursued by the organization, and more than five members register their opposition.

An example of a low level of consensus can be seen at the Tenth Meeting of Foreign Ministers in 1965. When the United States presented a proposal to send an Inter American Peace Force to the Dominican Republic, Mexico, Chile, Ecuador, Peru, and Uruguay voted in opposition, and Venezuela abstained. The level of consensus is assessed both during the debates held by the Council or Foreign Ministers based on public statements and meeting minutes, and at the conclusion of the meetings based on votes and official statements attached to the resolutions. As noted earlier, the strong desire for consensual action often results in all members reaching a general agreement on the final resolutions that are issued by the Council or Foreign Ministers. Thus, it is important to assess not only the final outcome as indicated by voting and member statements, but also the variety of proposals put forth and the context of the debate on these proposals.

Organ of Consultation/Principles

The third factor to consider when comparing cases of conflict resolution is which Organ of the OAS is responsible for handling the case (i.e., Council or Meeting of Foreign Ministers), and which Treaty/Articles are invoked (Rio Treaty or Charter). These characteristics are linked to the hypothesis concerning regional principles. Each article invoked establishes that certain principles are at stake in a given conflict. The conditions in each case largely determine the organ and instruments that are used. For example, Article 19 of the Charter, which prohibits coercive measures against another member state, will only be invoked if there is evidence of such actions being taken (as in the Ecuador–U.S. case in 1971). These institutional characteristics determine the set of procedures to be followed when a dispute occurs. It is important to identify which articles are invoked in each case because they specify which regional principles are at stake, shape organizational responses, and set the tone for the meeting. The articles that are invoked are also indicative of the level of military (or other) threat to the region. Some articles are intended to convoke a meeting of consultation when there is a general threat to the region, while others set more specific justifications for a meeting, such as when an unprovoked armed attack has occurred.

Four different articles of the Rio Treaty have been invoked historically (6, 8, 9, 11). Article 6 of the Rio Treaty is the most commonly invoked article. It states,

> If the inviolability or the integrity of the territory or the sovereignty or political independence of any American State should be affected by an aggression which is not an armed attack or by an extra-continental or intra-continental conflict, or by any other fact or situation that might endanger the peace of America, the Organ of Consultation shall meet immediately in order to agree on the measures which must be taken in

case of aggression to assist the victim of the aggression or, in any case, the measures which should be taken for the common defense and for the maintenance of the peace and security of the Continent. (Inter-American Treaty of Reciprocal Assistance, 1947, Article 6)

Article 9 (Rio Treaty) is invoked far less frequently. It further characterizes aggression as an unprovoked armed attack by a state against the territory, the people, or the land, sea, or air forces of another state; or invasion by the armed forces of a state, of the territory of an American state, through the trespassing of demarcated boundaries. Article 8 (Rio Treaty) is occasionally invoked when calling for a Meeting of Consultation. It lays out the measures that the Organ may apply to enforce compliance with the Treaty. These measures include: recall of chiefs of diplomatic missions, breaking diplomatic relations, breaking consular relations, partial or complete interruption of economic relations, of rail, sea, air, postal, telegraphic, and telephonic communications, and use of armed force. Article 11 (Rio Treaty) states, "the consultation to which the Treaty refers shall be carried out by means of the Meeting of Ministers of Foreign Affairs of the states which have ratified the treaty, or in the manner or by organ which may be agreed upon in the future." It is invoked when a member specifically wants the Foreign Ministers to handle a case rather than the Council.

Three articles of the OAS Charter have been invoked when calling for a meeting of an Organ of Consultation (19, 39, 40). Article 39 of the Charter resembles Article 6 of the Rio Treaty since it lays out the circumstances for when a Meeting of Consultation may be called. It states that a Meeting of Consultation of Foreign Ministers shall be held in order to consider problems of an urgent nature and of common interest to the American States. Article 40 of the Charter specifies that any member may request that a Meeting of Consultation be called. The request shall be addressed to the Council, which shall decide by an absolute majority whether a meeting should be held. Article 19 has only been invoked once (by Ecuador against the United States). It states that no country may use or encourage the use of coercive measures of economic or political character to force the sovereign will of another state to obtain advantages from it. Sanctions can only be applied multilaterally through a majority vote in the OAS. Although the invocation of certain principles does not have any direct implications for the ability of the United States to influence decisions made within the OAS, the principles do shape the tone of the debates within a Meeting of Consultation. Certain actions may be considered more or less appropriate based on the principles invoked. For example, when Article 8 (Rio) is invoked, laying out specific provisions to enforce compliance, it is likely that the Organ will take measures beyond diplomatic mediation to remedy the dispute. Identification of the principles within the Rio Treaty and Charter that justify a Meeting of Consultation also indicates what the threshold is for a matter to be brought before the organization.[27]

One factor that shows little variation is the level of resources employed by the organization. It is analyzed in chapters 5 and 6 in the case studies, but is not included in the historical examination because of the lack of variation. When looking at the resources employed in carrying out decisions, I found that there was a range of resources utilized, from diplomatic actions and pressures to military mobilization. In most cases, however, the instruments of choice were nonmilitary, reflecting a relatively low investment of resources.[28] This diplomatic emphasis suggests that the organization has few extra resources for military operations. A high level of resources is indicated by the use of military resources to carry out the resolutions of the Organ of Consultation. A mid-level use of resources is measured by one or more committees carrying on activities following the conclusion of the Meeting of Consultation (i.e., monitoring committees, research committees, etc.). If no committee work continues after the meeting and no military resources are used, the level of resources used is considered low.

By assessing the threat level, the type of conflict, the level of consensus within the organization, and the responsive organ and article invoked, I identify patterns of interaction that reveal organizational changes over time and help to explain the changing levels of U.S. influence within the organization in different cases. The following section will begin this comparison by examining early efforts at conflict resolution by the OAS.

The Decade of Consensus: Conflict Resolution from 1948–59[29]

Six of the seven cases handled by the OAS during this first decade have a number of characteristics in common including the types of disputes that were brought to the Council and the way they were handled by the organization. The conflicts were, for the most part, disputes between democracies and dictatorships and were perceived as mid- to low-level threats to the region. There was a relatively high degree of consensus among members in addressing these conflicts (see table 4.1). All the disputes were handled by the Council acting as provisional Organ of Consultation under the Rio Treaty. The one exceptional case is

Table 4.1 Cases invoking the Rio Treaty or the OAS Charter in chronological order (1948–89)

Cases	Date	Council or FM	Resources	Threat level	Consensus U.S.-LA	Consensus LA-LA	Brief description
Costa Rica–Nicaragua	1948	C	Mid	Mid	High	High	Costa Rica alleges invasion by Nicaragua; Pact of Amity signed; troops withdrawn
Caribbean	1949	C	Low	Mid	Mid	Mid	General instability in the region; active rebel forces
Guatemala	1954	C	NA	Mid	Mid	Mid	Coup removes Guatemala President Arbenz before Council can act
Costa Rica–Nicaragua	1955	C	High	Mid	High	High	Each country accuses the other of intervention; exile activity; governments sign conciliation agreement
Honduras–Nicaragua	1957	C	Low	Low	High	High	Territorial dispute; cease-fire signed; case to Int'l Court of Justice
Panama	1959	C	High	Low	High	High	Small invasion force, mostly Cuban; persuaded to surrender by OAS intermediaries
Nicaragua	1959	C	Low	Mid	Mid	Mid	Anti-Somoza rebels from Costa Rica/Honduras; CR/Hon pledge to restrain exiles

	Year	Case					Description
Caribbean	1959	FM 5	Low	Mid	Mid	High	DR charges Cuba and Ven of plotting invasion; general regional instability
Dominican Republic–Venezuela	1960	FM 6	Mid	Mid	Mid	High	DR attempt to assassinate Ven President Betancourt; DR condemned, sanctions imposed
Cuba	1960	FM 7	Low	Mid	Low	High	Cuban intervention; Soviet/Chinese condemnation
Cuba	1962	C	High	High	High	High	Soviet intervention; missile crisis
Cuba	1962	FM 8	Low	High	Low	Low	Cuban activities viewed as threat to the peace; Cuba effectively ousted from OAS
Dominican Republic–Haiti	1963	C	Low	Low	Mid	High	Each country accuses the other of illegal exile activities; governments agree to negotiations
Cuba	1964	FM 9	Low	Mid	Mid	Low	Sanctions expanded against Cuba for continued intervention activities
Panama–U.S.	1964	C	Low	Low	Mid	High	"Flag Riots" over refusal to fly Panamanian flag in the Canal Zone
Dominican Republic	1965	FM 10	High	Low	Low	Low	Coup; countercoup; multilateral peacekeeping; elections
Cuba–Venezuela	1967	FM 12	Low	Mid	High	High	Cuban intervention in Venezuela; sanctions expanded

Table 4.1 Continued

Cases	Date	Council or FM	Resources	Threat level	Consensus U.S.-LA	Consensus LA-LA	Brief description
El Salvador–Honduras	1969	FM 13	High	Mid	High	High	"Soccer War"; immigration disputes; cease-fire, withdrawal, dispute settlement procedures
Ecuador–U.S.	1971	FM 14	Low	Low	Mid	High	Fishing rights dispute; territorial waters; negotiations recommended
Cuba	1974	FM 15	Low	Low	Low	Low	Proposal to lift sanctions does not receive two thirds vote
Cuba	1975	FM 16	Low	Low	Mid	Mid	Economic sanctions no longer enforced
Nicaragua	1978	FM 17	Mid	Mid	Low	High	Sandinista revolution; proposed peacekeeping force rejected
Costa Rica–Nicaragua	1978	FM 18	Low	Low	Mid	Mid	Nicaragua invasion of CR territory; observers placed on border
Ecuador–Peru	1981	FM 19	Low	Low	High	High	Territorial dispute
Argentina–U.K.	1982	C > FM 20	Mid	Low	Low	High	Falklands/Malvinas conflict; Council supports Argentina and calls for a cease-fire
Panama–U.S.	1989	FM 21	Low	Low	Low	High	U.S. removal of President Manuel Noriega

Guatemala (1954) that least resembles the other cases during this time, dealing instead with the threat of communism to the region.

Shortly after the OAS was created, it faced its first challenge to resolve a dispute between members in accordance with the provisions of the recently signed Rio Treaty. On December 11, 1948, an armed incursion into Costa Rica from Nicaragua occurred. The Council met quickly at the request of the Costa Rican ambassador, convoked itself as the provisional Organ of Consultation, and sent an investigating committee to the two countries.[30] Based on the committee's reports, the Council unanimously approved a resolution calling on both governments to eliminate the conditions that led to the dispute, to abstain from further hostile acts against each other, and to observe the principle of nonintervention. A committee of military experts was sent to the border to ensure the effective fulfillment of the Council's resolutions. Another special committee of the provisional Organ of Consultation helped draft a Pact of Amity, which both sides signed on February 21, 1949. The handling of the Costa Rican–Nicaraguan case (1948) closely resembles the processes adopted for the latter cases that were handled during this early period.

The second case raised in the OAS addressed the "Caribbean situation" in 1949, which involved accusations and counteraccusations of intervention from the Dominican Republic against Haiti, Cuba, and Guatemala. In the end, the Council issued a series of resolutions that severely criticized the Dominican Republic, Cuba, and Guatemala. Only Haiti was not criticized for engaging in subversive activity. The Council recommended that all the parties engage in mediation and sent a monitoring committee to report on the progress of such talks. Sanctions were threatened if the peace was not kept. The next case brought to the OAS was Guatemala (1954). In this case, President Jacabo Arbenz of Guatemala, who some feared to be a communist, faced an invading force and was forced to resign and leave the country before any substantive actions were taken by the OAS. In 1955 the tensions between Costa Rica and Nicaragua came to the attention of the Council a second time when Costa Rican rebels who had trained within Nicaragua crossed into Costa Rica. The situation was resolved by a Special Committee of the Council that negotiated two agreements between Nicaragua and Costa Rica. The first one implemented the Pact of Amity signed in 1949 and the second one agreed to continued monitoring of the borders by the OAS. The only territorial dispute handled by the OAS during the 1950s was between Honduras and Nicaragua in 1957. The OAS investigating committee helped secure a cease-fire and troop withdrawal from the disputed region. A second committee worked with the parties to specify agreeable juridical procedures to conclusively settle the dispute. Both countries agreed to a ruling by the International Court of Justice.

In 1959 several cases arose. In April, Panama requested a Meeting of Consultation to deal with 87 armed men who had landed on the Panamanian coast and refused to surrender to the Panamanian military. An investigating committee gained the surrender of the soldiers and further landings were deterred by multilateral air and sea patrols authorized by the Council. In June, Nicaragua invoked the Rio Treaty requesting that the Council meet to address an invasion by approximately 400 rebels (many of them Nicaraguan exiles). The Council sent a special committee to investigate the situation. The neighboring states of Costa Rica and Honduras agreed to suppress any further insurgencies operating within their territory and the Council issued a final resolution urging members to uphold the principle of nonintervention.

Characteristics of Conflict Resolution from 1948 to 1959

In terms of relations between the United States and Latin American countries, the 1950s was a decade of consensus. In all seven cases there was a high- to mid-level degree of consensus among members in handling these conflicts. An example of a dispute where there was a high level of consensus is the case of Panama (1959). When Panama faced a force of largely Cuban invaders on its coast with the threat of additional invading forces, it requested a Meeting of Consultation. (Panama did not accuse Cuba because it believed the government had not aided the invaders.) The Council voted unanimously to invoke the Rio Treaty. Air and sea patrols were mounted quickly. The Cuban government even sent a representative to help negotiate with the invaders and secure their surrender. The Council was able to respond quickly and effectively, and members were in agreement on the actions to be taken to aid the victim of aggression (i.e., Panama). In two of the cases in which there was mid-level consensus (Caribbean, 1949 and Guatemala, 1954) the disagreement among members was based mostly on the juridical competence of the OAS and its governing bodies to handle the cases. There was not disagreement on the actions to be taken once the cases were addressed by the Council. In the Caribbean case (1949), Mexico and Argentina argued that the IAPC did not have juridical competence to deal with issues of a "general nature." Other members however, including the United States, wanted the IAPC to be involved in studying the unrest in the region. The IAPC did investigate and report back to the Council before the Council issued its final resolutions admonishing all sides in the conflict to observe their commitments to end their hostile propaganda and reestablish good relations.

Consensus was high during the 1950s because members agreed on the actions that should be taken to restore peace when conflicts broke out. L. Ronald Scheman (1988, 5) notes, "the machinery of the OAS functioned over the early years because of the underlying consensus among the member nations as to the values and kind of world they [wanted] for their people." Members believed that using the mechanisms established in the Rio Treaty and Charter for peaceful settlement was important for maintaining regional stability. The biggest point of contention among members during this period concerning application of the Rio Treaty was the degree to which the OAS should defend or condemn dictatorships when they were threatened by armed forces. For example, in 1959 many members were ambivalent about defending the Somoza dictatorship in Nicaragua when it faced a military uprising, but they were adamant about upholding the principle of nonintervention if these forces actually originated from outside Nicaraguan territory. This struggle was evident in the Nicaraguan case (1959) when the investigating committee delayed its departure for two weeks after being appointed. There was a reluctance to help Somoza defend his regime. In most cases, the committee is on the scene within a few days. By the time they had arrived in Nicaragua, Somoza had already arrested the rebels and no longer needed assistance from the OAS, thus negating their uncomfortable situation. Members continually struggled to determine the degree to which the OAS should be involved when dictatorships were threatened by rebel groups (either internal or external). This difficult issue would continue to be a problem for members into the next decade. Despite the tensions raised between democracies and dictatorships, however, relations among OAS members were remarkably consensual during this period.

The level of threat to the region from the conflicts during this first decade was mid- to low-level. Most cases involved disputes between dictators and democracies in the Central American and Caribbean regions. There was one territorial dispute between Honduras and Nicaragua in 1957, which was ultimately settled in the International Court of Justice. This case posed little threat to the region as a whole since only two members were involved on a very limited military scale. The other exceptional case was Guatemala in 1954, which was the first case in which the threat of international communism was raised. The

Guatemalan case was merely a hint at what was to come in the 1960s. Although most of the disputes during this period involved minor border incidents, the threats to the region were not incidental because the rebel groups involved were often sponsored by other governments in the region, thus violating the principle of nonintervention. Failure to respond to these violations would likely increase regional instability. Thus, the Council viewed these disputes as threats to the peace and security of the region.[31] In the Costa Rican–Nicaraguan case (1948), the Council stated that the "situation, which is abnormal and dangerous to inter-American peace, explains why the majority of the Central American and Caribbean Republics have, for some time, been living in an atmosphere of mutual distrust, constant anxiety, and open hostility" (Inter-American Treaty of Reciprocal Assistance vol. 1, 1948, 41). The situation in the Caribbean in 1949 was similarly characterized. The Council felt that solidarity had been seriously disturbed in the region (Council of the Organization of American States, Actas, April 8, 1950).

Another indication that the Council viewed these conflicts as a threat to regional peace is that in all of the cases Article 6 (Rio) was invoked. Article 6 states that if the integrity, the territory, the sovereignty, or the political independence of a state is affected by an aggression or situation that might endanger the peace of the Americas, the Organ of Consultation shall meet immediately to consider measures of common defense for the security of the continent.

Although the Council would eventually defer to the Meetings of Foreign Ministers to serve as the Organ of Consultation in later years, during the 1950s the Council chose to serve as the provisional Organ of Consultation in all the cases. The standard pattern of response during this time can be seen in the Costa Rican–Nicaraguan case (1955). Following the initial incident that provoked the request for a Meeting of Consultation, the Council met and formed itself into the provisional Organ. A call for a Meeting of Foreign Ministers was issued, but no date was set. An investigating committee was formed and sent to the scene to evaluate the situation and report back to the Council. The Council then issued its resolutions based on the recommendations of the committee. In this case, a special committee was established to monitor the situation and ensure that the Council's resolutions were carried out. Finally, the Council canceled its call for a Meeting of Foreign Ministers when the crisis was resolved.

The exception to this standard response to serve as Provisional Organ is the case of Guatemala. When Rio was invoked in the case of Guatemala, the ten members who called for a meeting raised Article 11, which states, "the consultation to which the Treaty refers shall be carried out by means of the Meeting of Ministers of Foreign Affairs of the states which have ratified the treaty..."[32] Thus, the Council met to set a specific date for a Meeting of Foreign Ministers (which never actually met), but chose not to constitute itself as the provisional organ. This decision resulted in the organization reacting too slowly to have any impact on the coup that ousted Guatemalan President Jacabo Arbenz. In the other cases, the Council responded rapidly, convoking the Organ of Consultation within one to three days of the member's request.

As is clear from the aforementioned discussion, the case of the Guatemalan coup in 1954 was unlike the other cases handled by the OAS during this period and consequently provoked a unique response from the OAS. It was the only case in which the threat of communism was raised, which contributed to an increased perception of a regional threat because of international communist connections. President Arbenz had been carrying out a series of land reforms that many U.S. companies opposed. The U.S. State Department had been concerned for several years that Arbenz was controlled by communists in the country and wanted him out of office.

Because of the supposed communist threat in the case of Guatemala, there was less consensus on this case than any of the others addressed in the 1950s. One of the biggest debates on the case, however, took place outside the context of OAS, in the UN Security Council. Guatemala, convinced that it would not receive a favorable hearing in the OAS, petitioned the UN Security Council.[33] The United States, supported by Brazil and Colombia on the UN Security Council, argued that the issue should be handled by the OAS, not the United Nations. The United States succeeded in getting the UN Security Council to reject the request of Guatemala. Guatemala then agreed to cooperate with the IAPC and the OAS. There was too little time at this point, however, for the IAPC to investigate or for the Foreign Ministers to meet before Arbenz was forced to resign two days later. The OAS Council did not move quickly, nor act decisively in this case as it did in the others. The Council instead moved cautiously, not only because of strong U.S. interest in the case, but also because of a desire to achieve consensus before acting. Its actions were further limited by the invocation of Article 11 (Rio) calling specifically for a Meeting of Foreign Ministers, and by the fact that Guatemala did not seek resolution through the OAS first, preferring the UN forum. These unique conditions resulted in a response from the OAS that was unlike its responses to other cases during this decade. The concern with international communism unique to the case of Guatemala in the 1950s would become much more pronounced in the next decade as the Cold War deepened.

The Impact of International Communism:
Conflict Resolution in the 1960s

The international environment and organizational environment underwent notable change in the early 1960s following the Cuban Revolution and the rise of Fidel Castro. The 1960s witnessed a shift from the Council handling cases of conflict resolution to the use of the Meeting of Foreign Ministers. The OAS Charter was used for the first time as an instrument for settlement instead of the Rio Treaty. In addition to the changes in the instruments and organ used to handle cases, the 1960s saw a shift in principles as well. Although members still voiced strong support for the principle of nonintervention, they also began to condemn dictatorships. At the Fifth Meeting of Foreign Ministers in 1959 addressing tensions in the Caribbean, the United States had argued strongly against any kind of intervention, fearing that it would cause further instability in the region. The United States notably shifted its position on this issue at the Sixth Meeting of Foreign Ministers in 1960 when it put forth a proposal for the OAS to monitor elections in the Dominican Republic. Although most Latin American members did not embrace this switch to intervention in order to promote democracy, they were willing to condemn dictatorships and even to sanction them for violations of the principle of nonintervention. For example, the Dominican Republic faced sanctions for over a year for intervening in the domestic affairs of Venezuela (1960). Cuba lost its right to participate in the OAS because members determined that Marxist–Leninist ideology of the Soviet type was not compatible with the principles of the Inter-American System. One other change during this decade was that consensus was not as strong as it had been during the first decade, facing considerable strain from the increasing number of cases dealing with communist intervention in the hemisphere.

The 11 cases handled in the 1960s were the Caribbean (1959)—consideration of the general tensions in the region; Dominican Republic–Venezuela (1960)—response to attacks by the Dominican Republic on Venezuelan sovereignty; Cuba (1960)—consideration of the international communist threat to the hemisphere; Cuba (1962)—exclusion of Cuba from OAS participation; Cuba (1962)—cooperation with United States on the missile crisis; Dominican Republic–Haiti (1963)—response to tensions between the two states; Panama–United

States (1964)—response to the "Flag Riots" in Panama in which U.S. high school students refused to fly the Panamanian flag in the Canal Zone; Cuba (1964)—extension of sanctions imposed in 1962 due to intervention in Venezuela; Dominican Republic (1965)—response to civil war; Cuba–Venezuela (1967)—further extension of sanctions on Cuba for intervention; and El Salvador–Honduras (1969)—response to border dispute (see table 4.1).

Characteristics of Conflict Resolution from 1959 to 1969
The Fifth Meeting of Foreign Ministers (1959) is illustrative of some of the changes in both the conflict environment and the way the OAS handled conflicts in the region throughout the 1960s. In August 1959, the Fifth Meeting of Ministers of Foreign Affairs was held in Santiago, Chile. It was convened to consider the "situation in the Caribbean," which included charges by the Dominican Republic that invasion forces had originated in Venezuela and Cuba, as well as other member concerns about extensive revolutionary activity in the region. Haiti and Ecuador had originally proposed a meeting to consider specific charges by the Dominican Republic against Venezuela and Cuba, but this request was withdrawn in favor of a broader agenda covering the Caribbean region as a whole. The Council called for a Meeting of Foreign Ministers, invoking Articles 39 and 40 of the Charter, which justified the meeting based on the urgent nature and common interest in the problems of the Caribbean. U.S. Secretary of State Christian Herter accurately stated that the central issue of the meeting was to reconcile the growing demand for democratic progress and social change in Latin America with the inter-American principles of peaceful relations and nonintervention in the internal affairs of others (Atkins 1997, 329). This agenda led to extensive debates in the plenary sessions of the meeting, which lasted six days.

After the debates ended, the meeting concluded with the Declaration of Santiago, which upheld the fundamental importance of free elections, freedom of the press, respect for human rights, and effective judicial procedures. The meeting also established the Inter American Commission for Human Rights. Despite these strides toward supporting democratic governance, however, most Latin American members were still reluctant to compromise on the principle of nonintervention. The United States also opposed intervention to overthrow oppressive regimes, fearing it would produce disorder and tension, and provide opportunities to communists.

Organs and instruments that had not been used during the first decade of conflict resolution were used for the first time in the

Caribbean case (1959). Although the Foreign Ministers had met in 1951 to address U.S. concerns during the Korean War, the Fifth Meeting was the first time the Foreign Ministers met in consultation to consider *inter-American* tensions since the founding of the OAS.[34] The Foreign Ministers handled eight of the 11 cases of conflict resolution during this period, leaving the Council to serve as the provisional organ of consultation in three cases (see table 4.1).

The invocation of the OAS Charter in the Caribbean case (1959), instead of the Rio Treaty, was also a first for resolving regional tensions.[35] The invocation of Article 39 of the Charter affected the tone of the meeting to be held, since the article states that a Meeting of Consultation may be held in order to consider problems of an urgent nature and of common interest to the American States. This provision contrasts to Article 6 of the Rio Treaty, which allows members to call for a Meeting of Consultation in cases of an armed attack or other threats to regional peace and security. The respective provisions in each document set a different tone for the subsequent proceedings. If the Charter is invoked, there is an apparent attitude among members that the stricter sanctions specified in the Rio Treaty will not be proposed at the meeting, although members are not technically restricted from calling for such sanctions under the Charter. An invocation of the Rio Treaty generally signals that the members are prepared to "get tough" on disputants by imposing various sanctions, possibly even militarized action. Furthermore, the overlapping, but different, membership of the OAS and Rio Treaty regime also means participants will differ based on which instrument is invoked. After many Caribbean states joined the OAS in the 1960s and 1970s, the voting membership was much broader on Charter issues than when the Rio Treaty was invoked since few of these new members signed the Rio Treaty. (By 2003, 23 of the 35 member states had ratified the Rio Treaty.) After the Cuban Revolution in 1959, the United States tended to argue for the application of the Rio Treaty, whereas most of the Latin American states preferred application of the "milder" Charter (Atkins 1997, 322).

The Charter was also invoked in the Cuban case (1960), the Dominican case (1965), and the Cuban–Venezuelan case (1967). In 1960, since Cuba was not directly involved in any military attacks on other members, there was no reason to invoke the Rio Treaty. The Foreign Ministers met under the Charter to consider the "strengthening of continental solidarity and the Inter-American System especially in face of threats of extracontinental intervention that might affect them" and to promote "inter-American cooperation . . . for the defense of democratic institutions against the subversive activities of any organization, government, or its agents" (Seventh Meeting of Foreign Ministers, Final Act, 2–3). There was no armed attack in the Cuban–Venezuelan case (1967) either. Venezuela accused Cuba of intervention by fostering subversion and terrorist activities with the deliberate aim of destroying the principles of the Inter-American System (Council of the Organization of American States, Actas, June 5, 1967). Thus, the Foreign Ministers met to consider a "problem of urgent nature and common interest to the American states" (OAS Charter, Article 39). The civil war in the Dominican Republic also resulted in action being taken under the Charter rather than the Rio Treaty.

The use of the Meeting of Foreign Ministers and the OAS Charter to resolve conflict were not the only changes seen during this era. During the turbulent 1960s, consensus among OAS members was not as high as it had been previously. Three cases had a low level of consensus between the United States and Latin American states, five were mid- level, and three were high based on the level of agreement on the actions to be taken by the OAS. When members faced a considerable threat to the hemisphere, such as the Cuban Missile Crisis (1962), consensus was high, supporting U.S. demands to have the missiles removed. Members could not appear to be divided on the issue of removal, even if they were not in agreement over the status of regional relations with Cuba, or else the Soviet Union might have gained negotiating leverage in its talks with the United States. Consensus was also high when ideology did not play a prominent role, such as in the "Soccer War" between El Salvador and Honduras in 1969. When violence at a World Cup Soccer tournament sparked border incidents between the two countries, the Foreign Ministers (Thirteenth Meeting) unanimously adopted resolutions to promote settlement of the dispute.[36] The dispute over immigration issues between the two countries did not produce any ideological sympathy from other member states. Whereas Latin American democracies were united in the form of the Caribbean Legion during the 1950s to oppose dictatorships, and anticommunists rallied against Cuban-inspired revolu- tions in the 1960s, the dispute between El Salvador and Honduras produced no such common support for either state.

During the 1960s, however, members were most often faced with challenging decisions concerning international communism and were divided on the issue of intervention. For example, consensus was low at the Seventh Foreign Ministers Meeting on Cuba (1960), when members debated whether to condemn Cuba explicitly for allowing Sino-Soviet influence in the region, or whether to condemn such intervention without naming names. The United States was at one extreme, wanting to identify Fidel Castro as a guilty party. Mexico chose to take the opposite position, stating its strong support for Cuba and refusing to condemn it. In the end, the Foreign Ministers did not name Cuba specifically in their condemnation of international communism. Consensus was also low in 1962 when the debate turned to whether Cuba could be excluded from participation in the OAS. There was sharp debate among all the members, again with Mexico being the strongest dissenter against Cuba's ouster. In the end, the Foreign Ministers determined that due to the nature of its current government, Cuba would not be allowed to participate in the OAS, although it would officially remain a member of the organization. The third case in which there was a low level of consensus concerned the Dominican Republic in 1965. This case raised some of the issues debated in the 1950s, since members were concerned about the overthrow of the democratically elected Dominican government. The intervention that occurred, however, with U.S. marines entering the Dominican Republic, reached a whole new level and sparked heated debates about the role of the OAS in restoring democracy. (The cases of Cuba [1960] and the Dominican Republic [1965] are discussed in greater detail in chapters 5 and 6). It is worth noting that consensus among members on the issue of Cuba during this era went from low (1960 when the Foreign Ministers condemned international communist intervention), to moderate (1964 when sanctions were increased), to high (1967 when Cuba meddled in Venezuelan affairs), then went to low again in the next era (1974 when members discussed ending sanctions).

Just as the level of consensus within the organization varied considerably during this time, so too did the perceived level of threat to the region. Two cases were considered to be a high level of threat, six were mid-level threats, and three posed only a low level of threat to the region. Some of the least-threatening situations included the "Flag Riots" in Panama (1964), a dispute between the Dominican Republic and Haiti (1963), and the U.S. intervention in the Dominican Republic (1965). In the Panamanian case, U.S. students in the zone refused to fly the Panamanian flag, provoking violence from Panamanians. The incident was isolated and posed no threat to other Latin American states. Similarly, the dispute between the Dominican Republic and Haiti over asylum issues did not threaten other member states. It is ironic that the incident that provoked the most militarized response from the OAS, in the Dominican Republic (1965), was not a great threat to the region. The conflict did not threaten other states, nor risk increasing regional instability. When the allegedly communist "Constitutionalists" tried to oust the military government, the United States quickly intervened unilaterally to prevent "another Cuba." The Constitutionalists, however, did not have a revolutionary agenda in mind that would have threatened regional stability. They wanted to restore democratically elected President Juan Bosch to power. Bosch had been ousted by a military coup in 1963. Consequently, most Latin American states did not find the justification by the United States of its action based on the presence of a communist threat convincing.

The majority of the cases posing high- or mid-level threats involved the Cuban government. Cuba's relations with the Soviet Union seriously threatened the peace and security of the region, with the Cuban Missile Crisis (1962) being the greatest threat during this time. Cuba's involvement in the domestic affairs of other Latin American states also threatened continental unity and placed democratic institutions in danger. Cuba was behind an assassination attempt on President Rómulo Betancourt of Venezuela in 1964. Bolivia and Uruguay repeatedly charged Cuba with intervention into the 1970s.

As is evident from the discussion mentioned earlier, the types of conflicts handled by the organization in the 1960s changed from tensions between democracies and dictatorships to issues of international communist intervention. At the center of over half the disputes was the Cuban government. Fidel Castro's efforts to export Cuba's revolution, along with U.S. fears of Soviet influence in the hemisphere, led to numerous clashes to be resolved by the OAS.[37]

The OAS in Decline: Conflict Resolution from 1970 to 1989

The next two decades (1970–89) saw the OAS become less active in the region on security issues. Several conflicts in the region could have been addressed by the OAS, particularly those in Central America throughout the 1980s, but these states preferred the Contadora and Esquipulas forums to the direct use of the OAS. The OAS had been unable to secure cooperation from the United States on the Falklands/Malvinas case in 1982, so Central American states believed that in 1983 Contadora was a more viable option for gaining cooperation from all actors involved in the conflicts, including the United States. The Contadora Group was organized by the presidents of Colombia, Mexico, Panama, and Venezuela in January 1983 to serve as mediator to the Central American conflicts. It was designed to facilitate discussions between the United States and Nicaragua, and in El Salvador between the government and insurgents (Atkins 1997, 59). Some states believed that the OAS was more likely to be influenced by the United States through its direct pressures and lobbying of other members to act on its proposals. In addition, the availability of other multilateral forums outside the OAS meant negotiations could occur without the formal binding of any legal protocols (such as the Rio Treaty or OAS Charter).[38] The lack of formal protocol would allow more flexibility in negotiations. The United States was also reluctant to use the OAS as a forum for negotiations because, ironically, it feared an anti-American response from other members, and the inability to gain support for its preferred policies in the region. Discussions proceeded through the Contadora Group until the parties reached an impasse in February 1987. A new formula was put forward by Oscar Arias Sanchez, president of Costa Rica, which became known as the Esquipulas II Accords. This formula was based on the concept of symmetry, simultaneity, and chronology and was regarded as innovative in the region. It provided for Central Americans to take the lead in bringing peace to their own region. Although the OAS as an institution was not actively involved in negotiating a settlement, its functionaries, including the Secretary General Joao Baeña Soares, were engaged in the peace process. In part due to the work and reputation of Soares, the OAS took a more active role in the implementation of the accords through the management of observation and verification forces.[39] Thus, the settlement of the largest conflicts in the region during this period were handled outside the OAS.

Because the Central American conflicts were handled by the Contadora Group and more multilateral forums were emerging in the region, only eight cases were raised in Meetings of Consultation from 1970 to 1989. During this time, several of the trends of the 1960s continued, while some of them shifted again to resemble the characteristics of cases handled during the first decade of conflict resolution by the OAS. Consensus, which had declined in the 1960s, continued its downward trend, reaching a low point during this period. Just as the Meeting of Foreign Ministers increasingly handled cases in the 1960s, all the meetings of the Organ of Consultation from 1970 to 1989 were Foreign Minister meetings. The level of threat posed by the cases from 1970 to 1989 was lower, just as it had been in the 1950s. Finally, the types of conflicts handled during this period were so diverse that they do not fall into any simple categorization and thus do not collectively resemble the cases of the 1950s or 1960s. The cases include such conflicts as a dispute between the United States and Ecuador (1971) over territorial fishing rights, an armed conflict between Argentina and the United Kingdom over the Falkland/Malvinas islands (1982), and a unilateral U.S. intervention in Panama to capture President (and drug lord) Manuel Noriega (1989). Because no single case can serve as an example of the way that the OAS handled conflict resolution during this time, the characteristics of the period are described later by referring to various representative cases rather than one specific case.

Like most of the cases handled in previous decades, none of the cases during this period presented a high-level threat to the region. The only mid-level threat was the Nicaraguan Revolution (1978) in which many Central American states were actively involved. The other seven disputes covered a wide range of issues, but posed only a low-level threat to the region as a whole. Although the dispute between Argentina and the United Kingdom involved military action (Argentina lost one of its naval vessels), the dispute was territorial and limited geographically. Likewise, the U.S. military action against Manuel Noriega (1989) was a strategic action that did not directly threaten other member states. The other disputes were clearly no threat to other member states. For example, the dispute over fishing rights between Ecuador and the United States did not threaten the peace and security of the region. In fact, the case was brought before the Fourteenth Meeting of Foreign Ministers under Article 19 of the OAS Charter that prohibits the use of coercion in relations between member states, rather than under the Rio Treaty.

Another indicator that the disputes during this period were not major threats to the peace and security of the hemisphere is that the Charter was invoked as often as the Rio Treaty. Articles 59 and 60 (revised, formerly Articles 39 and 40) are invoked to call a meeting to consider a matter that is urgent and of common interest to the American States. Article 6 (Rio), however, is only invoked when a matter of aggression is involved that threatens the sovereignty, territory, or independence of another member. Thus, the Rio Treaty is invoked when a more threatening attack is imminent or has been launched. To put the use of the Charter into context, the Charter was invoked in four of eight cases from 1970 to 1989, but in only four of 11 cases during the 1960s. This relatively frequent use of the Charter during this period also suggests that Latin American members exerted greater influence in the organization because in most cases Latin American states preferred to invoke the Charter instead of the Rio Treaty. As noted earlier, this preference is due to the "milder" nature of the Charter. The Rio Treaty is applied to more threatening situations when stricter sanctions or multilateral intervention is necessary. The lack of invocation of the Charter in the 1950s suggests that Latin American states did not have as much influence during this time. Cases were handled under the Rio Treaty even when threats were perceived as low level. In addition, two of the Rio cases handled during the 1970s (Cuba, 1974; Cuba, 1975) were actually held to *reconsider* (and possibly reverse) actions originally taken under Article 6. The passage of the Freedom of Action Resolution (1975) at the Sixteenth Meeting of Foreign Ministers suggested that a two-third majority of members no longer considered Cuba to be a threat to the region. The resolution allowed member states to determine individually whether they would continue to uphold the sanctions imposed against Cuba in 1964 and 1967 for its interference in the internal affairs of member states. Thus, the 1970s and 1980s had lower-level threats to the region compared to the previous period.

All the cases from 1970 to 1989 were handled by a Meeting of Foreign Ministers rather than the Permanent Council. The Council acted briefly as the provisional Organ of Consultation in 1982 with the Falklands/Malvinas crisis, but quickly convoked the Twentieth Meeting of Foreign Ministers to follow up on its initial efforts. This shift in the organ responsible for handling conflict resolution is indicative of larger institutional changes in the OAS, with the Permanent Council facing new responsibilities. After the revisions to the OAS Charter in 1967, the Permanent Council began serving as the preparatory committee for the new General Assembly. The Permanent Council prepared draft agendas and resolutions for meetings of the General Assembly. Although the Permanent Council inherited all the previous functions of the Council to serve as provisional organ of consultation, it is likely that its new responsibilities led to regular reliance on the Meeting of Foreign Ministers to serve as the Organ of Consultation (Ball 1969, 211). In addition, as the different organs of the OAS expanded in the 1980s, the Permanent Council's oversight of these organs took a considerable amount of time and expertise.

Just as the 1960s saw a decline in consensus among members on OAS reactions to regional conflicts, the 1970s and 1980s were also an era of disagreement. The only case that saw a high level of consensus among members concerned a flare-up in the long-term border dispute between Ecuador and Peru (1981). The Nineteenth Meeting of Foreign Ministers readily agreed to turn the matter over to the Guarantor States (Argentina, Brazil, Chile, United States) that had been arbitrating the dispute for several decades and to ask the parties to refrain from further violence. Other cases such as the war between Argentina and the United

Kingdom over the Falkland/Malvinas islands (1982), and the Nicaraguan Revolution (1978), saw the members strongly divided, with the United States taking a position at odds with that of most Latin American states. Consensus was also affected by the fact that there were two cases dealing with the Castro regime during this period that provoked considerable debate within the organization, just as Cuban issues had during the 1960s. The two meetings addressing Cuba (1974 and 1975) indicated that Latin American views were changing on the issue of sanctions while U.S. views remained unaltered. The United States resisted relaxing the isolationist sanctions against Cuba. Eventually, however, when faced with a clear two-thirds majority, the United States voted to release OAS members from their obligation to enforce sanctions against Cuba (1975). The United States was also party to two disputes (Ecuador–United States, 1971; Panama–United States, 1989) which, by definition, weakened consensus within the organization. As noted earlier, in terms of consensus between Latin American states and the United States, a dispute between the United States and any other member that comes before the organization will result in a low level of overall consensus.

In sum, the OAS played a less active role in conflict resolution from 1970 to 1989. This was a period of decline when compared with the 1960s. Some of the characteristics observed in the 1960s continued during this period, including the predominant handling of cases by the Foreign Ministers and the decline in consensus within the organization. The level of threats to the region was lower, more closely resembling the cases of the 1950s. The variety of cases handled during this period did not resemble either of the previous eras.

Application of Hypotheses

The exploration of the historical cases of peaceful settlement efforts in Latin America provides the necessary background knowledge to explore in more detail the impact of a variety of institutional factors on power relations within the OAS. The previous sections have looked at trends over time and at individual cases. A look at the cases as a whole will now be used to test the hypotheses derived in chapter 2. Chapters 5 and 6 apply these hypotheses in a detailed analysis of eight case studies that illustrate the decisionmaking processes and member dynamics within the OAS.

Organizational sociology provides three different approaches for explaining organizational activities and outcomes (see chapter 2). Adaptation of these approaches along with a constructivist approach provide a theoretical framework to explain the behavior of the OAS (see table 2.1). This framework includes the structural perspective, which examines the resources necessary to carry out the resolutions of the organization; the normative perspective, which explores the impact of regional principles; the internal relational perspective, which focuses on the degree of consensus among members; and the environmental perspective, which considers the type of conflict and the perceived threat to regional stability.

Not all these variables are significant in every case. By applying each of them, it is possible to determine which ones offer the best explanation for the apparent autonomy of the OAS from U.S. pressure in some cases. Some of the variables are most influential when paired with others, but do not have enough independent impact to result in organizational autonomy.

The first hypothesis is based on a structural factor, organizational resources. I hypothesize that the more resources that are needed to support the Meeting of Consultation and carry out the resolutions of the Organ of Consultation, the more influence the United States has on those resolutions. There are five cases where a high level of resources have been used to carry out the resolutions of the Organ of Consultation. These cases are Costa Rica–Nicaragua (1955), Panama (1959), Cuba (1962 missile crisis), Dominican Republic (1965), and El Salvador–Honduras (1969). In each of these cases military equipment was needed. The Dominican case was by far the most militarized, with several thousand U.S. marines participating in a multilateral peacekeeping force. The missile crisis also involved significant U.S. naval power in the blockade of Cuba. In both these cases the United States wielded a considerable amount of influence within the OAS even when it was facing Latin American opposition in the Dominican case. Half of the cases handled by the OAS, however, used only a low level of resources. The United States did not dominate the organization in any of these cases where a low level of resources was used. This is not to say that the United States did not gain support for its preferred policies; in many cases the United States and Latin American members were in agreement on the actions to be taken. There is support for the hypothesis on resources.

On the issue of consensus, I hypothesize that the greater the disagreement among Latin American members, the greater influence the United States has. In the 18 cases where there is mid- or low-level of consensus in the organization overall, I have examined the degree of unity among Latin American members only. In eight of the cases Latin American members were in disagreement with each other (in the other ten cases, the Latin American members were unified in their opposition to the U.S. policy position). In all except one of the cases when Latin Americans were divided in their preferences, the actions taken by the OAS were those preferred by the United States. In other words, when there was not a common Latin American policy preference, the policy preferences of the United States were adopted by the organization. Two examples are the cases of Cuba: 1962 when it was excluded from participation in the OAS, and 1964 when sanctions were tightened against it. In both cases there were Latin American members who were opposed to the U.S. proposals (particularly Mexico, Chile, and Bolivia), but the U.S. proposals were the ones that passed by a two-thirds majority. In the cases where the Latin American majority was united against the United States (Cuba, 1960; Nicaragua, 1978; Argentina–United Kingdom, 1982; and Panama–United States, 1989), the U.S. proposal was either rejected or revised to be acceptable to the Latin American members. When Latin Americans are unified, the United States wields less influence within the organization. Thus, the hypothesis is supported on the factor of consensus.

When considering the impact of regional principles, I hypothesize that any proposal or unilateral action by the United States (or other member state) that does not clearly uphold the principles of the organization will have less support than a proposal that is based on principled action, and will face strong opposition in the Council/Meeting of Foreign Ministers. Evaluation of this hypothesis is difficult at a macro-level. In every case different principles were raised and different justifications made for action. As noted in chapter 3, some of the principles of the Inter-American System can be contradictory. When one member advocates intervention based on the principle of supporting representative democracy or human rights, it must also address the violation of the principles of nonintervention and state sovereignty. A detailed evaluation of the hypothesis on regional principles is made in each of the case studies in chapters 5 and 6. The evaluation helps to trace the impact of regional principles on OAS action, as well as how priorities have shifted within the OAS membership over the years, with support for democracy and human rights gradually starting to outweigh nonintervention.

Finally, considering the factor of regional instability, I hypothesize that the greater the threat to regional stability, the greater influence the United States has within the OAS. Since this is a challenging factor to measure and almost half of the cases fall into the middle range on the perceived level of threat, conclusions are difficult to draw. There are, however, some trends and specific cases that support the hypothesis.

Throughout the 1970s and 1980s, the level of U.S. influence was declining in the OAS. Several resolutions passed during this time by Meetings of Foreign Ministers were contrary to U.S. policy preferences. In 1975, the Foreign Ministers voted to give members the freedom to determine individually whether sanctions would continue to be imposed against Cuba. In 1978, the Foreign Ministers rejected a U.S. proposal for a multilateral peace force to restore order in Nicaragua. The Foreign Ministers even went so far as to condemn U.S. actions in Panama in 1989 when U.S. military forces arrested President Manuel Noriega. Throughout these two decades, the perceived level of threat to the region posed by the cases brought to the OAS was also lower than at any other time. Such a low level of risk to regional stability gave Latin American members more leeway in accepting or rejecting U.S. proposals during this time since they were not dependent on the United States to protect the region in these cases. Looking at the two cases in which there was a high level of threat to the region also supports the hypothesis (Cuba, 1962; Cuba, 1962 missile crisis). In both cases the United States had considerable influence within the organization as it sought to defend the hemisphere from external threats (international communist subversion and nuclear missiles).

Summary

This chapter has traced the conflict resolution activities of the OAS over four decades in an effort to illustrate the changing nature of organizational relations and responses to handling regional disputes. The international environment, organizational environment, and member preferences have shifted over time, as reflected in the level of threat perceived, the organ and instrument invoked, and the level of consensus attained. In the first decade, threats were mid- to low-level stemming from struggles between democrats and dictators. The Council handled every case under the Rio Treaty achieving a high- to mid-level of consensus. This was a period in which Latin American states and the United States were largely in agreement with each other in terms of resolving regional conflicts. Members struggled with the contradiction between supporting the principle of democracy while upholding the principle of nonintervention. The United States sided with Latin American members in support of nonintervention until the Cuban Revolution in 1959 when it reversed its policy at the Sixth Meeting of Foreign Ministers.

Throughout the 1960s, the level of threats varied considerably, but were mostly linked to communist threats to the region. The Foreign Ministers took on the responsibility of handling more cases and the

OAS Charter was invoked for the first time. There was a lower level of consensus during this period, reflecting disagreements between Latin American members as well as with the United States over responses to regional disputes. In most cases the United States achieved its desired policy preferences, but not without protests from some Latin American states (Mexico in particular). This period marked an era of increased tensions, but few open challenges to the United States.

From 1969 to 1989 the region faced mainly low-level threats of a varied nature. The Foreign Ministers handled all the cases, which included a relatively large percentage of Charter invocations, suggesting a weaker U.S. influence within the organization. Consensus reached an historic low during this period. Latin American members challenged U.S. proposals on numerous occasions, reversing the embargo on Cuba (1975), refusing to get actively involved in Nicaragua (1978), denouncing the actions of the United Kingdom in the Falklands Malvinas (1982), and condemning U.S. intervention in Panama (1989).

A testing of the hypotheses over all 26 cases indicates that some are more strongly supported that others. There is limited support for the hypothesis on the perceived level of threat to the region. When the threat level was high, Latin American members tended to support U.S. leadership on the issue, as in the Cuban missile crisis. The characterization of many disputes as mid-level threats to the region, however, makes it difficult to draw strong conclusions. The variable of regional threat is traced in detail in the case studies in chapters 5 and 6. Support is strongest for the hypotheses on consensus among Latin American members and on organizational resources. In cases where Latin American members were unified in opposition to the United States, the United States was unable to exert much influence within the OAS. When the organization required extensive resources (i.e., military resources) to carry out its resolutions, the United States had more influence within the organization.

Now that these factors have been examined broadly for all the cases, a more detailed analysis of how these factors specifically affect U.S. influence and how they interact is needed. This is taken up in the case studies in the next two chapters that examine the decisionmaking process and member dynamics within the organization.

CHAPTER 5

CONFLICT: THE EBB AND FLOW OF
U.S. DOMINANCE

Introduction

Chapter 4 provided an overview of the 26 cases of conflict resolution handled by the OAS from 1948 to 1989, and emphasized the changes over time in the types of cases that were addressed and the mechanisms used to resolve them. It is evident from the examination of the resources needed, the perceived level of threat, and the level of consensus that a number of factors potentially affect the level of influence the United States is able to exert within the OAS. An examination of all these cases reveals some interesting patterns of decisionmaking in the organization. By focusing on the degree of consensus among member states and the actions taken by the organization, four different decisionmaking outcomes can be identified. First, there were ten cases where all member states were in agreement concerning the means to address the conflict and acted in a united fashion.[40] Second, there were five cases in which compromises were reached despite disagreements between the United States and Latin American members over what actions should be taken by the organization. Third, there were five cases in which the United States played a dominant role and strongly influenced the decisions that were made, despite opposition by some Latin American states. Finally, and perhaps most unexpectedly, in five cases, Latin American members successfully rejected controversial U.S. proposals or ignored U.S. policy preferences (see table 5.1).[41] Two of these outcomes are particularly interesting in terms of membership dynamics because the most powerful member state was forced to compromise or see its proposal rejected by the Latin American members. Classifying outcomes by U.S. dominance, Latin American unity, consensus, or compromise is useful for comparing the 26 cases and for further testing the four hypotheses to see which ones best explain these varying outcomes.

Table 5.1 Cases invoking the OAS Charter, Rio Treaty, or Resolution 108...

Case	Date	Council or FM	Resources	Threat level	Consensus U.S.-LA	Consensus LA-LA	Consensus	
Costa Rica–Nicaragua	1948	C	Mid	Mid	High	High	Consensus	Costa Rica ... invasion by Nicaragua; Pact of Amity signed; troops withdrawn
Costa Rica–Nicaragua	1955	C	High	Mid	High	High	Consensus	Each country accuses the other of intervention; exile activity; governments sign conciliation agreement
Honduras–Nicaragua	1957	C	Low	Low	High	High	Consensus	Territorial dispute; cease-fire signed; case to Int'l Court of Justice
Panama	1959	C	High	Low	High	High	Consensus	Small invasion force, mostly Cuban; persuaded to surrender by OAS intermediaries
Cuba	1962	C	High	High	High	High	Consensus	Soviet intervention; missile crisis
Dominican Republic–Haiti	1963	C	Low	Low	Mid	High	Consensus achieved	Each country accuses the other of illegal exile activities; governments agree to negotiations

Cuba–Venezuela	1967	FM 12	Low	Mid	High	High	Consensus	Cuban intervention in Venezuela; sanctions expanded
El Salvador–Honduras	1969	FM 13	High	Mid	High	High	Consensus	"Soccer War"; immigration disputes; cease-fire, withdrawal, dispute settlement procedures
Costa Rica–Nicaragua	1978	FM 18	Low	Low	Mid	High	Consensus	Nicaragua invasion of CR territory; observers placed on border
Ecuador–Peru	1981	FM 19	Low	Low	High	High	Consensus	Territorial dispute
Haiti	1991	FM	High	Low	High	High	Consensus	Coup overthrows President Aristide; returned to power in 1994
Peru	1992	FM	Low	Low	High	High	Consensus	"Self-coup" by President Fujimori
Guatemala	1993	FM	Low	Low	High	High	Consensus	"Self-coup" by President Serrano
Paraguay	1996	FM	Low	Low	High	High	Consensus	President Wasmosy challenged by General Oviedo

Table 5.1 Continued

Case	Date	Council or FM	Resources	Threat level	Consensus U.S.-LA	Consensus LA-LA	Outcome	Brief description
Venezuela	2002	C	Mid	Low	Mid	Mid	Consensus	Brief removal of President Chavez from power
Caribbean	1949	C	Low	Mid	Mid	Mid	Compromise	General instability in the region; active rebel forces
Nicaragua	1959	C	Low	Mid	Mid	Mid	Compromise	Anti-Somoza rebels from Costa Rica/Honduras; CR/Hon pledge to restrain exiles
Caribbean	1959	FM 5	Low	Mid	Mid	High	Compromise	DR charges Cuba and Venezuela with plotting invasion; general regional instability
Cuba	1960	FM 7	Low	Mid	Low	High	Compromise	Cuban intervention; Soviet/Chinese condemnation
Argentina–U.K.	1982	C > FM 20	Mid	Low	Low	High	Compromise	Falklands/Malvinas conflict; Council supports Arg and calls for a cease-fire

Guatemala	1954	C	NA	Mid	Mid	Mid	U.S. dominance	Coup removes Guat President Arbenz before Council can act
Cuba	1962	FM 8	Low	High	Low	Low	U.S. dominance	Cuban activities viewed as threat to the peace; Cuba effectively ousted from OAS
Cuba	1964	FM 9	Low	Mid	Mid	Low	U.S. dominance	Sanctions expanded against Cuba for continued intervention activities
Dominican Republic	1965	FM 10	High	Low	Low	Low	U.S. dominance	Coup; countercoup; multilateral peacekeeping; elections
Cuba	1974	FM 15	Low	Low	Low	Low	U.S. dominance	Proposal to lift sanctions does not receive two third vote
Dominican Republic–Venezuela	1960	FM 6	Mid	Mid	Mid	High	Latin American Unity	DR attempt to assassinate Ven President Betancourt; DR condemned, sanctions imposed
Panama–U.S.	1964	C	Low	Low	Mid	High	Latin American Unity	"Flag Riots" over refusal to fly Panamanian flag in the Canal Zone

Table 5.1 Continued

Case	Date	Council or FM	Resources	Threat level	Consensus U.S.-LA	Consensus LA-LA	Outcome	Brief description
Cuba	1975	FM 16	Low	Low	Mid	Mid	Latin American Unity	Economic sanctions no longer enforced
Nicaragua	1978	FM 17	Mid	Mid	Low	High	Latin American Unity	Sandinista revolution; proposed peacekeeping force rejected
Panama–U.S.	1989	FM 21	Low	Low	Low	High	Latin American Unity/ Unilateral U.S. action	U.S. removal of President Manuel Noriega
Ecuador–U.S.	1971	FM 14	Low	Low	Mid	High	No win; unresolved	Fishing rights dispute; territorial waters; negotiations recommended

The cases when the OAS Charter or Rio Treaty have been invoked are categorized in this chapter and chapter 6 based on OAS policy outcomes. In addition, these two chapters focus particularly on the level of consensus within the organization. Because one of the primary purposes of the research is to determine under what conditions the OAS is able to exhibit some degree of autonomy from U.S. influence, it is important to contrast those cases in which the United States was not in agreement with Latin American members with those where they were in agreement on policy options. This chapter explores two cases in which the United States dominated the organization, and two cases where Latin American unity led to the rejection of U.S. policy preferences. Chapter 6 examines cases of consensus and compromise among members that provide additional insights into the member dynamics within the organization.

Examination of cases where there is disagreement among member states is crucial because assessing U.S. influence within the OAS when there is general agreement on policies is almost impossible. There are no indications of the United States using pressure to gain passage of the proposals that the United States favors when others support similar policies. Evidence of U.S. preferences can also be more difficult when the United States has another member make proposals for it so that the United States does not appear to be dominating the policymaking arena. Thus, only when the United States must present a proposal on its own in contrast to those presented by other members is there evidence of U.S. exertion of influence to gain its passage. In chapter 4, the examination of the level of consensus indicated that although members are not often in full agreement, neither are they frequently in strong disagreement.[42] Only seven of the 26 cases under examination have a low level of overall consensus (see table 5.1). By examining the cases in which U.S. and Latin American preferences diverge, the conditions under which the United States does—or does not—get its way can be identified. Only in the cases where the United States faces opposition from other members is there evidence of U.S. efforts to influence the organization.

In five cases, the United States has successfully dominated the organization despite opposition, resulting in actions based on its own policy preferences. These cases are: Guatemala (1954), Cuba (1962), Cuba (1964, Dominican Republic (1965), and Cuba (1974). These cases most closely resemble the stereotypes of the United States using the OAS to pursue its own policies (as realism would predict). In the Guatemalan case (1954), the United States successfully delayed OAS action in response to a coup against the leftist President Jacobo Arbenz Guzmán. The United States won support for the effective ouster of Cuba from the OAS in 1962.[43] Two years later (Cuba, 1964), the United States pressured Latin American members to increase the sanctions that had previously been imposed on Cuba at the Eighth Meeting of Consultation held in 1962. In the Dominican Republic, the United States actively intervened without permission from the OAS, then proceeded to gain OAS approval post hoc for an Inter-American Peacekeeping Force despite considerable protest from some members. When a proposal came before the Foreign Ministers in 1974 to lift the sanctions against Cuba, the United States achieved the rejection of the proposal (only to face its passage when raised again in 1975). This chapter examines the cases of Cuba (1964) and the Dominican Republic (1965) in detail.

The case of the Dominican Republic (1965) is a "most likely" case in which the factors that give the United States influence within the organization are most evident (Eckstein 1992). It provides a model case for the way the United States occasionally dominated the organization to achieve its goals. The cases of Latin American resistance (discussed in a later section) are anomalies and are selected based on the "most different" system design that promotes a comparison between dissimilar cases to find commonalities (Przeworski and Teune 1970, 34). The cases of Latin American unity do not follow the pattern of behavior predicted by realism where the most powerful state dominates the organization. These cases differ in terms of outcome from the Dominican and Cuban cases, and have several factors in common with each other that explain the divergent outcomes and that are illustrated by comparing them to cases of U.S. dominance. Specifically, this comparison tests whether an institutional analysis offers a better explanation for why the United States was unable to dominate the organization than realism does.

Evolving Member Relations

Before examining the cases of U.S. dominance and Latin American unity, some contextual background of U.S.–Latin American relations following the creation of the OAS is useful. In the 1950s, there was considerable consensus among OAS members in dealing with security concerns in the hemisphere (as discussed in chapter 4). Throughout the 1960s, there was a growing divide between the United States and Latin American states over the effect of economic development on regional security and a traditional political security focus. In the early 1960s the efforts to reform the Charter began, culminating with the Protocol of Buenos Aires in 1967, which made some basic organizational changes to the OAS. The reforms also included making economic development an integrated part of the Inter-American System. In 1973, the General Assembly of the OAS created a special committee to draft amendments to the Rio Treaty. These amendments were approved in 1975 at a Conference of Plenipotentiaries, but never received enough ratifications from member states to come into effect. Nevertheless, the amendments indicated general Latin American dissent from the anticommunist alliance. The Latin American perception of U.S. coercion and intransigence over issues relating to Cuba led to most of the amendment proposals (Atkins 1997, 273). Throughout the 1960s and 1970s, there was a gradual reduction of U.S. influence in the organization that was especially evident in the Nicaraguan case (1978) (Wilson 1977). There was a growing power of Latin American consensus. When the United States faced a majority in opposition to its proposals, it would often back down to vote with the majority. For example, in 1975, when Latin American states wanted to release OAS members from their obligation to enforce the sanctions against Cuba, the United States chose to vote in favor of the resolution when it became clear that there was the necessary two-thirds votes for it to pass.

The cases of the Dominican Republic (1965) and Cuba (1964) are examples of U.S. dominance prior to its waning influence in the organization in the 1970s. A detailed examination of these cases reveals that certain institutional factors proved essential to the United States being able to dominate the organization and achieve favorable policy outcomes.

United States Dominance

The Dominican Republic (1965)
Summary of Events. The context of the diplomatic crisis in the Dominican Republic in 1965 dates back to 1961 and the assassination of President Trujillo. Trujillo was replaced by democratically elected President Juan Bosch. In 1963, Bosch was overthrown in a military coup. On April 24, 1965, a pro-Bosch army faction (the "Constitutionalists") deposed the existing military government. A "Loyalist" anti-Bosch faction attempted a countercoup, thereby precipitating an armed conflict. The United States sent in over 500 marines on April 28, ostensibly to protect U.S. and foreign nationals. The justification of the mission, however, rapidly shifted to include establishing a neutral zone, and then to guarding against communism in the Western hemisphere.

The United States contended that the Constitutionalists were influenced by international communist agents and would thus pose a threat to the region if they gained power in Santo Domingo. On April 29, Chile requested a Meeting of Foreign Ministers. The Tenth Meeting of Foreign Ministers was held on May 1 and dispatched a Special Committee to reestablish peace and normal conditions, to secure a cease-fire, and to evacuate those wishing to leave (Tenth Meeting of Consultation of Ministers of Foreign Affairs, May 1, 1965, 9). These goals were nominally accomplished with the signing of the Act of Santo Domingo on May 5. The United States, however, continued to push for greater OAS involvement and succeeded in creating the IAPF on May 6. The IAPF was to act under the general supervision of the newly created Ad Hoc committee, which was established June 2. The OAS secretary general, José Mora, began negotiating a settlement with the two factions in June. Negotiations continued through the summer and concluded with the signing of the Institutional Act and the Act of Dominican Reconciliation. A provisional government was established in September 1965, headed by Hector Garcia-Godoy. The IAPF remained in the Dominican Republic to stabilize the provisional government until elections could be held in June 1966, sponsored by the OAS. The IAPF was finally withdrawn when Joaquin Balaguer, who had defeated Juan Bosch in the election, was inaugurated in September 1966.

Structural Perspective. In chapter 2, I identified one structural aspect that provided the United States with the potential to influence the decisions made by the Organ of Consultation when considering how to handle a regional conflict: level of resources needed to carry out the resolutions of the Organ of Consultation. I predict that the more resources that are needed to carry out the resolutions of the Organ of Consultation, the more influence the United States has on those resolutions. It is important to note that this predicted impact on resolutions includes not only the initial commitment to engage in pacific settlement procedures, but also those subsequent resolutions made by the Organ of Consultation until the dispute is settled. The use of military forces and the duration of the operation classify the case of the Dominican Republic as one of only a handful of cases that have used a high level of resources. In the case of the Dominican Republic, the initial decision to commit the amount of resources necessary to implement the IAPF was made by the United States and later approved by the Organ of Consultation. After the United States committed itself to providing the bulk of the resources for the OAS operation, it still maintained a strong influence within the organization over decisions on how those resources were used.

When the Organ of Consultation met shortly after U.S. marines entered the Dominican Republic, the Foreign Ministers struggled to determine what role the OAS should play in restoring democracy to the Dominican Republic. Since the United States had acted unilaterally, the Foreign Ministers were faced with the decision of whether to legitimize U.S. actions by creating a multilateral force, or to find alternative solutions to the Dominican crisis (and the presence of over 10,000 U.S. troops). The Foreign Ministers decided to utilize both military and diplomatic resources in an effort to restore normal conditions in the country. Once the decision was made to create the IAPF, Latin American members were requested to contribute troops to the multilateral effort. Since there had been disagreement among members in creating the IAPF, it was difficult to recruit troops to the force (the disagreement among member states is discussed in greater detail later). In the end, Brazilian General Hugo Panasco Alvim was named commander of the force, with United States General Bruce Palmer Jr. serving as his second in command. Troops from Brazil, Costa Rica, El Salvador, Honduras, Nicaragua, and Paraguay participated in the IAPF (Palmer 1989, chapter 4). Even though the IAPF was a multinational force with a Brazilian commander, the United States dominated it. General Palmer writes, "as the international deputy and US commander, I had sufficient leverage to get IAPF decisions that were compatible with US desires" (Palmer 1989, 73).

In addition to using many military assets in this operation, the OAS also used diplomatic channels to promote settlement. It empowered Secretary General José Mora to act decisively to gain the cooperation of the factions and restore peace. The use of the secretary general in this role was unprecedented. It is possible that this power was bestowed in order to counter the overwhelming presence of the United States military forces in the Dominican Republic.

The implication from the hypothesis concerning resources and U.S. influence is that the OAS will turn to the United States in order to gain resources for large operations, thereby giving the United States more influence over the organization. In this case, however, the link between OAS resolutions and the level of resources necessary to carry them out is distorted. The commitment of significant resources by the United States was made before the OAS even considered its options in the case of the Dominican Republic and what resources might be necessary. Thus, the United States did not gain additional influence based on OAS recognition that a high level of resources would be needed to carry out a particular resolution. The fact that the United States had already contributed significant resources, however, gave it de facto influence over the IAPF throughout its operations even though it was nominally an OAS force. The Foreign Ministers apparently tried to use a second resource available to them, the diplomatic services of the secretary general, to counter the influence of the United States stemming from its military contributions. Even with his augmented authority, however, the secretary general did not wield enough influence to counter U.S. dominance of the operation through its military command.

Internal Relational Perspective. The variable considered by this perspective is the degree of consensus among members within the organization. I predict that the greater disagreement among Latin American members, the greater influence the United States has within the organization. It is evident in this examination of the Dominican case that there was considerable disagreement among Latin American members concerning U.S. intervention and subsequent organizational responses. When the United States acted unilaterally, the Foreign Ministers were faced with the decision of whether to legitimize U.S. actions by creating a multilateral force, or to find alternative solutions to the Dominican crisis. Several members were strongly opposed to the presence of U.S. troops and denounced U.S. actions (Chile, Uruguay, and Mexico). These members as well as Ecuador and Peru voted against creating the IAPF. (Chile, Uruguay, and Mexico were also opposed to the creation of the Ad Hoc Committee whose role it was to provide the IAPF with the directives necessary to carry out the resolutions of the Organ of Consultation and to restore normal conditions to the Dominican Republic.) A number of members simply wanted to resolve the crisis as quickly as possible and did not criticize U.S. actions. Colombia, Haiti, and Paraguay were openly supportive of U.S. actions and denounced international communism. Thus, preferences ranged across the board in terms of support for the U.S. actions in the Dominican Republic. Additional tensions among members were evident in the composition of the IAPF. Argentina did not contribute troops because it refused to have its troops serve under a Brazilian commander. Since there was no consensus on any alternative plan of action, the United States was able to gain the necessary two-thirds majority to pass its proposal to create the IAPF. Those that disapproved of U.S. intervention, but wanted action to be taken, supported the proposal. The lack of unity among

Latin American members gave the United States greater influence in the organization.

Normative Perspective. The normative perspective considers the influence of regional principles on member state relations. From the historical development of the OAS discussed in chapter 3, it is evident that regional principles have had a profound effect on states in the Western hemisphere. I hypothesize that any proposal or unilateral action that does not clearly uphold the principles of the organization will face strong opposition in the Organ of Consultation. At first glance, it appears that the case of the Dominican Republic does not support this hypothesis since a valued principle of the Inter-American System, nonintervention, was violated by the United States without repercussions. A closer look, however, reveals that the principles of the Inter-American System still played a role in the case of the Dominican Republic, shaping the actions and responses of member states, just not to a large enough degree to prevent or reverse the U.S. violation of the principle of nonintervention.

When the United States first intervened in the Dominican Republic, U.S. President Lyndon B. Johnson declared that the U.S. troops were there to protect foreign nationals. He later stated that the troops were there to establish a neutral zone in Santo Domingo, acting on a resolution by the OAS Council. The Council, however, noted that it had not specifically asked the United States to establish a neutral zone, it had merely called for one. As Johnson sent in more troops, he again changed the justification for their presence. U.S. troops were guarding the Western hemisphere against communist subversion. The United States contended that the Constitutionalists were influenced by communists and thus posed a threat to the region if they obtained power in Santo Domingo. Recognizing that it had clearly violated the principle of nonintervention, and that its justifications for doing so were weak, the United States rapidly pushed for the creation of an IAPF. The United States was thus influenced by the norms of the Inter-American System to try to legitimize the presence of its troops by the creation of such a multilateral force for which OAS Charter provisions allow, but not influenced enough to resist intervention at the outset.

Although the unilateral intervention by the United States blatantly violated the principle of nonintervention, the process by which the IAPF was created did adhere to the legal guidelines laid out in the OAS Charter. The United States invoked the Charter, Articles 39 and 40, calling the situation a problem of an urgent nature and of common interest to the American states. The United States was quick to base its justification for intervention on regional principles, stating that the conflict posed a threat to the region because of international communist involvement, and that the democratic government must be restored. Not all members, however, found U.S. justifications compelling.

Regional principles also influenced the mission of the force as seen in the wording of the resolution creating the IAPF. The resolution of the Foreign Ministers established that the IAPF's "sole purpose, in a spirit of democratic impartiality, [was] . . . cooperating in the restoration of normal conditions in the Dominican Republic, in maintaining the security of its inhabitants and the inviolability of human rights, and in the establishment of an atmosphere of peace and conciliation that [would] permit the functioning of democratic institutions" (Tenth Meeting of Consultation of Foreign Ministers, May 6, 1965, 11).

Even if the United States were simply espousing the principles of the Inter-American System to suit its own purposes, the principles still had an impact on the actions the United States took and the responses of the OAS. The hypothesis, however, also predicts strong opposition by member states to proposals or unilateral actions that do not clearly uphold OAS principles. Several states readily condemned U.S. actions, but did not have enough support within the Council to issue a formal condemnation by the OAS. The lack of enough opposition to condemn U.S. actions and block the U.S. proposal stems from the tensions within the organization over the issue of communist threat and the appropriate response of the organization. As noted in chapter 4, the potential threat of communist subversion in the region divided members of the OAS as early as 1954 and throughout the 1960s. The threat posed by international communism to the region had been officially established at the Tenth Inter-American Conference in 1954 where most members signed the Declaration of Caracas. At the Eighth Meeting of Foreign Ministers (1962), members had voted to suspend Cuba's participation in the OAS because its communist practices were antithetical to regional principles. These actions, however, had not been taken without reservations and objections by some members. Mexico and Argentina, in particular, had been in opposition, based on the implications such declarations would have for the principles of sovereignty and nonintervention. Consequently, in the case of the Dominican Republic, members were not in agreement that a potential communist threat merited the creation of an intervention force. Based on a report from the investigating committee and on the proposal presented by the United States, the Foreign Ministers established the IAPF with barely the two-thirds votes required.

Chile, Ecuador, Peru, Mexico, and Uruguay voted against the proposal and Venezuela abstained. In the Dominican case there was a majority to pass resolutions, including creation of the IAPF, but the dissension among members weakened their ability to oppose the most obvious violation of principles, namely U.S. intervention in the Dominican Republic.

Environmental Perspective. The environmental perspective focuses on the impact of the type of conflict being handled and the level of perceived threat to regional stability. I hypothesize that the greater the risk of regional instability that is perceived by member states, the greater influence the United States has within the organization. This argument is based both on the Latin American recognition that the United States has the necessary resources to protect the region when threatened, and that the United States frequently takes a leadership role in such situations because it views a threat to the region as a threat to itself. The perceived level of threat is closely linked to the different options that are available to member states to respond to a crisis. The OAS has both military and diplomatic mechanisms available should it choose to invoke them. If a situation involves a mid- or low-level threat, Latin American members prefer diplomatic efforts to the use of military force.

Although the OAS ultimately decided to establish the IAPF in the Dominican Republic, Latin American members were actually reluctant to pursue the military option. The conflict in the Dominican Republic is classified in this study as a low-level threat based on the fact that only one state was involved (i.e., it was a civil war), and there was little risk of the conflict provoking regional instability. In fact, member states only became concerned with the conflict after the U.S. military chose to intervene to restore order. Because military actions were taken prior to any decisions being made by the Organ of Consultation, however, the policy options available to the Council were limited once it met. The OAS had no ready alternatives to replacing U.S. troops and resolving the conflict, even if the United States could be persuaded to withdraw its forces. In the hope of establishing some influence over the military forces in the Dominican Republic, Latin American members agreed to create the IAPF. A few other nonmilitary options were briefly considered, but the IAPF soon became the preferred instrument to resolve the conflict. The day after U.S. troops entered the country, the Dominican representative in the OAS requested a special meeting to ask the Papal Nuncio to help establish a cease-fire. The secretary general was sent to help him. The secretary general ended up playing a prominent role in the diplomatic efforts to reestablish a democratic government in the Dominican Republic. In this case, by acting unilaterally, the United States preempted Latin American members' consideration of the level of conflict when determining the appropriate organizational response. Latin American states were forced to accept the existing militarized response and manage it as best they could.

Because the Dominican case did not pose a significant threat to the region in the eyes of most Latin American members (the Organ was not even convened to address the conflict until after the United States intervened), one would not expect the Latin American states to turn to the United States, and in fact they did not seek U.S. leadership in this case. The United States, however, took the matter into its own hands because of its exaggerated concern with an international communist threat. Thus, in the case of the Dominican Republic, Latin American perceptions of a threat to the region were not linked to the level of influence the United States wielded within the organization.

Results. The case of the Dominican Republic (1965) provides several good examples of the ways the United States is able to exert its influence within the OAS. The hypothesis that is most strongly supported is the one concerning consensus among members. It is clearly evident that the degree of disunity among Latin American members allowed the United States greater influence within the organization. Additionally, although the hypothesis concerning resources is not supported in the initial phase because U.S. actions preceded OAS decisionmaking, it is supported later through the duration of the mission in the Dominican Republic. The need for extensive resources, especially military, led to strong U.S. influence of the latter resolutions affecting the use of those resources.

The hypothesis on regional principles provides less conclusive explanations concerning U.S. influence within the OAS. On the issue of regional principles, there is limited support for the hypothesis that proposals or actions that do not uphold regional principles will face strong opposition. U.S. unilateral actions and its IAPF proposal did face opposition, but as noted earlier, it was not unified and thus not strong. Regional principles had their most notable impact on structuring U.S. justifications and proposals to conform nominally with regional norms.

The one hypothesis for which the Dominican case showed no support was the one concerning the threat to regional stability. Even though the conflict was perceived to be a low-level threat, Latin American members had little opportunity to oppose the militarized response because the United States chose to act unilaterally before consulting the organization. The question of turning to the United States for leadership based on the level of threat was not relevant in this case since the United States was already actively involved. This final hypothesis emphasizes one highly influential factor over which the OAS has little control: unilateral U.S. action. In the Dominican case, the organization was forced to respond to, rather than to initiate, action. The United States dominated within the OAS initially and throughout the operation. The OAS simply could not force the United States to take back actions to which it had already committed.

Cuba (1964)

Summary of Events. In the case of Cuba (1964), the issue before the Ninth Meeting of Foreign Ministers was whether the sanctions imposed on Cuba in 1962 ought to be expanded based on Cuba's continued acts of aggression and intervention in the region. An investigating committee verified the charges brought by Venezuela against Cuba and reported back to the Foreign Ministers. In their final resolutions, the Foreign Ministers warned Cuba that any continued acts of aggression could invite armed force against it, and called on member states to end their diplomatic relations with Cuba, to suspend all trade except food and medicine, and to suspend all sea transport. Mexico and Chile were the most outspoken in their opposition to these resolutions. Both argued that such sanctions were neither appropriate to the case, nor justified in the provisions of the Rio Treaty. The United States and Venezuela, however, were adamant that the sanctions be expanded to punish and prevent future Cuban intervention. Between the evidence gathered by the investigating committee indicting Cuba for intervention, and the pressure put on member states by the United States, the majority of member states voted to expand the sanctions. Thus, the United States was able to achieve one of its prime foreign policy objectives in the hemisphere by isolating Cuba through the multilateral actions of the OAS.

Structural Perspective. In the Cuban case, the level of resources needed to carry out the resolutions of the Foreign Ministers was low, thus one would not expect evidence of strong U.S. influence based on this factor. The Investigating Committee sent to verify the charges made by Venezuela against Cuba required few resources. In addition, the proposal to increase sanctions did not require many resources because it was a passive response to Cuba's revolutionary actions, not an active one. Member states were called upon to end their diplomatic relations with

Cuba, to suspend all trade except food and medicine, and to suspend all sea transport with Cuba. The final part of the resolution, however, suggested the potential for greater U.S. influence if Cuba did not cease its interventionary activities. Cuba was warned that any continued acts of aggression would invite the use of armed force against it in unilateral or collective self-defense. If the OAS was to credibly threaten to use armed force against continued aggressions, U.S. support would be needed. Thus, although only a low level of resources was needed to carry out the resolutions of the Ninth Meeting of Foreign Ministers, the threat of future militarized action unexpectedly gave the United States greater influence in shaping the organization's response to Cuban aggressions.

Internal Relational Perspective. When considering the degree of consensus among OAS members, there was little unity among Latin American states, and disagreement as well with the U.S. position. Mexico and Chile were the two Latin American members with the strongest reservations about the actions taken at the meeting. Other Latin American states also expressed concerns about the strong anticommunist position of the United States, but wanted to restore stability to the region by restraining the Castro government. The meeting produced two final documents: the Application of Measures to the Present Government of Cuba and the Declaration to the People of Cuba. The first document was in response to the report of the investigating committee. The Foreign Ministers resolved in paragraphs 1 and 2 to condemn emphatically the Government of Cuba for its acts of aggression and of intervention against Venezuela. Paragraph 3 laid out sanctions to be imposed according to the provisions of Articles 6 and 8 in the Rio Treaty. Paragraph 4 authorized the Council to discontinue the sanctions by two-thirds vote when Cuba no longer constituted a danger to regional peace and security. Paragraph 5 warned the Government of Cuba that further acts of aggression might provoke a militarized response by members in self-defense. Mexico and Chile both took exception to these resolutions. Chile abstained from voting on paragraphs 1 and 2, and voted against paragraph 3 because it did not believe the sanctions were consistent with the Rio Treaty. Finally, Chile voted against paragraph 5 because it believed there were discrepancies between that paragraph and Article 51 of the Charter of the United Nations concerning states' rights to self-defense until actions could be taken by the UN Security Council. Mexico had similar reservations and voted against paragraph 3 because it did not believe the Rio Treaty provisions were applicable to the current situation in Cuba.

The second document adopted by the Foreign Ministers, the Declaration to the People of Cuba, was directed at Cuban citizens and expressed sympathy for their loss of liberty. In the Declaration member states expressed their "deepest hope that the Cuban people . . . [would] be able . . . very soon to liberate themselves from the tyranny of the communist regime that oppresse[d] them." This essential call to action by the Cuban people was based on the support for democracy expressed in the Declaration of Santiago (1959) that "the exercise of representative democracy is the best vehicle for the promotion of . . . social and political progress." There were, however, also differing opinions among members about this second declaration. Not all members shared the same view of communism although it had been a topic of discussion for over a decade. Previous discussions within the OAS on the impact of communism in the hemisphere had led to a declaration at the Ninth International Conference of American States (1948) that condemned "international communism or any other totalitarian doctrine." Further anticommunist resolutions were adopted in 1954 in addressing the coup in Guatemala. The Declaration of Caracas (1954) linked communism to the issue of regional security, noting that "the domination or control of the political institutions of any American State by the international communist movement . . . would constitute a threat to the sovereignty and political independence of the American states, endangering the peace of America." The Declaration in 1954 was quite controversial, but as Cuba intervened in the 1960s in the affairs of other states to spark revolutions, more Latin American states came to support this anticommunist position. Chile and Mexico were the exceptions. Chile chose to abstain from voting on the Declaration to the People of Cuba because it believed the Declaration violated the principle of nonintervention. Mexico, likewise, expressed its disagreement with this strong anticommunist position on the basis of its interference with the domestic politics of Cuba.

The United States was able to exploit disagreements among Latin American members to eventually rally support for its policy proposals. The sanctions imposed at this time held for a decade. A proposal put forward in 1974 to end the sanctions failed to receive the two-thirds vote required. Only in 1975, at the Sixteenth Meeting of Foreign Ministers, did Latin American members gain enough support to end the enforcement of sanctions against Cuba as perceptions about the threat posed by communism declined.

Normative Perspective. The United States was able to justify its proposal for increased sanctions against Cuba by invoking Articles 6 and 8 of the

Rio Treaty. Article 6 establishes provisions for the Organ of Consultation to meet if the territory, sovereignty, or political independence of any state is threatened by an aggression that is not an armed attack, or by any situation that endangers the peace of the Americas. Article 8 establishes the measures that the Organ can take to sanction states and uphold the treaty. These include severing diplomatic and economic relations, interrupting communications and transportation, and the use of armed force. The proposed sanctions were within the scope of the Rio Treaty, despite the disagreement of Mexico and Chile on this point. The United States thus did not face strong opposition because its policy preferences were not contrary to the principles of the organization.

In addition to the resolutions being clearly based on provisions within the Rio Treaty, the two documents adopted by the Foreign Ministers also made reference to the norm of representative democracy and the incompatibility of communism with the principles of the Inter-American System. In the Declaration to the People of Cuba, members invoked the Charter—noting the fundamental rights of individuals; the Declaration of Santiago (1959)—advocating representative democracy; and the Ninth International Conference of American States (1948)—condemning international communism.

The opposition to the proposed sanctions, voiced by Mexico and Chile, was based on concerns about sovereignty and nonintervention. The support among member states for these arguments, however, was not as strong because the investigating committee had reported that Cuba was clearly behind the subversive attacks on the Venezuelan government. Cuba was thus already guilty of intervention and subject to punishment for its violations. Sanctions were also favored because they were viewed as less interventionary than direct military action, which was an alternative response to Cuban activities in the region. The U.S. position was based on regional principles and eventually won the support of a majority of Latin American members.

Environmental Perspective. By invoking Article 6 of the Rio Treaty and declaring the acts of Cuba against Venezuela to be acts of aggression and intervention, the Foreign Ministers indicated that they believed there was a serious threat to the peace and security of the region. The threat was not a high-level one because it did not involve widespread violence or place all members at risk. It was greater than a low level of threat, however, because Cuban actions were directed at destabilizing several regimes, particularly that of Venezuela. Despite the initial sanctions imposed on Cuba in 1962 by the Eighth Meeting of Foreign Ministers, the Castro government was still interfering in the affairs of other states. Members believed that further actions needed to be taken to reestablish regional stability. The United States was thus able to promote its proposal for increased sanctions in a favorable light. Not all Latin American states felt as strongly as the United States that communism was a major threat to the region, but most perceived Cuba's specific activities as destabilizing and were willing to support increased sanctions. In this case, the United States did not gain additional leverage because of the perceived level of threat, but did have support because many member states agreed with the U.S. position about the means to be used to restore stability.

Results. In this case, the United States succeeded in getting the OAS to adopt its preferred policy proposals despite opposition by some members. This case differs from the Dominican Republic (1965), however, because there was considerable support among many Latin American members for the U.S. proposals. The case cannot be classified as a case of compromise or consensus because there was no compromise with the positions of Mexico and Chile, nor was there consensus. The label of "U.S. leadership" rather than "U.S. dominance" might best fit this Cuban example. The factors of consensus and regional norms had the greatest impact on the level of influence the United States was able to exert in its "leadership" efforts in this case. A majority of Latin American states favored the U.S. position and did not need to be persuaded to expand sanctions against Cuba. Only a few states expressed disagreement with the U.S. proposal. The United States was able to provide leadership because there was no strong unified opposition. Although opponents to the U.S. proposal invoked the norms of sovereignty and nonintervention, the call for sanctions had stronger support because Cuba had already violated the principle of nonintervention and was thus subject to punishment.

Resources and the perceived threat to the region had little impact on the level of influence the United States was able to exert. The United States did not gain extra leverage based on the resources needed because the need was not significant. It did have the potential for greater influence, however, based on the possible need for military force in the future if Cuban aggressions continued. The Cuban situation was perceived as a mid-level threat and states were largely in agreement about means to address the threat. Members preferred sanctions to military action at the time. The United States used anticommunist rhetoric to try to raise security concerns, but didn't need to do too much to convince Latin American states of the threat and need for action.

Latin American Unity

In clear contrast to the cases of U.S. dominance discussed earlier, there are five cases in which the United States failed to dominate the organization despite efforts to do so. Successful Latin American resistance to U.S. pressure is evident in the cases of the Dominican Republic–Venezuela (1960), Panama–United States (1964), Cuba (1975), Nicaragua (1978), and Panama–United States (1989) (see table 5.1). In the Dominican Republic–Venezuelan case (1960), the Dominican government was accused of and condemned for trying to incite a coup in Venezuela. The case of the "Flag Riots" in Panama (1964) arose when American students refused to permit the flying of the Panamanian flag in the Canal Zone causing civil unrest between American and Panamanian citizens. The Meeting of Foreign Ministers in 1975 to consider lifting the sanctions against Cuba resulted in the release of members from their obligation to enforce the sanctions imposed in 1964. The Nicaraguan case (1978) dealt with the overthrow of the dictatorship of President Anastasio Somoza and subsequent rise of the Sandinistas to power. Finally, the case of Panama–United States (1989) addressed the U.S. military invasion of Panama to arrest President Manuel Noriega for drug trafficking. A closer look at the cases of Dominican Republic–Venezuela (1960) and Nicaragua (1978) reveals how the structural, internal relational, normative, and environmental factors resulted in reduced levels of U.S. influence in contrast to the cases above.

The Dominican Republic–Venezuela (1960)
Summary of Events. The Sixth Meeting of Foreign Ministers met in August 1960 to consider a conflict between the Dominican Republic and Venezuela. The meeting was preceded by three inflammatory events, each of which prompted Venezuela to request inter-American assistance. In November 1959, when a plane accidentally dropped pamphlets to incite rebellion among the Venezuelan armed forces on the nearby island of Curaçao, Venezuela requested that the IAPC investigate. In February 1960, Venezuela requested an IAPC investigation of the flagrant violations of human rights in the Dominican Republic that were aggravating tensions in the Caribbean. An assassination attempt on

President Betancourt of Venezuela in June 1960 led to a request for a Meeting of Consultation under the Rio Treaty. The Council called for a Meeting of the Foreign Ministers, which convened in August. The decision of the Foreign Ministers to condemn the Dominican Republic and impose sanctions was based on the reports from the IAPC and the Investigating Committee. The two IAPC reports on the leaflets and human rights violations indicated that the Dominican government under Rafael Trujillo was guilty of complicity and of human rights violations. Similarly, the Investigating Committee reported that the attack on Betancourt could not have been carried out without "the moral and material assistance of high officials in the government of the Dominican Republic" (Rio Treaty Application vol. II, July 8, 1960, 26).

Based on these reports the Foreign Ministers determined that Dominican actions justified collective action under Article 6 of the Rio Treaty. They did not, however, determine that further intervention was merited in this case. Latin American members believed sanctions were an adequate response based on Dominican aggression and intervention. The Foreign Ministers briefly considered a proposal by the United States to force the Dominican Republic to hold elections under the supervision of the OAS. This proposal was rejected by Latin American members, however, based on their concern about nonintervention. The United States then chose to abandon the proposal and supported the final resolution issued by the Foreign Ministers. The Foreign Ministers, by a vote of 19-0, condemned the Dominican government and declared it guilty of intervention and aggression. They imposed sanctions on the Dominican Republic by breaking diplomatic relations and suspending trade in arms. After a later report from the Special Committee sent to observe the effects of the sanctions, additional sanctions were imposed on petroleum and petroleum products, trucks, and spare parts. Sanctions were not lifted until January 1962, after Trujillo was assassinated.

In this case, the United States failed to significantly influence the actions of the OAS. The U.S. proposal for an electoral supervision mission was rejected by Latin American members, resulting in U.S. support for the Latin American proposal for sanctions alone.

Structural Perspective. The resources expended on this case were moderate, based on the number of committees involved and the extent and duration of their activities. The committee that investigated most extensively was the IAPC. The IAPC first investigated the dropping of antigovernment leaflets over Curaçao. It next looked into alleged violations of human rights in the Dominican Republic. Because the IAPC carried out its investigations prior to the Sixth Meeting, however, the decisions made by the Council (acting as provisional Organ of Consultation) and by the Foreign Ministers, did not reflect a consideration of the resources used by the IAPC.

Once the Organ of Consultation met, a third investigation was undertaken by the Investigating Committee, to examine the assassination attempt on President Betancourt. In addition to the investigating committee, the Organ also created the Special Committee, which visited the Dominican Republic three times (June, September, and November 1961) to determine the impact of sanctions on the island and whether the government still posed a danger to the peace and security of the region. After each visit, the committee reported back to the Council acting under the directive of the Foreign Ministers. The Council determined, based on the reports of the Special Committee, whether to impose new sanctions or to cancel them pending a change of behavior by the Dominican government. The U.S. proposal to monitor elections would have called for considerably more resources. Although this was not the main reason the U.S. proposal was rejected, it may have had an impact on the decisionmaking of the Foreign Ministers. The hypothesis on resources is supported in this case. There was no need for significant resources to be used to carry out the sanctions, and thus the United States was unable to wield significant influence by offering to provide extensive resources.

Internal Relational Perspective. On the issue of consensus, the United States faced a unified Latin American membership in opposition to its proposal for electoral monitoring and was unable to exert significant influence in the OAS. There was no dissension among Latin American members for the United States to exploit. There was a viable proposal for sanctions to be imposed, thus there was no need for U.S. leadership to provide a plan of action. Faced with a united opposition, the United States quickly abandoned its proposal and supported the imposition of sanctions against the Dominican Republic. Mecham (1961) notes that the United States had hoped to convince Latin American members that it disapproved of both right and leftist dictatorships by supporting the sanctions against Trujillo. In addition, the United States hoped that by supporting the Latin American proposal for sanctions, it would gain Latin American support against Castro at the Seventh Meeting of Consultation to follow. The United States, however, did not gain the support it had hoped for at the Seventh Meeting, settling instead for a compromise agreement (Wilson 1977, 14). (This case is discussed in detail in chapter 6.)

After the initial imposition of sanctions, there was some disagreement among Latin American members, as expressed by Brazil, on the value of the sanctions. When the Special Committee reported back to the Council on the effects of the sanctions and recommended an expansion of sanctions to include suspension of trade on petroleum products, trucks, and spare parts, the Brazilian representative wrote a dissenting opinion. He stated, "the real solution in such cases does not lie in the progressive application of coercive measures, but at the higher, more constructive, long-range level of moral sanctions and persuasion, which will not endanger inter-American solidarity but preserve the unity of the system ..." (Rio Treaty Application vol. II, Dissenting Vote of Brazil, 13). A majority of Council members, however, rejected this argument and voted to increase the sanctions as the committee had recommended.

Normative Perspective. On the issue of regional principles, the hypothesis states that any proposal or unilateral action by the United States that does not clearly uphold the principles of the organization will face strong opposition. In this case, the United States did face opposition based on regional principles to its proposal for electoral monitoring. Initially, the issue of nonintervention was not raised because the Trujillo dictatorship was universally detested and because the Dominican Republic was already guilty of intervention and thus subject to the consequences under the Rio Treaty. As the Foreign Ministers began to discuss the specific consequences for the Dominican actions, however, disagreements became evident. Latin American members saw a clear distinction between imposing sanctions based on violation of the Rio Treaty, and actively intervening in the government of the Dominican Republic in order to correct human rights violations and antidemocratic behavior (Rio Treaty Application vol. II, Dissenting Vote of Brazil, 13). In addition to their normative concerns about upholding the principle of nonintervention, Mecham (1961, 420) notes that Latin American members wanted to punish Trujillo and believed that sanctions would do so more decisively than promoting a transition to a representative democracy.

The United States attempted to use the IAPC report to rally support for its proposal. The IAPC reported that the international tensions in the Caribbean region had been aggravated by flagrant and widespread violation of human rights that had been and continued to be committed in the Dominican Republic (Report of the Inter-American Peace

Committee to the Seventh Meeting of Ministers of Foreign Affairs, August 5, 1960). It noted that the international tensions would continue as long as violations in the Dominican Republic continued. The United States interpreted this to be a strong reason to remove the existing government in order to end the violations and reduce international tensions. Latin American members, however, could not be persuaded that such measures would be appropriate for the OAS to take based on inter-American principles. The United States was unable to wield its considerable influence due to united Latin American opposition to its proposal, which was interpreted to contradict the principle of nonintervention and was seen as being "soft on Trujillo."

Environmental Perspective. I hypothesize that the greater the threat to regional instability, the greater influence the United States has within the OAS. In this case there was a moderate-level threat to the region given that two states were involved, and that several episodes of aggression and intervention had occurred. Regional tensions were high over the issue of Trujillo's disregard for human rights within the Dominican Republic, and his violations of other states' sovereignty in the region. The debates that occurred within the Meeting of Consultation would resemble those of the Cuban case (1960) (discussed in chapter 6) over the appropriate means to address the given threat. Latin American members favored sanctions as a justified response to Dominican intervention based on provisions in the Rio Treaty. They believed they could reduce the threat posed by the Dominican Republic by isolating it and cutting off its access to armaments. The United States, however, wanted a longer-term solution. Secretary of State Herter argued that the transition to representative democracy could best be achieved by resorting to orderly and peaceful processes (i.e., elections, not sanctions). This proposal, however, involved a degree of intervention that was unacceptable to Latin American members. The United States wanted to end the threat by removing the source. Latin Americans simply wanted to reduce the occurrence of Dominican interventions in the region through isolation. In this case, the threat level was moderate, but not high enough to merit a military solution. Thus, based on the perceived level of threat to the region, the United States did not have considerable influence on the final resolutions of the Meeting of Consultation. Both Latin American members and the United States wanted diplomatic solutions, but the U.S. proposal was more extensive than Latin Americans were willing to support.

Results. In the case of Venezuela–Dominican Republic (1960), three variables played an important role in reducing the level of U.S. influence within the OAS. The hypotheses on regional principles, consensus, and threat to regional stability were supported by the evidence in the case. When considering regional principles, Latin American members determined that sanctions were justified based on the acts of aggression committed by the Dominican Republic, but that intervention in the form of electoral monitoring was not. Thus, the U.S. proposal for elections ran counter to the regional principles of state sovereignty and nonintervention, and faced strong opposition from Latin American members. The United States was also unable to exert influence by dividing Latin American members over the issue of elections. Latin American states remained united in their support for sanctions over elections. On the issue of threat, Latin American members clearly did not feel that the Dominican situation posed enough of a threat that they needed to rely on U.S. leadership or military forces to counter it. Thus, Latin American states pursued the issue of sanctions and gained U.S. support for the measure rather than yielding to U.S. pressure.

The hypothesis on resources affecting influence was supported by the evidence in the case, but did not appear to be as significant in terms of affecting U.S. influence within the organization. Moderate resources were needed to carry out the extensive investigations, but several of these were completed before the Foreign Ministers even met on the issue. The resources used by the Special Committee to monitor the effects of the sanctions in the Dominican Republic were minimal. Thus, the United States could not offer to provide extensive resources in order to gain greater influence over their use. The U.S. proposal for an electoral monitoring team would have used more resources and likely given the United States more influence, but it was rejected by the Foreign Ministers.

Nicaragua (1978)

Before presenting the specifics concerning the revolution in Nicaragua in 1978, some general background on reforms within the OAS is necessary. In the late 1960s and early 1970s, Latin American members of the OAS began to push strongly for changes within the organization. Specifically, the members wanted to strengthen the economic and social mission of the OAS and its machinery to serve better the needs of economic development. The goal was to incorporate the Alliance for Progress commitments and then expand the multilateral activities of the OAS by committing the United States to specific long-term pledges supporting economic development and additional financial obligations.

Cognizant of U.S. preeminence in the OAS, Latin American members also wanted to limit the expanding political role of the Council (Wilson 1977, 14). The United States was resistant to such proposals, and remained preoccupied instead with Cuba and regional security issues. Despite U.S. reluctance to reform, however, the Protocol of Buenos Aires was passed in 1967 and resulted in an amended charter taking effect in 1970. The amended charter addressed Latin American members' concerns about fostering economic development in the region, and expanding the economic and social mechanisms of the organization by creating several new bodies, including the Inter-American Economic and Social Council. This reorganized economic Council promoted and coordinated OAS economic and social activities, as well as cooperated with other IOs to facilitate technical assistance.

In addition to passing economic reforms in the OAS (despite U.S. resistance), Latin American members also disregarded U.S. preferences concerning sanctions on Cuba. In 1974, the Foreign Ministers considered lifting sanctions, but just fell short of the necessary two-thirds votes to do so. In 1975, at the Sixteenth Meeting of Foreign Ministers, the Freedom of Action resolution was passed that allowed individual member states to resume relations with Cuba as they saw fit. Thus, following the Dominican case (1965), Latin American members asserted themselves in a variety of ways. They did not let U.S. preoccupation with security concerns thwart their efforts to either expand the economic focus the OAS, or to effectively lift the sanctions imposed on Cuba. This new Latin American assertiveness, along with diminishing concern about communist threats to the region, is quite evident in the Nicaraguan case.

Summary of Events. In September 1978, fighting in Nicaragua between the Sandinistas (FSLN) and the Somoza dictatorship increased dramatically, provoking Venezuela to call for a Meeting of Foreign Ministers under Articles 59 and 60 of the Charter (an issue of an urgent nature and common concern to all American states). The developing popular revolution initially had garnered support from Costa Rica, Honduras, Mexico, Panama, and Venezuela, and thus had significant regional repercussions. Violations of Costa Rican borders and attacks on civilians resulted in the Costa Rican representative requesting an Ad Hoc Committee to observe its borders with Nicaragua. The Council sent a committee to Costa Rica and, after two weeks of deliberations, called for the Seventeenth Meeting of Consultation by the Foreign Ministers. The Foreign Ministers issued a resolution on September 23, 1978 that urged the various governments to refrain from any actions that might aggravate the situation. They also sent the Inter-American Commission on Human Rights (at the invitation of Nicaraguan President Anastasio Somoza) to investigate alleged human rights violations. No further action was taken until June 1979 when the United States requested that the Foreign Ministers reconvene to consider the "critical situation" in Nicaragua. The United States presented a proposal to establish a government of national reconciliation with the presence of an inter-American peacekeeping force to support the process. Latin American members rejected the proposal, fearing it would serve as a justification for direct U.S. intervention. The final resolution passed by the Foreign Ministers was unprecedented. Based on the critical report of the human rights commission, the Foreign Ministers essentially called on the people of Nicaragua to replace the Somoza government and establish a representative democracy through elections:

> The Seventeenth Meeting of Consultation of Ministers of Foreign Affairs declares that the solution of the serious problem is exclusively within the jurisdiction of the people of Nicaragua. That in view of the [ministers] this solution should be arrived at on the basis of the following:
> 1. Immediate and definitive replacement of the Somoza regime.
> 2. Installation in Nicaraguan territory of a democratic government . . .
> 3. Guarantee of the respect for human rights of all Nicaraguans . . .
> 4. The holding of free elections as soon as possible that will lead to the establishment of a truly democratic government that guarantees peace, freedom and justice. (Seventeenth Meeting of Consultation of Ministers of Foreign Affairs, June 23, 1979)

In July 1979, Somoza fled Nicaragua and the provisional government pledged to the OAS secretary general to install a representative democratic government. This was the end of the Seventeenth Meeting of Consultation's involvement in Nicaragua (Walker 1985).

The ability of the United States to influence the decisions made by the Organ of Consultation in this case was surprisingly ineffective. Thomas Walker (1982) has noted that the reaction to U.S. Secretary of State Cyrus Vance's proposals "may well have marked the nadir of US influence in the OAS." Anatoly Glinkin (1990, 141) also remarks, "United States had lost its control . . . it was no longer able to use [the OAS] for pursuit of its own interests, or to bring pressure to bear via [the organization] on the foreign policies of the Latin American countries or to carry out armed intervention in the region under the OAS flag." This case provides an excellent example of how institutional factors explain why the United States was unable to exert its influence and Latin American members were able to prevail within the OAS.

Structural Perspective. On the matter of resources needed to carry out the resolutions of the Organ of Consultation, the Foreign Ministers chose an option that would require few resources from the organization. By stating specifically that the "solution of the serious problem is exclusively within the jurisdiction of the people of Nicaragua," the Foreign Ministers made the Nicaraguan people responsible for taking action against Somoza, rather than undertaking multilateral actions as the United States had proposed (Seventeenth Meeting of Consultation of Ministers of Foreign Affairs, June 23, 1979, 1). By rejecting the proposal by the United States that would have required a considerable contribution from the United States, the Foreign Ministers denied the United States the ability to influence the actions of the OAS in this case through its contribution of resources.

Internal Relational Perspective. On the issue of consensus, Latin American members were unified in their opposition to the U.S. proposal for an inter-American force to be sent to Nicaragua. Most Latin American states were actively supporting the Sandinistas, although Argentina was selling arms to Somoza. These members were in agreement in their call for the overthrow of Somoza. The United States had little to no opportunity to exploit divisions among Latin Americans to gain support for its position.

Recognizing that the United States would not have much influence with Latin American members on this issue, President Jimmy Carter was not committed to using the OAS to address the conflict in Nicaragua. Rather than working to persuade Latin American members to support the U.S. position on Nicaragua, Carter worked unilaterally to try to achieve a negotiated settlement between the Sandinistas and Somoza. The United States no longer wanted to support the Somoza government with its numerous human rights abuses, but had few other alternatives available. Carter's negotiation efforts sought to create a government of national reconciliation that would include elements of the Somoza government as well as other opposition factions. The United States did not support Sandinista participation, however, because of their links to Cuba and their communist tenets. President Carter hoped that by including opposition factions other than the Sandinistas in a government of national reconciliation, they could minimize the influence of the Sandinistas and still remove Somoza from power. Carter's efforts were met with a lack of cooperation from and rejection by Somoza.

A lull in the fighting in early 1979 falsely reassured the United States that the Somoza regime would be able to remain in power until the scheduled elections in 1981 when a new, non-Somoza regime could come to power. The United States proceeded in its negotiations with Somoza to accommodate his timetable for leaving office (Morley 1994, 309). In May 1979 the Sandinistas initiated their second revolutionary wave that would topple Somoza in July. On June 11, at an interagency Policy Review meeting in Washington, State Department representatives suggested that the proposal for an IAPF should be quietly discussed with Latin American governments (Lake 1989, 220). By a second meeting on June 19, members of the State Department reported that initial soundings suggested that the chances of gaining support for a peace force were slim. No further efforts were made to gain support from Latin American members because memories of earlier U.S. interventions were still vivid among Latin Americans and further efforts would likely backfire (Lake 1989, 220). Alternative plans were made to form a government of National Reconciliation that could request the support of the United States. Based on the victories attained by the Sandinistas, however, the State Department determined that calling for an inter-American peace "presence" was their best chance to maintain some control over events in Nicaragua (Lake 1989, 223). When the United States put forth its proposal on June 23, Latin American members rejected it outright, believing it to be the last effort of the United States to gain control over the situation in Nicaragua before the Sandinistas came to power.

Because President Carter had chosen to pursue negotiations bilaterally and had not been active in OAS efforts at resolution, the United States was in no position to assert itself when it finally chose to participate through the forum of the OAS. In the Nicaraguan case, the hypothesis on consensus is supported. The United States was unable to gain influence within the organization because of the unified rejection of its proposal by Latin American states.

Normative Perspective. On the issue of principles, the Nicaraguan case proves to be anomalous. In this case, the U.S. proposal was based on the precedent of the Dominican case (1965) and the resolution of the Foreign Ministers was unprecedented in terms of advocating the overthrow of a sovereign head of state. The Foreign Ministers based their decisions on the reports of two committees. The Ad Hoc Committee investigated the border violations reported by Costa Rica at the request of the Permanent Council. They found the Nicaraguan National Guard guilty of attacking civilian villages in Costa Rica. The Foreign Ministers chose to keep the Committee intact to continue its duties and provide updates on the situation. Shortly thereafter, the Foreign Ministers sent the IACHR to investigate violations of human rights within Nicaragua. Its highly critical report was issued in October and found that the Somoza government had been responsible for "serious, persistent and generalized violations of human rights" (IACHR Report, October 1978, 77). The resolutions issued by the Foreign Ministers in June 1979 reflect the conclusions of these reports. Whereas the "inhumane conduct of the dictatorial regime governing the country, as evidenced by the report of the IACHR, is the fundamental cause of the dramatic situation faced by the Nicaraguan people," the Foreign Ministers declared that the people of Nicaragua should install a democratic government that reflects the free will of the Nicaraguan people. Acknowledging the involvement of other member states in the conflict, the Foreign Ministers resolved to urge member states to facilitate an enduring and peaceful solution of the Nicaraguan problem by scrupulously respecting the principle of nonintervention and abstaining from any action that might by incompatible with a peaceful solution (Seventeenth Meeting of Consultation of Ministers of Foreign Affairs, June 23, 1979, 2).

Although such a proposal was unprecedented, and appeared to contradict regional principles, the resolution reflected larger changes in the organization as a whole and among member states shifting toward domestic democratic regimes. It could even be argued that principles *were* upheld in the Nicaraguan case. Nonintervention was still a key principle and was raised in reference to the U.S. proposal for an intervention force. The inclusion of democracy was a new priority, however, and the means recommended by the Organ of Consultation to the Nicaraguan people were unprecedented.

The decisions of the Foreign Ministers resemble decisions made more recently in the 1990s in support of democratic government in the region than any case preceding the Nicaraguan crisis. The Nicaraguan case is perhaps a turning point in the organization, with members choosing to support the principle of democratic government even to the point of overlooking issues of sovereignty. This shift illustrates that priorities and principles do evolve over time. Although the principle of representative democracy had been a part of the OAS since it was founded, it had not received such primacy prior to the Nicaraguan crisis.

The hypothesis that any proposal or unilateral action by the United States that does not clearly uphold the principles of the organization will face strong opposition is not supported in this case. The U.S. proposal did not violate any principles of the organization, and in fact offered the least radical response of the proposals presented in terms of principled actions. Given that the U.S. proposal was not contradictory to regional principles, it should not have faced such strong opposition. As noted earlier, however, this was a low point in U.S.–Latin American relations. Latin American assertiveness combined with American disinterest in OAS multilateralism may well have meant that any proposal by the United States, whether upholding the principles or not, likely would have been rejected by Latin American members. Although the U.S. proposal did not oppose regional principles, Latin American members clearly viewed the U.S. proposal for a peacekeeping force, which would consist of mostly U.S. troops, as a regionally sanctioned unilateral action. In other words, it would be very much like the force that entered the Dominican Republic, consisting of mostly U.S. troops with an OAS approval of their presence. Such action, in this case, was not supported by Latin American members.

Environmental Perspective. The level of influence that the United States was able to exert based on the perceived threat to regional stability was not strong in the case of Nicaragua. The perceived threat level in the Nicaraguan case was moderate because of the number of neighboring governments involved in the civil war. There was some regional instability stemming from incursions into Nicaragua from across the Costa Rican border. There was not a large risk of escalation, however, because the situation was an internal conflict, and all neighboring countries opposed the Somoza dictatorship. Because there was no support for Somoza, there was little risk of escalation among Latin American states that supported opposing sides in the civil war. Latin American members did not feel that they needed to depend on the U.S. military to ensure security in the region. Despite U.S. efforts to arouse the fears of member states by linking the Sandinistas to Castro, members did not perceive the Sandinistas as a regional threat. The Sandinistas did not have a revolutionary agenda in terms of spreading the revolution to their neighbors as Cuba had had when the OAS acted against it in 1960. Latin American members did not believe the Nicaraguan situation called for a militarized OAS response.

The United States had made several diplomatic efforts to resolve the conflict before they proposed the multilateral peacekeeping force, but failed to gain Somoza's cooperation. The United States had participated with Guatemala and the Dominican Republic on a tri-national commission authorized by the OAS to mediate with Nicaraguan elites and Somoza (but which excluded the Sandinistas). The goal of the mediators was to help establish an interim government before the 1981 elections were held and to keep the National Guard in place. The Nicaraguan elites refused to accept keeping the National Guard in power and left the negotiations, leaving only Somoza with whom to negotiate (Walker 1982). Carter tried, unsuccessfully, to use economic and political pressure to get Somoza to reach reconciliation. As it became more evident that the Sandinistas were gaining the upper hand, the United States made its peacekeeping proposal in an effort to establish a multiparty government of reconciliation that would bring non-Sandinistas to power and yet remove Somoza. The U.S. representative to the OAS made a persuasive argument (particularly in retrospect) that in order for a democratic government to take root in Nicaragua, greater international help would be needed in the form of a peacekeeping force, in addition to economic and humanitarian aid.

Despite U.S. arguments, however, Latin American members were not persuaded of the necessity for a military response. By the time the Foreign Ministers issued their unprecedented call for the ouster of Somoza by the Nicaraguan people, the Sandinistas were close to claiming victory and thus no extensive multilateral action was necessary to secure Somoza's ouster. The United States was unable to gain greater influence within the organization by portraying the situation as a serious regional threat that would require greater intervention on the part of the OAS with U.S. leadership.

Results. The Nicaraguan case provides a stark contrast to the actions and events surrounding the Dominican case in 1965. There are a number of similarities between the conflicts, but the reaction of the OAS and of individual member states was quite distinct. Both cases constituted civil wars with communist elements among the factions. Both were fought in an effort to overthrow authoritarian leaders in power. Both caused regional instability and raised security concerns for other OAS members. Whereas as many states were almost disinterested in the Dominican case until the United States intervened, in the Nicaraguan case, neighboring states were actively involved in the conflict itself. Furthermore, the ability of the United States to influence the decisions made by the Organ of Consultation was surprisingly ineffective.

Three of the four variables had a significant impact on the level of influence the United States was able to exert in the Nicaraguan case. Just as in the Dominican/Venezuelan case (1960), consensus among Latin American members played an important role in reducing the level of influence of the United States within the organization. Members were united in their opposition to the U.S. proposal for an inter-American force in Nicaragua. The perceived level of threat to the region also played an important role in reducing U.S. influence. Without a significant threat to the region, the United States was unable to justify a militarized response to the Nicaraguan conflict, nor to exercise any kind of leadership stemming from such a response. The third variable, resources, was linked to the policy choices of the organization. Because the Foreign Ministers chose not to send in a multilateral peacekeeping force to establish democratic government in Nicaragua, they did not need to request the extensive resources of the United States. This gave the United States little opportunity to exert its influence through the provision or control of resources.

Surprisingly, the hypothesis on regional principles was not clearly supported. The significant role that regional principles played in the Dominican/Venezuelan case (1960) is not seen in this case. Latin American members chose to uphold the principle of democratic government while essentially disregarding the principle of sovereignty by calling for the replacement of Somoza. The U.S. proposal was not in opposition to regional principles, and was in fact, based on the precedent of the Dominican case (1965).

Summary

An examination of two cases in which the United States dominated the OAS, and two cases where Latin American unity led to the rejection of U.S. preferences, reveals the impact of four different institutional factors on the level of influence the United States is able to exert within the organization. Consensus among members, or the lack thereof, was a key factor in each of the organizational decisionmaking outcomes. Unity among Latin American members gave them the strength they needed to resist U.S. pressure when they were opposed to U.S. proposals. In the Dominican case (1965), the United States wielded considerable influence within the OAS because of the inability of Latin American members to agree on an alternative response to the IAPF proposal. In the Dominican–Venezuelan and Nicaraguan cases, where the United States was faced with a unified Latin American membership with a preferred plan of its own, the Latin American states rejected the U.S. proposals. The need for significant resources gave the United States greater influence in the Dominican case (1965), while the lower level of resources needed in the Dominican/Venezuelan (1960) and Nicaraguan (1978) cases reduced U.S. influence.

The impact of regional principles on U.S. influence was evident, but less predictable than with the other factors because of the contradictions between some of these norms, and the changing priorities given to them by member states. Whereas support for nonintervention and sovereignty led to the rejection of electoral intervention in the Dominican Republic in 1960, these principles were downplayed in the case of Nicaragua in deference to promoting representative democracy. At times the United States was able to rally support for its position based on normative arguments, at other times it failed in such endeavors. Even when principles did not significantly restrict U.S. actions, however, as in the Dominican case (1965), they did influence the United States enough that it attempted to justify its actions and proposals based on regional principles in order to gain Latin American support. Norms thus affected U.S. influence by pressuring the United States to adhere to regional principles in order to gain Latin American support for its policies. Uncertainty arose, however, when it was unclear which norms would be given top priority within the OAS when the norms conflicted with each other. Regional principles were crucial to providing Latin American members with justifications to resist U.S. proposals in the Dominican Republic–Venezuela (1960) case. By presenting U.S. proposals as inattentive to or contrary to certain regional principles, Latin American members were able to strengthen their position in opposition to the United States around a unifying factor.

The threat level, when linked to consideration of diplomatic versus military options, also affected the U.S. ability to gain support for its proposals. None of the cases provided the United States with the opportunity to exert its influence based on a high level of threat to the region. The United States attempted to portray the situations in each case as a serious threat to the region in an effort to gain support for its proposals. But in both cases with reduced U.S. influence in the organization, Latin American members were unconvinced by such arguments and rejected U.S. interventionist proposals. When Latin American members did not feel greatly threatened by the security issue under consideration, they maintained greater flexibility in their response options and did not have to rely on U.S. military might to secure the region. Latin Americans preferred to use other available means to restore order to the region.

Consideration of the perceived level of threat offers an additional insight. In cases where there is a mid-level threat, it is important to make a distinction between an overt military threat and a less obvious ideological one when considering the level of influence the United States is able to exert. Latin American members often rejected the U.S.

interpretation of level of threat posed by communism and its proposed militarized responses. Overt military threats are more likely to result in increased U.S. influence than more subtle ideological ones.

It is evident that these structural, internal relational, normative, and environmental factors each affect decisionmaking and U.S. influence within the OAS, but it is also important to determine how these variables interact with each other. Overall, in comparing the four cases in this chapter, the variable that directly resulted in the United States not gaining passage of its proposals was consensus among Latin American members. Unity among Latin American states resulted in a majority vote that overruled U.S. policy proposals. The ability of Latin American members to achieve a unified consensus, however, is linked to resources and the level of threat to the region (and the military/diplomatic options available). In order for Latin American states to be able to reject a U.S. proposal, an alternative plan must be presented if actions are to be taken. In the Dominican/Venezuelan case (1960), Latin American members proposed sanctions as opposed to electoral monitoring. Latin American members encouraged an internal solution rather than a multi-lateral response in the case of Nicaragua (1978). Alternative policy options involve consideration of both military and diplomatic options and the available resources. By having an alternative to a U.S. proposal, and one that did not require extensive resources, nor rely on the United States for military support, Latin American members were able to resist U.S. pressure to pursue U.S. proposals.

Formulating an alternative response to crises also requires an evaluation of the conflict and an assessment of options based on the type of conflict and its threat to the region. A variety of diplomatic options are available to members when a threat does not necessitate a militarized response. These options resulted in a reduced level of U.S. influence when threats were low or moderate in three of the four cases. The Dominican case (1965) was the exception. Although the threat was low, the United States essentially overreacted militarily, but still succeeded in gaining OAS justification for its continued presence.

In order to present their policy alternatives to a crisis, Latin American members need to justify them in terms of OAS principles. Reference to principles is also useful in justifying a rejection of U.S. proposals. For example, Latin American members rejected electoral monitoring in the Dominican Republic in 1960 based on the principles of sovereignty and nonintervention. By being able to argue against the U.S. position based on principle, Latin American members weaken U.S. influence in the organization. These variables can work together to produce outcomes that are not those preferred by the United States. Norms are used to justify opposition to the United States, or to support alternative plans. Alternative plans, often requiring fewer resources, can be formulated to unite Latin American members and to resist U.S. proposals.

Chapter 6 continues exploring the impact of these institutional factors on U.S. influence, and further examines the organizational decisionmaking process by looking at cases that resulted in compromise or consensus.

CHAPTER 6

CONSENSUS AND COMPROMISE: COOPERATION BETWEEN MEMBER STATES

Introduction

In contrast to chapter 5, which examined organizational outcomes when there was disagreement among OAS member states that resulted in one side or the other dominating the policymaking process, this chapter looks at those less extreme cases where there was consensus or compromise among members. As noted earlier, relations between the United States and Latin American members have often been cooperative rather than conflictual. Between 1948 and 1989 there have been ten cases where all member states were in agreement concerning the means to address the conflict and acted in a united fashion, and five cases in which compromises were reached despite disagreements between the United States and Latin American members over what actions should be taken by the organization (see table 5.1). Although the cases where there are significant disagreements among members provide strong test cases for the hypotheses, an examination of the cases where there is consensus or compromise among members provides important insights into the member dynamics within the organization. This chapter explores two cases where there was consensus among OAS members, and two cases where the member states reached a compromise on the actions to be taken. The cases of Costa Rica–Nicaragua (1955) dealing with anti-Somoza rebels, and Panama (1959) removing a small invasion force from the country, serve as examples of consensus within the organization. The Cuban (1960) and Caribbean (1959) cases reveal an outcome of compromise between members. In the Cuban case (1960), the United States and Latin American members come to a compromise agreement on the final wording of the resolution issued by the Seventh Meeting of Foreign Ministers that condemns international communist intervention in the hemisphere. The Caribbean case (1959), dealing with extensive revolutionary activities in the region, is representative of many cases in which there is a moderate level of disagreement among members. The differences of opinion in these cases are not as stark as some of the cases with a low level of consensus (discussed earlier in chapter 5). Many of the mid-level consensus cases result in a compromise agreement that incorporates the preferences of all members, including the United States, so that there is full support for the final resolution.

Organizational Consensus

Although the cases where there is considerable disagreement among member states (particularly when the United States is challenged by Latin American members) receive the most attention, the most common outcome is a consensual agreement on the actions to be taken by the OAS. In ten of the 26 cases under consideration, the outcome has been consensual with high levels of agreement among member states on how to address the security concern. States in the hemisphere have long valued consensus when taking multilateral actions. Not only does agreement of all member states strengthen the influence of the organization, but also reinforces solidarity among members. Consensus is understood in this study to mean that members are in agreement about the interests of the organization in a particular case, and the means used to achieve them. In cases where "compromise" is the decisionmaking outcome, members frequently achieve a consensual agreement after debate and discussion of their different preferences on an issue. In those cases where there is a difference of opinion, it is usually over the means to an agreed-upon end. In these cases the difference of opinion usually results in a compromise in which some of the concerns of each party are addressed. The following examples illustrate two cases of consensus in which members were united in their response to security threats to the region. Because there are no indications of the United States using pressure to gain passage of the proposals when there was general agreement on policies, there is no way to test the individual hypotheses. The United States had no need to exert pressure to achieve its policy objectives in these cases. Thus, the cases in this section are discussed without specific reference to the hypotheses concerning the level of U.S. influence in the organization.

Costa Rica–Nicaragua (1955)

In early 1955 President José Figueres of Costa Rica and Anastasio Somoza of Nicaragua were openly feuding. In January, an invasion of

Costa Rica took place from Nicaraguan territory. The OAS Council quickly convened as the provisional Organ of Consultation under the Rio Treaty and sent an investigating committee to the border to determine the conditions there. The conflict escalated when three Nicaraguan planes strafed Costa Rica. The Council authorized an air observation patrol and the sale of four U.S. aircraft to Costa Rica for its self-defense. The Council also issued a series of resolutions: (1) condemning the acts of intervention in Costa Rica; (2) requesting the Nicaraguan government (and all American governments) take the necessary measures to prevent the use of their territories for any military action against the government of another state; and (3) appealing to both Costa Rica and Nicaragua to sign the bilateral agreement in the Pact of Amity that had been negotiated in 1948 after a series of earlier border clashes. Negotiations eventually produced the implementation of the Pact of Amity in 1956.

Consensus among member states is evident in this case in several ways. When the case was brought before the Council, there was no disagreement that the Rio Treaty ought to be invoked. Members recognized the need to take action based on the violation of the principles of sovereignty and nonintervention. Members were united in their resolve to take action quickly to maintain the solidarity (and security) of member states. The Council helped provide the means for Costa Rica to defend itself, but upheld the principle of pacific settlement by encouraging both sides to negotiate and implement the Pact of Amity already agreed upon.

Panama (1959)

The case of Panama (1959) produced a similarly consensual response from OAS member states. In April 1959, 87 armed men, mostly Cubans, landed in Panama. The Panamanian military surrounded them but they refused to surrender. The Panamanian government invoked the Rio Treaty, but did not specifically bring charges against Cuba for intervention. The Council, acting as provisional Organ of Consultation, sent out an investigating committee, followed by air and sea observers to make sure no further invasion forces were in the area. Castro denied any connections to the invasion force and Panama believed that the Cuban government had not assisted the expedition. The Cuban government sent a representative to Panama to help negotiate a surrender by the invaders. By being united in their resolve to address this threat to Panama, the Council was able to respond quickly and cooperatively. In both these cases, member states were in agreement concerning the actions to be taken by the organization.

The hypotheses concerning institutional factors that affect U.S. influence are not applicable in these cases where there was consensus among member states. The hypotheses are based on the assumption that, given a difference of opinion about the actions the organization should take, the United States or Latin American states will attempt to influence members to adopt policies supporting their preferences. Because there is no disagreement among members in these cases, there is no need for (nor evidence of) any member state exerting itself to persuade others to support its position. Members agreed that a threat to the region existed and also agreed on how to address that threat. This level of cooperation was achieved most frequently during the 1950s prior to increased Cold War tensions.

Member State Compromises

Although member states in the OAS value consensus, it is no surprise that from time to time members do not agree about the degree of threat facing the region, or the appropriate means to respond to that threat. In most cases when there has been disagreement, the United States has put forth a proposal for which it has only partial support among Latin American states. It is up to member states to determine whether to support the U.S. proposal, to put forth their own counterproposal, or to negotiate a compromise between the different positions on the issue. In five cases, OAS member states have negotiated a compromise with the United States in order to address security concerns in the region. The cases of the Caribbean (1959) and Cuba (1960) serve as examples of how compromises have been reached between member states. An examination of each hypothesis in these cases helps to determine how much influence the United States was able to wield and to what effect.

Caribbean (1959)
Summary of Events. When the Fifth Meeting of Foreign Ministers convened in August 1959, it met to consider a broad range of events causing instability in the Caribbean. Tensions between dictatorial regimes and democracies had been on the rise, with both sides engaged in covert acts of intervention. There was considerable debate about how to address these tensions. Venezuela and Cuba both favored assertive OAS action to promote democracy and protect human rights, even if this meant compromising the principle of nonintervention. The United States and a majority of other Latin American states were reluctant to

sacrifice nonintervention even in support of democracy. The United States argued that overthrowing oppressive regimes would produce more disorder and tension in the region than already existed, and would provide an opportunity for communists to move into the region.[44] Cuba and Venezuela argued that more democratic governments would result in improved relations among member states. The concerns of both sides were addressed in the meeting. No interventionary actions were approved by the Foreign Ministers to promote democracy, but they did adopt the Declaration of Santiago, which addressed many of the priorities of those states that advocated greater democracy. The Declaration laid out specific principles that characterized representative democracy. The Foreign Ministers also created the IACHR, and strengthened the IAPC, which investigated disputes among members. The compromise reached addressed both the concerns of those promoting democracy, and those that did not want to compromise the principles of nonintervention and state sovereignty.

Structural Perspective. In order to carry out the policies adopted by the Fifth Meeting of Foreign Ministers, the OAS did not need a high level of financial resources, and had no need for military resources. The IAPC had already been established in 1956 when its temporary statute was adopted as permanent by the OAS Council. The Fifth Meeting expanded the authority of the IAPC to act at the request of governments or *on its own initiative* rather than only with the prior consent of the parties involved. Because the financial support and staffing for the IAPC was already established and did not require additional resources from member states, the United States could not use the need for resources to influence the policy decisions concerning the situation in the Caribbean.

The Foreign Ministers also adopted Resolution VI that created the Inter-American Commission on Human Rights. The Commission was to "promote respect for such rights" as enumerated in the 1948 American Declaration on the Rights and Duties of Man. It was given authority to prepare studies and reports, and to organize lectures and seminars on human rights. Its powers did not extend, however, to investigating human rights violations or making policy recommendations directly to governments. The seven-member Commission did not require significant resources to carry out its limited mandate at this time. The United States thus did not gain significant leverage at the meeting with the decision to create the IACHR.

Internal Relational Perspective. Although member states placed different priorities on potential solutions to the tensions in the Caribbean, with some preferring active intervention and others resisting such proposals, relations between members remained relatively agreeable. In this case, the mid-level of consensus stemmed from a disagreement between a few Latin American states and the rest of the OAS membership, including the United States. The majority of Latin American members were unified in their support of the principle of nonintervention, and were in agreement with the position of the United States. Venezuela and Cuba wanted to actively promote democracy and human rights and sacrifice (to some extent) the principle of nonintervention. Although the majority could have adopted a final resolution without taking the preferences of Venezuela and Cuba into consideration, the compromise agreement that they reached strengthened the resolutions issued by the Foreign Ministers and succeeded in upholding the core principles of the organization. Because the United States was in agreement with a majority of members on how to deal with Caribbean instability, the United States did not have to exert significant influence to achieve its policy preferences. In this case, because a majority of states agreed with the U.S. position, the issue of consensus was less of a factor in explaining OAS actions than the consideration of regional principles.

Normative Perspective. The maintenance of regional principles is a consideration in each of the conflict resolution cases the OAS handles. OAS member states, including the United States, take particular care to frame their policy proposals in terms of support for the regional principles that have evolved over the past century. There are times, however, when these principles can be contradictory. The Caribbean case (1959) provides a good example of how the principles enshrined in the OAS Charter can lead to conflicting justifications. The United States and many other Latin American states wanted to stabilize relations in the Caribbean, but did not want to actively intervene in the sovereignty of other member states. They argued that such interventions would increase the risk of instability and might allow subversive communist elements to gain a foothold in the region. Venezuela and Cuba argued that the OAS ought to intervene in order to promote democracy and human rights in the region because it would lead to greater stability. Both sides justified their proposals based on regional norms.

State sovereignty is clearly established in Article 3 of the OAS Charter, which states, "every state has the right to choose, without external interference, its political economic and social system . . . and has the duty to abstain from intervening in the affairs of another State." The Charter upholds both the principle of democracy and nonintervention in Article 2: "The Organization of American States . . . proclaims the following essential purposes . . . to promote and consolidate representative democracy, with due respect for the principle of nonintervention." In Article 3 the organization further affirms, "the solidarity of the American States and the high aims which are sought through it require the political organization of those States on the basis of the effective exercise of representative democracy." Article 3 also establishes the "fundamental rights of the individual without distinction as to race, nationality, creed, or sex." These individual human rights are further elaborated in Article 33 in which members agree that "equality of opportunity, equitable distribution of wealth and income, and the full participation of their peoples in decisions relating to their own development are . . . basic objectives to integral development."

In this case, because contradictory norms were raised to justify proposals for both action and inaction, members needed to reconcile the contradictions so that none of the principles were devalued. This was essentially accomplished in the Declaration of Santiago that reaffirmed the value of representative democracy, but did not go so far as to intervene in members' domestic affairs to achieve democratic government. The Declaration noted, "the existence of anti-democratic regimes constitutes a violation of the principles on which the Organization of American States is founded, and a danger to united and peaceful relationships in the hemisphere" (Final Act 1960). The Declaration furthered specified that governments should be the result of free elections, and that there should be a separation of powers to ensure rule of law. The Declaration of Santiago also upheld human rights principles by declaring that governments should maintain a system of social justice based on respect for human rights, and that human rights should be protected by effective judicial procedures. The actions to be taken with regard to these declarations involved the commissioning of the IAPC to study the relationship between respect for human rights and the effective exercise of representative democracy, and the relationship between economic underdevelopment and political instability.

The policy outcome in this case was clearly affected by the existence of regional norms. Even though only a minority of states advocated actions based on the principles of democracy and human rights, the United States and the majority of Latin American states could not afford to ignore the invocation of these principles. The actions taken by the organization were thus a compromise based on the policy preferences of each group of states.

Environmental Perspective. The Fifth Meeting of Foreign Ministers was convoked pursuant to Articles 39 and 40 of the OAS to consider the "serious situation in the Caribbean area." Tensions between democracies and dictatorships, and revolutionary activities in the region, had led to instability and ongoing conflicts between member states. Growing demands for democratic progress and social change within oppressive regimes needed to be addressed. Although, in June 1959, Haiti and Ecuador proposed that a Meeting of Consultation be held to consider the Dominican allegation that invading forces had been organized in Cuba and Venezuela against it, the Meeting of Consultation was eventually convoked to consider a broader series of events causing regional instability. Because the Foreign Ministers were considering the general situation, not specific grievances, their policy response was also generalized. They sought diplomatic, not militarized, actions to promote regional security. Although there was a mid-level threat to security, members were largely in agreement that military actions would lead to greater instability, not increased security. There was no need for the United States to take a leading role based on the perceived threat to the region because members believed security could be strengthened through the diplomatic actions laid out in the Declaration of Santiago.

Results. In the Caribbean case (1959) the factor of consensus played a lesser role than in other cases where Latin American interests have been pitted against U.S. preferences. This is due, in part, to the fact that the disagreement among members was with a minority of Latin American states, with the majority agreeing with the U.S. position. The factor of regional norms was much more influential in shaping the policy outcome in this case. The need to consider sovereignty and nonintervention, as well as democracy and human rights, led to the inclusion of the positions of the majority as well as the minority (Venezuela and Cuba). Resources and perceived threat level had less of an impact on decisionmaking and policy outcome. The empowerment of the IAPC and the creation of the Commission on Human Rights did not require significant resources. Furthermore, members felt that the threat could best be addressed through diplomatic actions rather than a militarized response.

Cuba (1960)
Summary of Events. The Seventh Meeting of Foreign Ministers was convoked on August 22, 1960, immediately following the Sixth Meeting

of Foreign Ministers held in San José, Costa Rica. The Sixth Meeting had dealt solely with the Dominican Republic–Venezuela (1960) conflict (discussed in chapter 5). The Seventh Meeting was to focus entirely on Cuba and the question of external communist influence in the hemisphere. The Castro government was actively trying to export its communist revolution to other states in the circum-Caribbean and thus provoking violent unrest in several countries. Peru requested the meeting under Article 39 of the Charter, considering the effects of Cuban actions to be of "an urgent nature and common concern to the American states." After receiving a report of the IAPC and engaging in much discussion, the Foreign Ministers unanimously (19-0) adopted the Declaration of San José. The Declaration: (1) condemned all forms of "extracontinental intervention" that could endanger inter-American solidarity; (2) rejected Sino-Soviet efforts to destroy hemispheric unity; (3) reaffirmed nonintervention, including ideological intervention; (4) reaffirmed the incapability of totalitarianism with the Inter-American System; (5) requested members to submit to OAS discipline and principles; and (6) declared that all controversies between members should be resolved by peaceful measures (Seventh Meeting of Consultation of Ministers of Foreign Affairs, August 22–29, 1960, 4–5).

In this case, Latin American members did not support the proposal presented by the United States that explicitly condemned Cuba for intervention in the region. The U.S. proposal read as follows:

[The Seventh Meeting of Consultation of Ministers of Foreign Affairs]
Condemns the efforts of the Sino-Soviet powers to extend their political influence over the sovereign American states through political and economic subversion, and that exploit, for their ends, the determination and dreams of the American people to succeed in reaching higher economic and cultural standards of living;

Manifests its profound concern for the declarations of high government officials in Cuba to admit the possibility of intervention by powers within the Sino-Soviet block in Inter-American affairs;

Declares that the encouragement and acceptance on Cuba's part of the intervention by Sino-Soviet powers in Inter-American affairs constitutes a direct break with the basic principles of the Inter-American system and a threat to the peace and security of the American States; and

Exhorts the Republic of Cuba
1) to repudiate and reject every effort of the Soviet Union, of the People's Republic of China and all other powers associated with them, to interfere in Cuban affairs or those of other countries in this hemisphere; and

2) that it pursue its goals of political, economic and social development according to the democratic principles of the Inter-American
system; and

3) that it conform, in its international relationships, to the purposes
and principles outlined in the Charter of The Organization of
American States and in other Inter-American treaties and conven-
tions. (Seventh Meeting of Consultation of Ministers of Foreign
Affairs, Documents, August 25, 1960)

The wording of the final resolution constituted a compromise between
the United States and Latin American members in which the Soviet
Union and China were mentioned, but Cuba was not. An examination
of the four institutional variables offers insight into why Latin American
members resisted U.S. pressures to the point that the United States was
forced to compromise on its preferred wording of the resolution.

Structural Perspective. The resources necessary to carry out the final resolutions of the Seventh Meeting of Foreign Ministers were of a low level. Most
of the resolutions were condemnations of the intervention in the hemisphere of the Soviet Union and China, and requests of members to observe
inter-American principles. These resolutions were based on the findings of
the IAPC, which effectively served as the investigating committee in this
case. The IAPC report presented at the Seventh Meeting stated that international tensions in the Caribbean had been "considerably heightened as a
result of increasing desire during recent months on the part of the Soviet
Union and other extracontinental powers to intervene more actively in
inter-American affairs" (Seventh Meeting of Consultation of Ministers of
Foreign Affairs, 1960). It also highlighted the importance of continental
solidarity and support for democracy and human rights. Furthermore, it
stated that collaboration for socioeconomic development was significant
for regional security. Although the report supported U.S. claims concerning the threat the Soviet Union posed to the hemisphere, the inclusion of
democracy, human rights, and socioeconomic development raised issues
that greatly concerned many Latin American members. Consequently, the
report helped serve as a foundation for the compromise reached between
the United States and Latin American members in the Declaration of
San José.

The one resolution requiring organizational resources was the provision establishing an Ad Hoc Committee. The Committee was created to
clarify facts and to offer its good offices to facilitate settlement of bilateral

controversies between the United States and Cuba. These bilateral issues included violations of the rights (personal and property) of United States citizens. Latin Americans did not see these as issues of serious concern to themselves, but recognized the need to reduce tensions between the United States and Cuba (Ball 1969, 461). The resources necessary for such action were minimal, involving only the travel expenses of the diplomats. (The expenses were, in fact, non-existent since the committee never met.) There was no need for military resources, nor was the United States asked to provide any special resources. Thus, the United States was not able to gain any leverage within the organization, in this case, through the provision of resources. This case is quite a contrast to the Dominican case (1965) (discussed earlier), in which extensive military, diplomatic, and logistic resources were necessary for an extended period.

Internal Relational Perspective. In the case of Cuba (1960), unity among Latin American members weakened the influence the United States had within the organization. From the beginning of the meeting, there was general agreement among Latin American members to condemn communist intervention but not on whether to name those states involved in provoking regional instability (i.e., Cuba, Soviet Union, and China) (Seventh Meeting of Consultation of Ministers of Foreign Affairs, August 22–29, 1960, 4). Latin American states did not want to specifically condemn Cuba. Some had not even wanted to mention the Soviet Union specifically. These members soon recognized, however, that the United States would never agree to such a resolution, and the lack of agreement would weaken, and possibly endanger, the Inter-American System. Yet the unity among Latin American members in opposing specific condemnation of Cuba left the United States with little influence (Seventh Meeting of Consultation of Ministers of Foreign Affairs, August 22–29, 1960, 4). There was no division among the majority for the United States to exploit, nor the lack of a plan for which the United States could provide leadership. Because the United States felt so strongly about Cuba, and because the Latin American members recognized the need for complete consensus on the resolution, they reached a compromise on wording. The final resolution, passed by a vote of 19-0, clearly implicated Cuba through its deeds even though it only specifically rejected Sino-Soviet powers:

> The Seventh Meeting of Consultation of Ministers of Foreign Affairs condemns energetically the intervention or the threat of intervention . . .

by an extracontinental power in the affairs of the American republics . . .
[The meeting of foreign ministers] rejects, also, the attempt of the Sino-Soviet powers to make use of the political, economic, or social situation of any American state, inasmuch as that attempt is capable of destroying hemispheric unity and endangering the peace and security of the hemisphere. (Seventh Meeting of Consultation of Ministers of Foreign Affairs, August 22–29, 1960, 4)

The resolution also reaffirmed the principle of nonintervention by any American state in the internal or external affairs of another, and reaffirmed the incompatibility of totalitarianism with the Inter-American System.

Although Latin American members showed a united front in their resistance to U.S. preferences at the meeting, there is some evidence that not all members were in complete agreement. Two statements issued by Mexico and Guatemala in response to the Declaration of San José reflect the range of different opinions held by Latin American states on the issue of Cuba. Mexico stated that the resolution was in no way a condemnation or a threat against Cuba, whose aspiration for economic improvement and social justice had the fullest support of the people of Mexico (Seventh Meeting of Consultation of Ministers of Foreign Affairs, August 22–29, 1960, 13). Mexico's statement also reaffirmed the principles of sovereignty and self-determination. Guatemala, on the other hand, stated that it was convinced that the actions of Cuba, by adopting a policy favoring the Soviet Union, threatened the hemisphere and that the American states would have been justified in assuming a stronger attitude (Seventh Meeting of Consultation of Ministers of Foreign Affairs, August 22–29, 1960, 13). Despite these starkly different attitudes toward Cuba, the Latin American members were unified in their resistance to accept the U.S. proposal condemning Cuba. Since most Latin American members agreed with the United States, however, that intervention in the hemisphere by the Soviet Union and China was detrimental to regional security and unity, they were able to reach a compromise on the final wording of the resolution.

Normative Perspective. The principles raised in the Cuban case (1960) largely resemble those advanced in Caracas in 1954, when most members reluctantly signed the Declaration of Caracas dealing with the Guatemalan coup. The Declaration defined international communism as a threat to the region:

The domination or control of the political institutions of any American State by the international communist movement extending to this

Hemisphere the political system of an extracontinental power, would constitute a threat to the sovereignty and political independence of the American States, endangering the peace of America, and would call for a Meeting of Consultation to consider the adoption of appropriate action in accordance with existing treaties. (Cited in Atkins 1997, 201–202)

At the Seventh Meeting of Consultation, Latin American members continued to uphold the principles of self-determination and nonintervention despite efforts by the United States to condemn Cuba specifically based on an extracontinental communist threat. Mexico, in particular, defended the Cuban regime as an indigenous communist movement and argued it was thus not subject to inter-American intervention (i.e., condemnation or additional actions). Although many Latin Americans had been enthusiastic about the Cuban Revolution shortly after Fidel Castro took power, his expropriation of private property, suppression of civil rights, and postponement of constitutional government eventually had led to distrust of the new regime. When Castro sought closer ties with the Soviet Union, including trade relations, the United States canceled its Cuban sugar imports. U.S. actions brought the charge of economic aggression from Cuba and Mexico, which was very supportive of the Cuban Revolution. After Soviet President Nikita Khrushchev declared Cuba a communist protectorate, many Latin American states viewed this increasingly extracontinental involvement in the hemisphere as a threat to the peace of the Americas and called for a Meeting of Consultation. Based on Castro's increasingly threatening attitude toward other Latin American regimes, the United States believed that Latin American members would not hesitate to condemn Cuba in addition to the Soviet Union and China. The United States did not anticipate that Latin American members would view its dispute with Castro as a bilateral issue to be solved by the two countries, not the OAS (Mecham 1961, 461).

When the Foreign Ministers met, the debates essentially pitted the principles of democracy and regional security against nonintervention and self-determination, with most Latin American states supporting the latter. Latin American members largely considered the dispute the United States had with the Cuban regime over sugar exports and the expropriation of private property to be a bilateral issue, to be resolved through negotiations. The dispute did not merit multilateral intervention on the part of the OAS. The one issue on which the United States and most Latin American states agreed was the threat of Sino-Soviet intervention in the hemisphere. Latin American members, however, did not want to make an explicit link between Sino-Soviet influence in the hemisphere and the Cuban regime. The U.S. proposal went beyond what Latin American members believed was necessary and thus threatened other fundamental principles of the Inter-American System on which they were unwilling to compromise given the existing situation. All members were worried about the security of the circum-Caribbean, but did not agree on the means to resolve the problems in the region. In this case the United States was largely alone in its desire to condemn Cuba, the Soviet Union, and China explicitly. The United States faced determined opposition to its proposal because many members were concerned about its disregard of other regional principles.

Environmental Perspective. As with the Caribbean case (1959), the Meeting of the Foreign Ministers in the Cuban case (1960) was not called to address a specific conflict in the hemisphere, but to remedy certain conditions of regional instability. Sanctions were not an issue, nor was establishing or observing a cease-fire. There was no need for military options to be considered at this time (although the United States would have been interested in unilateral actions to protect its citizens and their property in Cuba). Although there was no need for U.S. leadership in a militarized operation, the United States did attempt to exert its influence concerning the perceived level of threat to the region. By emphasizing the ideological threat from Cuba, the United States attempted to gain support for a harsh diplomatic response to Cuban actions. U.S. Secretary of State Christian Herter made a strong case that the installation of a communist regime in any American republic would automatically involve the loss of the country's independence (Mecham 1961, 460). He pointed to the obvious loss of independence by Eastern European countries to support this contention. He stated that subversion was as much of an intervention as an armed attack and thus was a grave security concern for all in the hemisphere (Ball 1969, 459). The U.S. argument was persuasive in so far as all members believed Cuba's acts of intervention were threatening to the region. Despite this portrayal of the great risk to the region by Cuba and the Soviet Union, the United States was unable to gain enough support for its proposed condemnation of Cuba. Although the Foreign Ministers were holding a Meeting of Consultation, signifying a threat to the region, Latin American members disagreed with the United States on the appropriate response to Cuba's actions because of their concerns about regional principles. Specific condemnation of Cuba raised issues of sovereignty and self-determination. By attempting to present the situation as highly threatening, the United States hoped to exert enough influence to support specific condemnation of Cuba. Because the situation was only a mid-level threat and did not present a direct military threat to any member, however, the United States was forced to compromise on its proposal.

Results. In the case of Cuba (1960), the United States was forced to compromise with Latin American members over the wording of the final resolution at the Seventh Meeting of Foreign Ministers. The level of influence the United States was able to exert was considerably lower than in the Dominican case (1965). The two variables that most obviously reduced the U.S. level of influence were the level of consensus among Latin American members, and Latin American support of regional principles. A unified Latin American membership on the issue of not condemning Cuba specifically led to a compromise solution that only condemned the Soviet Union and China. Latin American members were also united in upholding the principles of nonintervention and self-determination. Although the United States based its arguments on the principles of regional security and democracy, Latin American members believed the United States was disregarding other fundamental principles of the Inter-American System and opposed the U.S. proposal.

The hypothesis based on the perceived threat to regional stability was generally supported by the Cuban case, although it pointed to some additional factors to consider. The moderate level of threat corresponded with a moderate level of U.S. influence. The United States was able to make a persuasive case that Cuban actions were threatening to regional security, but its proposed response did not meet with the approval of Latin American members. Even though Latin American states agreed that Cuba posed a threat to the region, this did not result in an increase in U.S. influence in this case. The United States retained sufficient influence to produce a compromise rather than a rejection of its proposal, but proved unable to dominate the organization as it had in the Dominican case (1965). Although members were convinced that Cuba did pose a threat to the region, they did not turn to the United States to provide leadership in the face of this threat. In addition, the United States was unable to use its extensive resources to gain influence within the organization because no special resources were needed in this case to carry out the resolutions of the Foreign Ministers.

In the cases where the outcome was a compromise between the United States and Latin American states, Latin American members were able to exert enough leverage to resist U.S. dominance. These cases are the most difficult to explain since no member state was dominant in the debates where a number of different policy preferences were being put forward. Several factors, however, apparently contributed to the compromise outcomes in the OAS. In the case of Cuba (1960), most Latin American members were unified in their desire not to condemn Cuba specifically.[45] They had the majority of votes necessary to reject the U.S. proposal. They also had an alternative proposal available on which to vote. An alternative proposal is important if the U.S. proposal is objectionable to member states. If no alternative actions are proposed, then there is a greater likelihood that the U.S. proposal will be supported rather than facing the option of taking no action at all. Latin American members were able to unite behind the alternative resolution because it did not require considerable resources to be carried out and thus they were not dependent on the United States to provide such resources. The United States maintained some influence based on the fact that the Cuban case presented a mid-level threat to the region with the potential for continued regional instability. Member states recognized the need to address the actions of Cuba and did not want to alienate the United States on this issue. Agreement on normative issues brought member states together in this case. Members reaffirmed the principle of nonintervention and reaffirmed that the Inter-American System was incompatible with any form of totalitarianism.

In the Caribbean case (1959), similar factors had an influence on the outcome. There was no need for a high level of resources to carry out the resolutions, thus giving member states some freedom from U.S. influence. The threat was only mid-level, providing some space for members to address the problem without resorting to a militarized U.S. response to guarantee regional security. The effect of regional principles also played a role in helping Venezuela and Cuba persuade the United States and other members to support the Declaration of Santiago. The United States would not have wanted to oppose supporting representative democracy as long as the proposal did not advocate intervention. The different positions of member states were thus able to be accommodated in these compromise cases based on less dependence on the United States for resources, on only a mid-level threat to the region, and on a normative culture supporting regional principles including representative democracy, nonintervention, and sovereignty.

Summary

Because the majority of decisionmaking outcomes are either consensual, or are compromises when the Rio Treaty or OAS Charter have been invoked for conflict resolution, it is important to examine these cases in order to better understand the decisionmaking dynamics within the OAS. Cases of consensus and compromise illustrate the impact of structural, internal relational, normative, and environmental factors on the decisionmaking process and outcome. In cases of consensus, members were in agreement on the desired means and ends to address the security issue confronting the organization. Members were able to act quickly and effectively to resolve the problem peacefully. In the Panamanian case (1959), the invading force was persuaded to surrender. In 1956, both Nicaragua and Costa Rica were pressured into implementing the Pact of Amity. In a number of cases when there was some disagreement among members about how to peacefully resolve the tensions in the region, the need for resources and the threat level were not high enough to allow U.S. dominance. Instead, members worked out a compromise that addressed the preferences of each side. In the Cuban case (1960), members agreed on an alternative wording that did not explicitly condemn Cuba, only external communist interventions in the region. Members also compromised on the Caribbean case (1959) by addressing member concerns about democracy, not just restoring political stability. These compromise agreements strengthened regional solidarity and the legitimacy of the actions taken by the organization. Members were able to come together to present a unified front that addressed the concerns of all, and to take action that promoted regional security.

CHAPTER 7

CHANGE AND CONTINUITY: HEMISPHERIC RELATIONS IN THE 1990S AND THE NEW MILLENNIUM

Introduction

The cases in chapters 5 and 6 illustrated the ways that structural, internal relational, normative, and environmental factors can affect decisionmaking within the OAS and the level of influence exerted within the organization by a dominant member. The 26 cases dating from the Cold War era depict not only the changing relationships between member states, but also the evolutionary changes of the organization. Chapter 4 outlined three different periods of OAS history (from 1948 to 1989) that illustrated changes in the international environment, the organizational environment, and the policy preferences of members over time. These shifts were evident in changes in the type of conflict being handled, the organ and instrument being invoked, and the level of consensus within the organization. The end of the Cold War resulted in both changes and continuities within the organization.

One change witnessed in the 1990s was the redefinition of and response to security threats in the region. In contrast to the 1960s when the organization was largely concerned with communist threats, OAS members have been focused on threats to democratic governance since the 1990s. Whereas the organization was less active in responding to regional security threats in the 1970s and 1980s, the OAS actively responded on a number of occasions when democratic government was at risk in the 1990s. The revitalized organization has been able to address these threats using several new mechanisms put in place in the early 1990s including Resolution 1080 and the Democratic Charter (both discussed later).

Another change that is evident is the shift in the priority given to the principle of representative democracy vis-à-vis the principle of nonintervention. The 1978 case of Nicaragua signaled the beginning of a normative shift within the OAS promoting the value of democratic government. The end of the Cold War brought this concern for democracy to the forefront as member states revised their perceptions of regional threats and revitalized the organization. A third change seen in the 1990s is the renewal of cooperation and consensus among members. The impact of Resolution 1080 and the Democratic Charter in restoring democracy has been notable based on the high level of consensus among member states. Members have been unified in their defense of democracy, and have responded rapidly when governments in the region have been threatened. The consensus achieved in the 1990s is quite a contrast to relations in the 1970s and 1980s, when consensus was low and threats did not invoke a unified regional response.

Rather than marking a distinct break from the past, however, the changes in normative priorities and member consensus can actually be viewed as part of a greater continuity seen in the organization. Although the priorities given to regional principles have shifted in favor of democracy over nonintervention, the impact of norms on organizational decisionmaking continues to play a significant role. The consensus seen in the 1990s is also not new, but closely resembles the relations between members in the 1950s prior to the intensification of the Cold War. As noted in chapter 6, the majority of decisions made historically by member states have been either consensual, or based on compromises to achieve consensus. This remained true throughout the 1990s with members striving to promote regional unity based on support for representative democracy. Despite this common goal and high level of consensus within the organization, some disagreements between members are still evident. In the cases where democracy has been threatened, members have been united on the desired *end* (restoration of democracy) but have sometimes been at odds concerning the *means* to achieve that end. For example, when Jean-Bertrand Aristide was ousted as president of Haiti in 1991, Argentina and Venezuela wanted the OAS to approve military action to restore him to power. Initially, however, the majority of members did not approve of military force and chose instead to impose sanctions to try to force General Raoul Cedras from power. Despite these different proposed means, members were in agreement on the desired end: the restoration of democracy in Haiti.

This chapter examines the changing nature and definition of security threats to the region and the structural adaptations in the OAS to address these redefined threats. The chapter then explores the actions taken by the OAS in the 1990s and the new millennium, and examines the cooperative relations between Latin American members and the United States in this "new" era.

Redefining Regional Security

One of the changes seen in the post–Cold War era is the redefinition of hemispheric "security" issues. The traditional concept of regional security based on geopolitical/strategic threats has gradually been expanded to include a number of concerns that had not previously been considered "security issues." The United States and Latin American states have developed a common agenda of security concerns that includes consideration of human rights, democracy, the environment, government reform, social equality, and a free-market environment (Wiarda 1995). These issues have been of nominal concern to Latin American states for many years, but until the collapse of the Soviet Union they were not considered genuine security issues. After a decade of discussion and redefinition, in the new millennium regional order and security have increasingly come to be defined in terms of collective defense of democracy, and the promotion of liberal economic reform and regional integration. As the number of democratic countries in the hemisphere has increased, a growing consensus supporting democratic government has emerged. Taking into consideration the broader definition of regional security issues, current concerns include not only traditional threats such as boundary disputes, but also threats to democracy (i.e., coups or other disruptions of the democratic process), and threats related to narco-trafficking.

New Normative Priorities and Institutional Structures

In addition to a broader concept of regional security, the end of the Cold War has led to a new prioritization of regional norms. The Western hemisphere has had a long history of support for norms such as state sovereignty, nonintervention, pacific settlement of disputes, consultation between states during crises, and representative democracy. All these principles are in the OAS Charter dating back to 1948. The priorities placed on these principles, however, have shifted over time. State sovereignty and nonintervention largely dominated security discussions from the 1940s to the 1990s. Recently, however, states have placed less emphasis on the principle of state sovereignty in conflicts in which democracy is threatened, thus allowing for greater multilateral intervention to address this concern. This new attitude toward intervention in support of democracy, combined with the broader definition of security concerns, has altered the security arena in the new century. It has allowed for a more active response from member states when regional security is threatened.

The redefinition of regional security has taken place at many levels and in many forums in the Western hemisphere, but has been largely institutionalized within the OAS. The OAS has been an ideal forum for the discussions that have resulted in the broader definition of security issues because it is the only regional organization in which all states of the hemisphere are members.[46] In addition, the organization has been revitalized in the 1990s after several decades of decline. Members have expressed renewed interest in acting multilaterally to address a number regional concerns including the promotion and protection of democracy. The first step taken regionally to promote democracy in the hemisphere was taken in 1990 when the OAS General Assembly established the Unit for the Promotion of Democracy (UPD). It was created to provide advisory services and technical assistance to member states on issues of democratic government. Its main objective has been to provide an effective and immediate response to OAS member states requesting advice or assistance in modernizing or strengthening their political institutions and democratic processes (www.oas.org). The UPD has strengthened democracy in two ways: (1) by helping members to develop solid, transparent, and efficient political institutions and (2) by promoting a democratic political culture in the societies of the Americas.

In its first five years the UPD was most active in the area of electoral observations. Early efforts usually included a few high-level observers who were present on election day. Later missions expanded considerably to include monitoring of the registration process, the campaign, the voting process, and the verification of results by electoral officials. Following the First Summit of the Americas (1994), the UPD was strengthened and restructured to carry out special programs in support of peace processes on the continent. One example of the work it has carried out can be seen in Guatemala where the UPD supported the reintegration of ex-combatants, promoted peaceful resolution of conflicts, and supported legislative and electoral reforms laid out in the Peace Accords (1996). In Nicaragua, the UPD has provided support to government agencies concerned with human rights, and to the peace commissions (www.upd.oas.org). In the 1990s, the Unit monitored over 50 elections in more than 20 member states. In its efforts to promote a democratic political culture, the UPD has developed a regional program to train young political leaders about the workings of democratic government. As an organization dedicated to the collection and management of information relevant to democracy and good government, the UPD has supported research, seminars, publications, and a database on democracy in the hemisphere.

A second step by the OAS to promote democracy was taken in June 1991 in Santiago Chile, when the General Assembly passed Resolution 1080 creating automatic procedures for convening an OAS Meeting of Foreign Ministers in the event of a coup or other disruption of constitutional order. Resolution 1080 has been invoked on four occasions: Haiti (1991), Peru (1992), Guatemala (1993), and Paraguay (1996). Under Resolution 1080, members have the authority to impose economic and diplomatic sanctions on states where the constitutional order has been disrupted, but are not able to take military action. Some members are more susceptible to such pressures than others. For example, when Haitian President Jean-Bertrand Aristide was ousted by General Raoul Cedras in 1991, the economic sanctions imposed by the OAS were ineffective in restoring Aristide. In the case of Peru in 1992, however, the threat of economic sanctions brought swift cooperation from President Alberto Fujimori to restore the constitutional order after a "self-coup." If economic and diplomatic sanctions are ineffective in restoring democracy after a coup, OAS members now have an additional option at their disposal to promote democratic governance. In September 1997, the Washington Protocol, an amendment of the OAS Charter, came into effect. The Protocol allows the organization to suspend membership of any state whose democratically elected government has been overthrown by force.

A third mechanism to promote democracy developed out of the Summits of the Americas where heads of state met in 1994, 1998, and 2001. At these Summits, members not only redefined the security agenda by placing new items such as drug trafficking, terrorism, corruption, and economic integration on the agenda, but they also gave democracy a high priority. They "reaffirmed hemispheric commitment to preserve and strengthen [the] democratic systems for the benefit of all people of the hemisphere . . . to strengthen democratic institutions and promote and defend constitutional democratic rule in accordance with the OAS Charter" (First Summit of the Americas, Declaration of Principles [1994]). Members strongly believed that regional security was closely linked to the maintenance of democracy and wanted to establish additional mechanisms for preserving democratic rule. The

2001 Summit held in Quebec, Canada, directed the OAS to further study ways in which the organization could strengthen democracy and respond when it was under threat. The Inter-American Democratic Charter was the organization's response to the directive given by the heads of state at the Summit. A draft of the Charter was presented and approved at the regular annual session of the General Assembly in June 2001. The Permanent Council then made suggested revisions and presented a final draft to a special session of the General Assembly. The General Assembly adopted the Democratic Charter on September 11, 2001.

The Democratic Charter is a comprehensive document that lays out the links between democracy and a variety of related topics including economic development, human rights, institutional development, and political culture. Section I of the Charter discusses democracy and the Inter-American System, establishing the rights of the people to democratic rule and the obligation of governments to promote and defend it. Democracy and human rights are linked in Section II, which states, "democracy is indispensable for the effective exercise of fundamental freedoms and human rights" (Inter-American Democratic Charter, Article 7). Section III declares, "democracy and social and economic development are interdependent and are mutually reinforcing" and that "poverty, illiteracy, and low levels of human development are factors that adversely affect the consolidation of democracy" (Articles 11 and 12). The Democratic Charter establishes procedures to respond not only when there is a formal disruption to democracy (as in a coup), but also when democracy is seriously altered and at risk (Section IV). Section V provides for electoral observer missions to ensure free and fair elections. Promotion of democratic culture is included in the final section that advocates programs for "good governance, sound administration, democratic values, and the strengthening of political institutions and civil society organizations" (Article 26). The Democratic Charter was first formally applied in April 2002 shortly after its adoption when President Hugo Chavez of Venezuela was temporarily forced out of office. It has also been used to guide the organization's actions in Haiti as that country continues to struggle to democratize.

Member Relations and Multilateral Actions

Given that relations between member states in the 1990s were largely consensual, an analysis of relations between member states based on different preferences is not particularly valuable. During the Cold War, the cases handled by the OAS under the Rio Treaty and OAS Charter illustrated the impact of organizational factors on the level of influence the United States was able to wield in the OAS, particularly those cases in which U.S. preferences differed from those of Latin American members. In the 1990s, however, there was little need for United States to take the lead or exert undue influence within the organization. Members were largely united in their perceptions and definitions of threats to regional security. The puzzle concerning whether the United States successfully dominated the organization was not an issue in the 1990s. In addition, the Rio Treaty was not invoked at all between 1989 and 2001 to address regional security concerns. The focus in this chapter thus shifts to disruptions to democracy and the use of the new mechanisms discussed earlier to protect and strengthen democratic governments. The organizational factors that provided insights into levels of influence exerted by members during the Cold War still provide useful insights into member relations during the period of consensus seen in the 1990s.

One aspect of member relations that is evident with the high level of consensus in the 1990s is the willingness of the United States to support OAS actions and, in many cases, to act multilaterally to achieve hemispheric goals (and security). Although the United States had participated in hemispheric deliberations in the OAS in the past, under the Clinton administration the United States demonstrated a new level of commitment to multilateralism not previously seen. President Clinton personally participated in the Summits of the Americas (1994, 1998) and reiterated U.S. support for a Free Trade Area of the Americas. This commitment to multilateralism was remarkable since the United States was in the privileged position, unlike many states in the region, to take effective unilateral action if it chose to do so. In the past, the United States has taken unilateral action on a number of occasions, the most notable recent case being the invasion of Panama and capture of its president, Manuel Noriega, in 1989 based on drug trafficking allegations. U.S. responses to disruptions to democratic rule in the hemisphere, however, have been largely multilateral, in cooperation with other OAS members.

A look at the factors of consensus, norms, resources, and perceived threat levels, offers insights into incentives for the United States to act multilaterally on many of the current challenges facing the organization. The same organizational factors that help explain the dynamic decisionmaking process in which the United States does not always dominate the OAS, also help explain why the United States might choose to work multilaterally rather than unilaterally in most situations when regional stability is threatened.

Strong consensus among member states provides several incentives for multilateral action. Consensus among members strengthens the legitimacy of the organization's resolutions and may weaken the leadership of a member state that faces hemispheric condemnation. Consensus also helps the organization respond rapidly to a crisis rather than engaging in a time-consuming debate about how to respond. In the context of threats to democracy, there is considerable agreement among member states embodied in the OAS Charter, Resolution 1080, and the Democratic Charter to protect and strengthen democratic government in the region. Consensus on this issue allows the organization to issue strong condemnations regarding disruptions to democracy. Unity against coup leaders weakens their position and helps convince them to restore democracy or face additional sanctions. Consensus promotes a swift response that can be critical when trying to support a fragile democratic regime that is facing a challenger.

A strong normative regime can also provide incentives similar to those of consensus among members for multilateral action on the part of the United States. Members are motivated when norm violations occur to take action to uphold the norm. Thus, violators face a strong prospect of sanctions in response to their actions. Members strengthen the norm if they all act together in opposition to violations, rather than responding haphazardly, or not at all. Multilateral action presents the strongest type of response inspired by united support of regional principles. An added benefit for the United States is that the United States is able to avoid the appearance of "imperialism" by engaging in multilateral instead of unilateral actions. The strength of the democratic norm in the region has led to unified multilateral responses from all member states when democracy has been threatened in the last decade. In each of the four cases when Resolution 1080 was invoked, the Foreign Ministers responded decisively to the threats to democracy.

The factor of resources needed to carry out the resolutions of the Foreign Ministers has also provided incentives for the United States to support multilateral actions. The OAS mechanisms that are in place to respond to threats to democracy are largely diplomatic and economic sanctions, and do not require significant resources. Thus, the United States does not have to contribute considerable resources in response to these threats. This low level of resources needed has allowed the United States to support multilateral action without much domestic controversy. An examination of the four cases in which Resolution 1080 has been invoked illustrates how these factors of consensus, norms, and resources have provided some incentives for the United States to take multilateral action.

The threats posed to the region by antidemocratic forces were not perceived as a direct threat to U.S. security in the 1990s. There was no longer the underlying ideological concern with communist subversion that once pervaded U.S. concerns in the region. Coups affected regional stability and perhaps had economic spillover effects that impeded regional trade, but did not directly threaten the United States. Thus the United States was willing to address these problems multilaterally based on the potential incentives described earlier. Given the terrorist attacks on September 11, 2001 and the American global antiterrorist campaign, it is possible that greater priority might be given to antidemocratic forces in the new millennium if they are relabeled as terrorist forces. With such a designation, the United States would likely consider them a greater threat to the United States and the region. It is uncertain whether the United States would continue to address such a security threat multilaterally as it has in the past, or if this higher security priority would lead the United States to take unilateral actions against threats to democracy. Recent events in Venezuela and Colombia provide unclear indications about the U.S. attitude toward multilateral action in the region. On the one hand, the long-running war against narco-traffickers and guerilla forces in Colombia has largely been addressed by the United States through bilateral cooperation with the Colombian government (although the United States continues to discuss the drug trafficking problems within the context of the Inter-American Drug Abuse Control Commission [CICAD]). On the other hand, the events in Venezuela following the temporary removal of President Hugo Chavez from office in 2002 indicate a continued willingness to work multilaterally, but also illustrate that the degree of unity and consensus among OAS members has declined in recent years.

Throughout the 1990s, however, the consensus that prevailed led to preferences for multilateral versus bilateral (or unilateral) action by the United States. There have been a number of incentives for OAS members, including the United States to take multilateral actions in response to threats to democracy. The unity behind these multilateral actions resulted in fairly successful outcomes in restoring democracy that might not have been possible if member states had been less unified. This unity and successful restoration of democracy is evident in the four cases when Resolution 1080 was invoked (Haiti, 1991; Peru, 1992; Guatemala, 1993; and Paraguay, 1996). The first invocation of the Democratic Charter (Venezuela, 2002) shows continued support for democratic norms and multilateral action, but also a weakening of unity among OAS members. Anti-narcotics operations carried out in Colombia reveal the limits of U.S. willingness to address security threats multilaterally.

Defending Democracy

Given the changing nature of security threats to the region, neither the OAS Charter nor the Rio Treaty was invoked for conflict management from 1989 (United States–Panama case) to 2001 (attacks on World Trade Center and Pentagon). The region's new commitment to defend democracy led to Resolution 1080 being invoked four times since it was adopted by the General Assembly in 1991. The steps taken to restore democracy in these cases closely resemble those taken in earlier decades under the Rio Treaty or the OAS Charter to resolve conflicts in the region. Immediately following the crisis, emergency meetings of the Permanent Council or the Foreign Ministers were called, then special committees were sent out to investigate and report on the situation, finally resolutions were issued condemning the disruption of democratic rule and calling for its restoration. Resolution 1080 established these procedures to help OAS members maintain and strengthen democratic regimes in the hemisphere. In each case, OAS members worked cooperatively through the organization to restore democratic government in the member state. The cases reveal several challenges facing the OAS even when there is consensus among members that action must be taken. In the case of Haiti (1991), economic and diplomatic sanctions were not enough to restore democracy. The organization had to work with the United Nations and eventually rely on the threat of military action to return Aristide to power. In the Peruvian case (1992), members were faced with a trade-off between reducing the threat of regional guerilla forces and strengthening democratic institutions.

Haiti (1991)

Resolution 1080 was first invoked following the Haitian coup in September 1991, a few short months after Resolution 1080 was adopted by the General Assembly. President Jean-Bertrand Aristide had been elected in December 1990 in an election deemed free and fair by international observers. A coup against him occurred on September 30, 1991, led by dissatisfied elements of the army and supported by many of the country's economic elites. Aristide fled into exile. The OAS secretary general, João Baena Soares, called for an emergency meeting of the Permanent Council on that same day. The Council condemned the events in Haiti and called for an ad hoc meeting of the Ministers of Foreign Affairs. The Foreign Ministers, meeting on October 3, also condemned the coup and refused to recognize the ruling military junta led by General Raoul Cedras. They called for diplomatic and economic sanctions against Haiti. Following an unsuccessful diplomatic mission by the OAS secretary general to restore democracy to Haiti, the Foreign Ministers recommended freezing Haitian assets. Sanctions were implemented in November 1991 with all trade embargoed except for humanitarian purposes. Although military intervention was proposed by Argentina and Venezuela, members opted instead to send another mediation team to negotiate with Cedras to return Aristide to power. The OAS also sent an IACHR team to investigate charges of human rights violations.

The Foreign Ministers met again in May 1992 to tighten the embargo and urge member states to "adopt whatever actions may be necessary for the greater effectiveness [of the measures]" (as cited in Atkins 1997, 208). When further negotiation efforts met with failure, the OAS decided to request assistance from the United Nations. The UN Security Council met in November 1992 and issued its own call for an economic embargo. The UN secretary general appointed a special representative to begin negotiations with the Haitian de facto government and worked closely with the OAS to try to restore Aristide to power. Progress toward restoring democracy was slow as Cedras refused to implement the Governors Island Agreement reached in July 1993. This agreement would have returned Aristide to power, promoted administrative and judicial reforms, modernized the army, and created a new police force. UN sanctions were to be lifted and Cedras would step down. UN and OAS human rights monitors would be allowed to enter the country and international forces would train new police forces, help rebuild infrastructure, and retrain the military for professional (i.e., non-political) roles. When the United Nations Mission in Haiti (UNMIH) arrived in Port-au-Prince in October 1993, they were met by violent crowds and were unable to dock. They left port the next day and sanctions were reimposed.

The situation was essentially an impasse for the next nine months. When no further progress was made in negotiations, the UN Security Council imposed a total trade embargo and authorized a naval blockade to enforce it in May 1994. In July the Security Council authorized the United States to put together a multinational force to restore democracy.

Finally, in September 1994, pending the imminent arrival of 20,000 U.S. troops acting under UN authority, Cedras capitulated and Aristide was restored to power. U.S. troops were replaced in March 1995, after a secure and stable environment was established, by a UN force of 6,000 troops who worked to restore law and order in the country. The democratic crisis ended following legislative and presidential elections in 1995. During both elections the OAS and the United Nations provided Electoral Assistance Teams to monitor the process. Although the legislative elections, held in June, were disorganized and disorderly, the presidential election in December was more efficient and resulted in the first peaceful transfer of power to a democratically elected successor (Atkins 1997, 214).

In this early effort by the OAS to restore democracy in Haiti, OAS members were united in their determination to see democratically elected President Aristide returned to power. OAS actions reflect this determination and unity throughout the struggle. Because of the high level of consensus, members were able to respond quickly to the crisis. The Permanent Council met the same day of the coup to call the Foreign Ministers into session just four days later. Both meetings invoked Resolution 1080 and condemned the coup. Members solidly affirmed the norm of representative democracy and used the resources at their disposal to restore democracy in Haiti by imposing diplomatic and economic sanctions, and eventually threatening the use of military force. With an estimated 40,000 refugees fleeing by boat to the United States, the United States had a strong interest in seeing the situation stabilized. Rather than acting unilaterally, however, it chose to act in cooperation with OAS members and the United Nations to resolve the crisis. Unlike previous cases such as the Dominican Republic (1965), in the Haitian case OAS members supported U.S. involvement because the United States was upholding a democratically elected government and following the procedures established by the OAS General Assembly in Resolution 1080. The United States was able to safeguard its own security interests and maintain the legitimacy of its actions because of its multilateral approach.

Peru (1992 and 2000)
Resolution 1080 was invoked a second time when Peruvian President Alberto Fujimori engaged in a "self-coup" in April 1992. The relatively unknown Fujimori had been elected in a surprise victory over the

center–right coalition candidate, Mario Vargas Llosa, in 1990. Fujimori had introduced "shock therapy" measures to reduce hyperinflation from 7,650 to 139 percent in one year (www.state.gov). He also took a hard-line against the guerilla movement, Sendero Luminoso, that had wracked the country with violence. When Fujimori began to face opposition to his reform efforts, he engaged in a "self-coup" with the support of the military to strengthen the position of the president vis-à-vis the other branches of government. He suspended the constitution and most civil rights, and ruled by decree. He closed Congress, intervened in the judiciary, established martial law, arrested several members of Congress, and censored the media (Atkins 1997, 410). He justified these measures by arguing that the legislature and judiciary had been hindering the security forces in their fight against the guerrillas (http:// news.bbc.co.uk).

One week after the coup, the OAS Foreign Ministers convened and issued a resolution "deeply deploring" Fujimori's actions and calling for the restoration of democratic institutions in Peru. The resolution also urged members to suspend financial assistance to Peru. Several states in the hemisphere, including the United States, withheld aid contributions until democracy was restored. The ministers appointed a special mission to initiate negotiations between the Fujimori government and the opposition to restore the democratic order. Although Fujimori initially proposed holding a plebiscite to validate his seizure of power (drawing on his popular support to legitimize his actions), he eventually yielded to pressure from the international community and presented an election plan to the OAS Foreign Ministers when they met in the Bahamas in May 1992. The election would be for a Democratic Constituent Congress (CCD) that would draft a new constitution and serve as an interim national legislature. The OAS provided technical electoral assistance and observation for the election of the CCD in November 1992 and for the election of municipal officials. A number of major political parties abstained from participating in the election claiming the process was not free and fair (Atkins 1997, 410).

Despite the protests of the opposition parties, at the Meeting of Foreign Ministers in December 1992, a majority of OAS members declared the elections free and fair, and viewed them as a step toward restoring democracy. Canada, Venezuela, and the United States disagreed with this endorsement, but because Fujimori maintained strong public support and was still faced with the threat of the Sendero Luminoso guerrillas, they did not take further actions against Fujimori. Despite the fact that OAS members had recently redefined security threats to include the disruption of democracy, members were faced with the difficult decision in this case. They had to consider whether the guerilla forces or Fujimori's self-coup posed a greater security threat to the region. The majority decided in favor of Fujimori, contingent on his plan to restore democratic institutions, and Peru was returned to good standing within the OAS in early 1993.

Had Fujimori not faced a united front in the hemisphere opposing his "self-coup," it is unlikely he would have acceded to the Foreign Ministers' call for the restoration of democratic institutions. The consensus among OAS members led to a swift response and considerable international pressure on Fujimori for violating the norm of representative democracy. The Peruvian case is somewhat unusual, however, because Fujimori actually faced more international condemnation than domestic opposition to his coup. This gave him some leverage in negotiating with the Foreign Ministers to restore democratic processes in Peru. In addition, his success in combating Sendero Luminoso guerrillas also gained him some room for compromise with OAS members.

The outcome in the Peruvian case, however, was not entirely satisfactory in terms of strengthening the democratic institutions in Peru. Fujimori made some concessions and held elections, but still maintained much autocratic authority. It became obvious throughout the rest of the 1990s that he was less committed to democracy than many OAS members had hoped. The actions Fujimori took in 1992 and 1993 were not the first steps toward greater democratization, but were essentially the *only* steps he took. In hindsight, those members who had reservations about Fujimori's commitment to democracy were justified in their suspicions. As the presidential elections of 2000 approached, Fujimori asserted that he had the right to run for a third term even though this was prohibited by the new constitution adopted in 1993. He justified his position by arguing that his first term was served under the old constitution, thus he had only served one term under the new one that limited him to two terms. Several judges were fired when they ruled against this interpretation of the constitution. In addition to this term-limit scandal, criticisms had been growing that Fujimori had been using his authoritarian power against his democratic political opponents, not just the guerilla forces. His security advisor, Vladimiro Montesinos, was accused of intimidating and spying on political opponents. Fujimori was accused of exerting unfair control on the mass media and the judiciary, and using government resources to support his own political campaign. Following the

June 2000 election, the OAS expressed concerns over irregularities in the electoral campaign (although it did not invoke Resolution 1080). Eventually domestic opponents and OAS members put enough pressure on Fujimori that he resigned and left the country in November 2000. President Alejandro Toledo took office in July 2001 following a new presidential election in April, which was monitored by the UPD.

The OAS was more successful in strengthening democracy in Peru in 2000 than it had been in 1992. Many of the institutional factors were the same at both times: members were still unified in their support for representative democracy and had the mechanisms and resources in place to promote democratic government. One factor that was different in 2000, however, was the reduced level of threat posed by Sendero Luminoso. Fujimori had captured the Sendero leader, Abimael Guzman, in 1992 and weakened the guerillas considerably. Although some OAS members had been willing to compromise with Fujimori in 1992 as he attempted to retain his autocratic position to deal with the guerillas, in 2000, states were not willing to tolerate continued authoritarianism because it was no longer justifiable based on security concerns. Members no longer felt like they had to make a trade-off between democracy and security. OAS members had not had to make this kind of trade-off in the Haitian case (1991) because democracy and security were clearly linked. The disruption to democracy in Haiti had caused a security problem in the region with a large flow of refugees heading to the United States. In Peru in 1992, there had *not* been an exodus of refugees, but there *had been* a continued guerilla threat. Fujimori thus retained many of his powers because members perceived the guerilla threat as greater than the threat to democracy and were satisfied with the changes Fujimori proposed to make. The situation was reversed by 2000, and OAS members were determined to see democracy fully restored.

The situation in Peru illustrates another challenge that the organization faces as it redefines security threats and seeks to uphold regional principles. Just as the concerns about sovereignty and nonintervention sometimes made it difficult for members to give priority to the norm of democracy in earlier decades, so do current security concerns when they run counter to promoting democracy.

Guatemala (1993)

In May 1993, a similar "self-coup" to that of President Fujimori was attempted by President Jorge Serrano of Guatemala. Serrano had faced difficult circumstances following his election in November 1990. When he was inaugurated in January 1991, he had pledged to improve Guatemala's human rights record and to reach a final peace agreement with the Guatemalan United Revolutionary Front (URNG) that had been engaged in guerilla activities since the 1960s. Talks began in April 1991, then became deadlocked at the end of the year. Negotiations were resumed in May 1992 and once again broke down. On May 24, 1993, President Serrano, supported by the military high command, suspended civil rights and other constitutional guarantees, discontinued the judicial system, dissolved congress, and censored the media (Atkins 1997, 198). Serrano had hoped to gain the power necessary to force a final peace settlement, but faced considerable opposition to his "self-coup" both at home and abroad.

The Permanent Council of the OAS met the day of the coup in accordance with Resolution 1080 and officially deplored the events in Guatemala. They convoked an ad hoc Meeting of the Ministers of Foreign Affairs who also condemned Serrano's actions and called for a constitutional resolution to the situation. The Foreign Ministers sent Secretary General João Baena Soares to meet with Serrano and threatened to impose economic sanctions if Serrano did not resign. Serrano initially refused. In the next few days, however, the United States and the European Community (EC) suspended all aid to Guatemala, and the United States threatened to suspend its trade relations as well. On June 1, the Guatemalan military withdrew their support for Serrano and forced him to resign. President Serrano fled into exile. Additional international pressure prevented the formation of a governing military junta. The Guatemalan Congress convened to elect Attorney General Ramiro de Léon Carpio as president to serve out Serrano's term until the next presidential elections in January 1996.[47]

Rapid international action as well as strong domestic opposition led to a quick restoration of democracy. Actions were much more harsh than with Peru in 1992. Domestic opposition made a big difference and left Serrano with little leverage to use against the demands of the OAS Foreign Ministers. The Foreign Ministers were determined to see democracy restored and acted in a united fashion to achieve that end. The United States fully supported the OAS call for imposing sanctions against Guatemala and did not need to take further unilateral actions for the successful restoration of democracy.

Paraguay (1996)

The most recent case when Resolution 1080 was invoked was in Paraguay in 1996 when the country's first civilian president in 40 years was challenged by Army Chief General Lino Oviedo. President Juan Carlos Wasmosy had been elected in May 1993 under a new democratic constitution (established in June 1992). This election was monitored by international observers, including OAS members, and was deemed free and fair. In April 1996, General Oviedo attempted to oust President Wasmosy. With the support of the international community and the Paraguayan people, Wasmosy stood up against Oviedo and called for the resignation of the General. Oviedo refused to comply and threatened to invade the presidential palace. The OAS Foreign Ministers met in an emergency session and unanimously condemned Oviedo's behavior and offered their support to President Wasmosy. Wasmosy successfully asserted his authority and Oviedo was arrested and imprisoned. He remained imprisoned until President Raul Cubas Grau (elected in 1998) commuted his sentence and released him, but was forced into exile when Cubas resigned in scandal in 1999.

In each of these four cases when democracy was threatened in the hemisphere, the OAS responded rapidly and took unified multilateral actions to successfully restore democracy (with strong U.S. actions and help from the United Nations in the case of Haiti). Involvement in Haiti has been the most prolonged and extensive, but the UPD has continued to monitor the situations in each of these countries and to help strengthen their democratic institutions. The OAS was revitalized in the 1990s because members agreed on their definitions of and responses to regional threats, particularly threats to democracy. The United States was a team player in these cases, choosing to act multilaterally through the OAS to pursue its regional policy preferences.

Venezuela (2002)

The constitutional order in Venezuela was threatened on April 11, 2002 when President Hugo Chavez briefly lost power in a 48-hour coup by top military officials. He was removed from the capital and held incommunicado at several different military bases. Although some media sources reported that he had given his resignation, others challenged this report. On April 12, Pedro Carmona, a former oil executive, was sworn in as interim president. He quickly moved to repeal dozens of controversial economic laws, and dissolved the Supreme Court and the National Assembly. He promised to hold a presidential election in one year (http://news.bbc.co.uk). The next day, the lower ranks of the army came to Chavez's rescue and crowds of supporters marched in the streets. He returned to office and promised not to seek revenge against those who overthrew him, acknowledging that both sides had made mistakes.

After returning to power, it was clear that the Chavez government would only achieve stability by engaging in dialogue with the opposition groups that had been protesting for months prior to the coup. He began bargaining with these groups with the OAS secretary general, César Gaviria, the UN Development Program, and the Carter Center facilitating the discussions. Negotiations between the Venezuelan government and opposition groups continued through the rest of 2002, with strikes in the oil industry occurring in late November and a number of street protests taking place. In January 2003, Jimmy Carter offered two proposals to the negotiating parties. One would be the adoption of a constitutional amendment that would cut the president's term to four years from six, ending Chavez's term in office in 2003 to be followed by new elections. The second option would be for a recall referendum to be held in August 2003 that would ask the people whether Chavez should be removed from office (www.nytimes.com; January 25, 2003). Chavez said that he would support the referendum and the opposition slowly came to support this option as well, but still made demands concerning protection for those oil executives who had shut down the state oil company in protest. In February, both sides signed the "Declaration Against Violence and in Favor of Peace and Democracy" and continued to work out a final settlement to the crisis. On May 23, 2003, the parties signed an Agreement that called for a referendum with the date to be determined as soon as all the legal and constitutional requirements had been met. The Agreement specifically expressed adherence to the Inter-American Democratic Charter, the OAS Charter, and the American Convention on Human Rights. It urged the National Assembly to form a Truth Commission to examine the events surrounding April 11, 2002. The parties also acknowledged the willingness of the OAS, Carter Center, and the United Nations to provide technical assistance for the upcoming referendum. After a tumultuous year, Venezuela was finally on track to return to a stable constitutional order.

Although the OAS was actively involved in helping to restore democracy in Venezuela, the crisis revealed a weakening of consensus in the region. The reactions of Latin American leaders to the coup spanned the spectrum from support for Chavez to condemnation of the Chavez government and implicit support for the coup leaders. On the one hand, President Vicente Fox stated that Mexico would abstain from recognizing the new government in Venezuela. The presidents of Paraguay and Argentina also called the new government illegitimate. On the other hand, President Francisco Flores of El Salvador stated, "we consider President Chavez's resignation as the culmination of a process of polarization, confrontation and abuses of democratic principles" (http://news.bbc.co.uk). The U.S. position closely resembled that of President Flores, with U.S. officials blaming the crisis on Chavez and accusing him of ordering his supporters to open fire on antigovernment demonstrators just prior to the coup. Some leaders, rather than offering support of Chavez or the coup leaders, stressed the importance of upholding the democratic process. Peruvian President Alejandro Toledo stated, "I wasn't the greatest fan of the Chavez government and I recognize that the people have the right to remove their government, but they have to do so through democratic channels in adherence to the rule of law" (http://news.bbc.co.uk). OAS Secretary General César Gaviria also urged Venezuelans to express their dissent constitutionally and not through coups.

This emphasis on the democratic process became the focus of OAS members as the Permanent Council met on April 13, 2002 to discuss the situation in Venezuela. The General Assembly met in a special session several days later on April 18 and issued a resolution in support for democracy in Venezuela. At a regular meeting in June 2002, the General Assembly issued a Declaration on democracy in Venezuela that invoked the Democratic Charter and reiterated the OAS's willingness to provide support to the Venezuelan government to consolidate the democratic process. It also encouraged the government to continue the national dialogue that had begun and to work toward national reconciliation (AG/Dec 28). The Permanent Council continued to support the process of dialogue between opposition groups and the government, issuing a resolution of "Support for the Process of Dialogue in Venezuela" in August 2002 (CP/Res 821). At a meeting in December 2002, the Council strongly stood behind the secretary general's efforts to negotiate a settlement. The members urged the Venezuelan government to promote a constitutional, democratic, peaceful, and electoral solution, and reiterated "the determination of the member states to continue applying, without distinction, and in strict accordance with the letter and spirit of the Inter-American Democratic Charter, the mechanisms provided therein for the preservation and defense of representative democracy, and the rejection of the use of violence to replace any democratic government in the hemisphere" (CP/Res 833; December 16, 2002).

Although OAS members eventually came together in their call for a democratic solution to the tensions in Venezuela, when democracy was first threatened, the response by OAS members was not as united as it had been during the 1990s. Members faced a difficult situation in which the democratically elected president, himself, had not been upholding democratic principles, so when he was removed from power through a coup, it was difficult to determine what the best course of action would be to fully restore democracy. These circumstances led to varied initial responses from member states. Although the United States joined with other members in the Permanent Council and General Assembly in condemning the coup, it did so only after issuing several statements that implied its support for the removal of Chavez. These statements cast considerable doubt on its commitment to democratic government in the eyes of many Latin Americans (Hakim 2002). The United States was initially unsympathetic toward Chavez, noting that his government had tried to suppress peaceful demonstrations. Secretary of State Colin Powell spoke before the special session of the General Assembly on April 18, 2002 and chastised the Chavez administration as well as the coup leaders. He remarked, "there is no justification for any government to prevent its citizens from exercising their fundamental rights . . . [and] democracies do not remain democracies for long if elected leaders use undemocratic methods" (www.oas.org/speeches).

Powell's speech to the General Assembly, however, also emphasized that "all elements of society [should] seek resolution of grievances through democratic means" and must come together to resolve their problems constructively and constitutionally. He invoked the Democratic Charter and declared, "the democratic principles that it enshrines must be our guide." This invocation of the Democratic Charter was what eventually drew OAS members together to promote the restoration of democracy in Venezuela. All members recognized that changes needed to be negotiated within the constitutional framework to restore stability and democracy, and they worked together to achieve these ends.

The United States chose to support the multilateral mechanisms for protecting and restoring democracy in Venezuela rather than seeking a unilateral solution that was most compatible with its own policy preferences. OAS members agreed upon the desired end, return to a constitutional order, even though initial reactions to the coup were quite different. It is difficult to predict whether future disruptions to democracy will have similar outcomes, or if the consensus of the 1990s has come to an end. It seems likely, however, based on the continued support for the norm of democracy that members will remain united in their efforts to consolidate democratic government in the region. The Venezuelan case indicates that members still face challenges to upholding this principle, however. Although there are a number of mechanisms in place to strengthen democracy, their effectiveness is by no means guaranteed. As Colin Powell noted in his speech to the General Assembly in April 2002, the Democratic Charter should have been invoked sooner in the case of Venezuela to prevent the coup from ever occurring. There were indications that the Chavez administration was violating democratic norms before he was removed from office, but the OAS did not respond to these violations. The OAS only got involved after the coup had occurred. Members acknowledge that there is still much work to be done to strengthen democracy, but also note that Venezuela was a successful case in the end.

Narco-Trafficking

The one security issue on which member states have not taken effective multilateral action is the issue of narco-trafficking. The drug trade affects every state in the hemisphere in numerous ways ranging from money laundering and government corruption, to cartel violence and drug-related crimes. On the issue of the drug trade, however, the United States has taken bilateral actions in cooperation with Colombia, rather than relying on the OAS to take multilateral action. Thus far the OAS has taken only a few small steps toward addressing this threat to the hemisphere. Members have been working through the Inter-American Drug Abuse Control Commission to design and implement a new Multilateral Evaluation Mechanism to measure national progress against narco-trafficking ("Strengthening Cooperation ...," March–April 1999). Progress has been slow, however, and successes have been limited.

Given the swift, successful, and unified multilateral actions taken in response to threats to democracy, what explains the lack of dynamic multilateral action on narco-trafficking concerns? On this issue, the United States has chosen to move ahead bilaterally, working closely with Colombia. On the issue of drug trafficking, the United States does not face the same incentives that promote multilateral actions when democracy is threatened.

In contrast to the cases where consensus was strong and the United States was motivated to support multilateral action when democracy was threatened, consensus among members is not as strong on the issue of narco-trafficking. Although many member states are negatively affected by the drug trade, Latin American states and the United States cannot agree whether the problems are supply- or demand-induced, or what the most effective strategies to address them might be. Without a strong consensus on a response to the threat, OAS actions have been limited and less timely. The lack of regional unity on the drug issue has limited the usefulness of the OAS and has led the United States to act bilaterally in cooperation with Colombia and other key states on this issue.

The violation of norms with regard to the drug war does not present members with a clear-cut decision as the cases of threats to democracy have. Arguably there is a need to respond to the violations of human rights norms. There are numerous reports and documentation of human rights abuses, but these are not limited to the guerilla forces or narco-traffickers (Robinson 1998). Paramilitary forces are also guilty of such abuses. OAS members are thus faced with a difficult decision to condemn not just the guerrilla forces (Sendero Luminoso and FARC), but also the state forces fighting them (thus undermining the legitimate state government). Support of human rights norms in this situation contradicts the norms of nonintervention and state sovereignty. Although members have indicated a willingness to override issues of nonintervention and sovereignty when democracy is threatened, states have not yet made this same level of commitment to human rights norms. This has reduced the willingness of OAS to act with regard to such violations in Colombia and other states challenged by narco-traffickers. This lack of regional commitment has led the United States to opt for bilateral solutions. Even within the United States, however, there is disagreement among policymakers on the importance of protecting human rights in the midst of the drug war. For example, Congress attempted to limit funding of the Colombian military until progress on human rights issues was evident. President Bill Clinton overrode this effort, however, declaring that the war on drugs was a national emergency and that the Colombian military needed the funding right away.

An effective regional response to narco-trafficking (if one is in fact possible) would require considerable resources, including military resources. Such a contribution on the part of the United States would require consensus among OAS members (particularly between Latin American states and the United States) on the type of resolutions issued and operations to be conducted. Since there is no agreement on how to best address the threat the drug war poses to the region, the United States has chosen to act on its own, responding to the requests of the Colombian government in particular. A multilateral approach to this transnational problem might ultimately be more efficient and effective, but only if there is agreement about the means to address the problem.

The contrast between OAS responses to interruptions to democracy and to the drug war illustrates a Cold War pattern that has continued in the post–Cold War era. The United States continues to play a leading role in those situations that pose the greatest threat to the region. The fact that the United States considers narco-trafficking to be a national threat increases the likelihood that the United States will continue to act bilaterally rather than multilaterally on the issue. Threats to democracy generally have less direct impact on the United States than narcotics-related problems. Since OAS members have not been in complete agreement about responses to the crisis in Colombia, however, the United States has chosen to act unilaterally rather than multilaterally through the OAS. The issue of narco-trafficking reveals the limits of U.S. willingness to work multilaterally, and also shows some of the weakening of the organization that occurs when there is not consensus among members.

The regional response to drug trafficking may serve as an indicator for what relations between the United States and the OAS will look like in the future if consensus is not maintained, or relations may continue to be more cooperative as they were in addressing the Venezuelan coup. Much depends on how the United States chooses to define threats in the region. Antidemocratic forces may be labeled as "terrorists," which would likely invoke a stronger unilateral U.S. response than was seen in the 1990s. The incentives remain, however, for the United States to pursue multilateral action even in responding to such "terrorist" threats. Multilateral responses provide added legitimacy to the actions; they allow for sharing the financial and personnel burden; and they uphold regional principles through the use of the security mechanisms that are already in place.

Summary

The end of the Cold War has led to some changes as well as continuities within the OAS. Security concerns have expanded beyond traditional geopolitical/strategic concerns to include protection of democracy and expansion of the liberal economic order. The OAS has adapted its structures and priorities to this changing security environment, creating the UPD, passing Resolution 1080, and signing the Democratic Charter to address threats to democracy. These new mechanisms reveal the changing priorities given to regional norms with greater emphasis on representative democracy than has been seen in the past. The strong consensus among member states concerning support for democracy has led to the OAS being fairly effective in responding to threats to democratic regimes in the region. The four invocations of Resolution 1080 in Haiti, Peru, Guatemala, and Paraguay eventually led to a restoration of democracy in all four cases. The first invocation of the Democratic Charter in Venezuela was also successful.

One aspect of the OAS that reflected a change from the 1980s, but resembled relations in the 1950s, was the high degree of consensus among members. As members sought to strengthen democracy, there were disagreements concerning the specific actions to be taken, but not on the end to be achieved. Members, including the United States, had incentives to act multilaterally on most issues with the exception of the threat posed by narco-trafficking. Despite the changes in the region toward supporting democratization, the issue of narco-trafficking has remained a more traditional security concern. The consensus among member states is much lower on this issue. The negative impact of narco-trafficking on states in the region remains high, with the United States strongly motivated to address the issue from the perspective of reducing drug supplies.

Examining the workings of the OAS in the post–Cold War era provides additional insights into member relations. High levels of consensus supporting the norm of democracy, and benefits to pooling resources provide incentives for members, including the United States, to work multilaterally to promote regional security. On the issue of narco-trafficking, however, these same incentives are absent, leading the United States to take bilateral action in cooperation with Colombia and other states to address this threat to U.S. security. Despite the lack of consensus and effective multilateral action on the threats posed by narco-trafficking, the OAS has performed well following the end of the Cold War. The ability of the OAS to redefine regional security concerns and adapt its institutional structure to address these concerns bodes well for the future of the organization. The value of the organization for member states and its future prospects are addressed in chapter 8.

CHAPTER 8
CONCLUSIONS AND FUTURE PROSPECTS FOR THE OAS

As the United States seeks to strengthen its alliances around the world following the attacks of September 11, 2001, it has turned to its formal alliance partners, including the members of the OAS, for support. The OAS, founded as a collective security organization, is structured to respond to security threats to its members. Historically, it has engaged in conflict resolution efforts through the invocation of its Charter or the Rio Treaty. More recently Resolution 1080 and the Democratic Charter have been invoked to defend democracy in the region. The OAS has served as a regional forum for dialogue between the United States and Latin American states on these security issues and has responded to over thirty regional crises in the past 50 years. A close examination of these responses reveals that some have been in line with policy preferences of the United States, others have not, and many have been based on regional consensus. An exploration of the unexpected outcomes when the organization does not simply adopt the policy proposals of its most powerful member reveals a number of interesting aspects about organizational processes and member relations. The analytical framework laid out in chapter 2 facilitates examination of relations within an IO, highlighting previously unexplored organizational factors and their impact on the influence member states exert within the organization. These factors also provide insights into members' motivations to pursue multilateral or unilateral actions in the post–Cold War era. The in-depth case studies in the latter half of the book illustrate the interactions between institutional factors and the ways that they affect organizational decisionmaking. This study of the OAS reveals some unexpected outcomes, including a surprising amount of cooperation among members when addressing security issues, and the inability of the United States to dominate the organization at all times. It is important to recognize and understand the relational dynamics within such an IO in order to assess its ability to respond to member requests and needs in the future. This chapter evaluates the usefulness of the analytical framework and the empirical findings of the case studies, and concludes with an assessment of the organization's future prospects and its ability to respond to the security needs of its members.

Analytical Framework

This book explores the decisionmaking process within the OAS as it is affected by structural, internal relational, normative, and environmental factors. These four perspectives help determine the conditions in which a hegemonic member exerts, or is unable to exert, its influence within the organization. A study of the OAS at the organizational level rather than the system level of analysis expands upon the realist and neoliberal institutionalist understandings of IOs. These theories provide useful, but incomplete, explanations for decisionmaking in IOs.

Realist theory portrays IOs as the tools of their most powerful members. Its focus is primarily on power relations between states. This perspective would anticipate that decisionmaking outcomes would frequently be categorized as "U.S. dominance" because of the hegemonic power of the United States, but cannot explain the anomalous cases in which the United States fails to dominate the OAS, nor the cases where members work consensually or achieve compromises. Realism might argue that cases where the United States is not dominant are explained by a lack of hegemonic interest, or by the hegemon choosing to act unilaterally, but in many of the cases examined here, the United States displayed a strong interest in acting multilaterally through the OAS. For example, in the Cuban case (1960), in which the United States and Latin Americans reached a compromise on the final wording of the Foreign Ministers' resolution, the United States was keenly interested in condemning the subversive behavior of the Sino-Soviet powers as well as Cuba. Furthermore, the United States recognized that a region-wide condemnation of Soviet subversion in the hemisphere would have more weight than a statement made solely by the United States. It was important for the United States to work within the OAS and compromise with Latin American members in order to achieve its goals.

The United States did initially attempt a unilateral solution to the Nicaraguan case (1978). When U.S. attempts at a negotiated settlement with Somoza and the non-FSLN rebels failed, however, the United States was forced to seek multilateral support for an Inter-American peace force. In each case, the multilateral forum of the OAS was the most effective and legitimate means for the United States to use to address regional concerns and to try to find support for its policy preferences. The significance of the regional organization for the hegemonic member, and the hegemon's inability to dominate the organization in every case are unexpected and unexplainable outcomes for realist theory. The realist explanation for decisionmaking in the organization based on power relations is oversimplified. The impact of additional factors must be examined.

Neoliberal institutionalism is equally unable to explain the inability of the United States to dominate the OAS. Neoliberal institutionalism helps to explain cases of compromise and consensus, but doesn't fully capture the impact of organizational factors on decision outcomes. In an effort to explain cooperative relations among states within an institutional context, neoliberalism focuses on bargaining and state interests. The key to achieving cooperation is for states to have some shared interests. An IO facilitates cooperation by helping states reach an equilibrium point when several exist. In the context of the OAS, Latin American members and the United States have had a number of shared interests that they have pursued within the organization. The point of contention in some instances was the means used to pursue a shared goal, rather than differing goals. For example, in the Cuban case (1960), Latin American members and the United States both wanted to reduce the influences of China and the Soviet Union in the region. The United States viewed Cuba as a conspirator in terms of allowing international communism to intervene in hemispheric affairs. The United States wanted to specifically condemn Cuba for its role in increasing regional instability. Latin American states believed that it was not necessary to condemn Cuba specifically in order to reduce Sino-Soviet intervention, so they chose only to condemn the Soviet Union and China. The situation was similar in the Dominican–Venezuelan case (1960) where Latin American members and the United States both wanted to establish a more democratic government in the Dominican Republic. They were divided, however, over the means of promoting democracy within the Dominican Republic. The United States preferred holding and monitoring elections. Latin American members, preferring a less interventionist option, chose to impose sanctions.

Although neoliberal institutionalism recognizes that an IO helps states reach compromise agreements when multiple equilibrium points exist, such as when members are divided over the means to pursue their common goals, it does not consider the impact of structural and normative factors on the diplomatic exchanges that occur in this bargaining process. (Internal relational and environmental factors are taken into account to some degree when considering the shared interests that bring members together within an IO in the first place.) What institutional mechanisms affect the choice of means adopted when states have common interests? An answer to this question requires a different level of analysis. The analytical framework developed in chapter 2 helps define and categorize previously unspecified organizational factors with the potential to impact the influence wielded by the United States within the OAS. The synthesis of these perspectives provides insights into relations among member states within the context of the OAS. The four organizational factors give more detail into the decisionmaking process than realism or neoliberalism alone can do. The next section on case comparisons shows the impact of each factor on the level of U.S. influence in the organization. The following two sections on regional principles and on consensus, resources, and threats to the region discuss the interaction of four factors and the way that they affect organizational decisionmaking.

Case Comparisons

The impact of resources, principles, consensus, and the perceived level of threat on decisionmaking within the OAS is evident in the case studies. The more resources that were needed to carry out the resolutions of the Organ of Consultation, the more influence the United States wielded. This was most evident in the case of the Dominican Republic (1965). U.S. military forces were the core of the IAPF created by the Foreign Ministers. The mandates and operations of the IAPF coincided with the policy preferences of the United States as it sought to manage the restoration of democracy in the Dominican Republic. In other cases, the OAS did not need such extensive resources to carry out its resolutions, and the United States had less influence in the organization. For example, in the Dominican–Venezuelan case (1960), a Special Committee was established by the Foreign Ministers to monitor the impact of sanctions and to recommend whether they should be increased or terminated. The Committee required few resources compared to the IAPF in the Dominican Republic.

The Dominican case (1965) also illustrated that the greater the disagreement among Latin American members, the greater influence the United States had. Consensus and unity among Latin American members were low in the Dominican case, and the United States was able to gain support for its proposals even though there was opposition to them from some members. In other cases such as the Dominican Republic–Venezuela (1960) and Nicaragua (1978) in which U.S. influence was reduced, there was a high degree of Latin American unity. Latin American members were in agreement on alternative plans to U.S. policy proposals.

Latin American members and the United States have regularly referred to regional principles to support their positions and justify their actions. Although the priorities given to these norms have shifted over time, they have remained a central factor affecting OAS decision-making during security crises. Any proposal that is not rooted in regional norms, or that is contrary to them, receives little support from OAS members.

The cases in which the United States failed to gain the support of Latin American members, or was forced to compromise with them, also support the contention that if there is a low- or mid-level threat, the United States has less influence. For example, in the Cuban case (1960) there was recognition among Latin American members that Sino-Soviet influence in the region was having a destabilizing effect in some member states, thus members were willing to compromise with the United States on condemning such intervention. There was not a great enough fear for regional security, however, that Latin American states would condemn a fellow member. The Dominican–Venezuelan case (1960) also did not pose enough of a threat to Latin American members that they felt compelled to turn to the United States for leadership. The imposition of sanctions was determined to be sufficient to reduce Dominican intervention in the region without resorting to other means. In the Nicaraguan case (1978), the conflict was not seen as threatening enough to request U.S. intervention for security purposes. Latin American members were resistant to the proposal for an IAPF, recognizing that such a force would lead to strong U.S. influence within the organization and in Nicaragua. In addition, Latin American members did not want to risk Somoza remaining in power if the United States took an active role in the conflict, so they rejected the U.S. peace force proposal.

None of the four factors alone is determinant. Each factor interacts with the others. The ability of Latin American members to achieve consensus is linked to their ability to formulate alternative proposals to those of the United States based on regional principles, with the use of limited resources. When there is a low-level threat, there are a number of diplomatic options available to the organization. A high-level threat may necessitate a militarized response, which leaves Latin American members more dependent on the United States for leadership and resources. The lack of an alternative proposal weakens Latin American members' unity and their ability to resist U.S. pressure. In each case of Latin American unity, there was an alternative plan that Latin American members supported, giving the United States less influence through policy leadership. For example, the Latin American proposal for a Nicaraguan solution to oust Somoza was based on the principles of representative democracy and self-determination. Furthermore, this proposed solution did not require extensive OAS resources.

Regional Principles
The significance of regional principles such as respect of state sovereignty and territorial integrity, peaceful settlement of disputes, nonintervention in the domestic affairs of other states, consultation in the event of a crisis, and representative democracy is introduced in chapter 3. The exploration of the origins of the Inter-American System and the OAS indicate that all these principles emerged before the United States took a more active role in the region and continued to evolve despite U.S. resistance throughout the 1920s and early 1930s. After a period of cooperation throughout World War II, the United States and Latin American states incorporated the evolving regional principles into the two instruments that have defined regional security responses for 50 years: the Rio Treaty and OAS Charter. The evolutionary history of regional principles supports the constructivist literature in IR that asserts that IOs can play a more significant role in IR than has previously been acknowledged by realism and institutionalism. Institutions can take on a life of their own following their creation. Through normative influences, IOs affect the preferences of member states as well as limit their policy options through threats of sanctions and diplomatic coercion (Finnemore 1996, Wendt 1992). Within the OAS, principles serve to place some constraints on U.S. actions in that the United States frequently feels obliged to justify its proposals (multilateral) and actions (unilateral) in terms of regional norms. Norms also serve to unite Latin American members when they are opposed to U.S. proposals. By making reference to regional principles, Latin American members are able to justify their opposition.

The cases of conflict resolution examined in chapters 4–7 provide further evidence that regional principles have been a fundamental part of the Inter-American System and have consistently shaped interstate relations in the region on security issues. The principles of pacific settlement and consultation have been the norms at the center of each case brought before the Council or Foreign Ministers. Members of the OAS have taken their responsibilities seriously to promote peaceful settlement of disputes in the region. They have been committed to promoting regional security through diplomacy rather than force of arms.

The principles of sovereignty and nonintervention have also been invoked often in an effort by Latin American states to resist U.S. hegemonic intervention. In the Cuban case (1960), Latin American members resisted U.S. pressures to include specific condemnation of Cuba in the Foreign Ministers' final resolution because they felt such condemnation was a violation of the principle of sovereignty and self-determination. In the cases of the Dominican Republic–Venezuela (1960) and Nicaragua (1978), Latin American members maintained that the actions proposed by the United States would violate the principle of nonintervention and thus justified their opposition on these grounds.

The frequent reference to these inter-American principles in such forums as the OAS, however, does not mean that they are unambiguous or unchallenged. In fact, several principles are essentially contradictory when taken to the extreme. Support for human rights and representative democracy in the form of condemnation of a regime (or other punitive actions) could be interpreted as an act of intervention, which violates the principles of sovereignty and nonintervention. Thus, regular debates occur among members about which principles ought to take precedence and how OAS actions might be interpreted juridically. These debates about principles are evident in the meetings of the Organ of Consultation when member states attempt to justify their policy proposals based on regional principles. In some cases, such as the Dominican–Venezuelan (1960) and Nicaraguan (1978) cases, members showed considerable disagreement concerning interpretations. The United States defended its proposals for intervention based on the principles of establishing and supporting democracy. Latin American members preferred options that did not result in a physical intervention in the countries (i.e., sanctions against the Dominican Republic, and action by the Nicaraguan people). In the Dominican–Venezuelan case (1960), Latin American members were able to unify and to give precedence to the principle of nonintervention over democracy. In the Nicaraguan case (1978), Latin American members supported the principle of democracy and nonintervention by calling for a Nicaraguan-based solution to the problem and thus rejecting the U.S. proposal for an intervention force. The principle of representative democracy has also been a key factor affecting actions taken in the 1990s to restore the constitutional order in Haiti, Peru, Guatemala, Paraguay, and Venezuela.

Latin American members have not been the only ones to use princi-pled arguments to support their policy positions. The United States has also justified its actions (even those taken unilaterally) and its policy proposals by referring to inter-American principles. In sum, principles are highly valued in the region, and have a long history of evolution and formal incorporation into regional institutions. Despite their ambiguity that gives rise to debate, they are used by both the United States and Latin American members to justify policy proposals in the OAS. They have also served occasionally as a unifying factor for Latin American members to oppose U.S. proposals.

Consensus, Resources, Threats to the Region

A second significant characteristic brought to light by a focus on orga-nizational factors is the issue of consensus among member states. The cases in chapters 4–6, reveal that when there was disagreement with the United States, ultimately it was consensus among Latin American members that resulted in reduced U.S. influence. By voting together as a unified block, Latin American members used their majority of votes to reject any proposal put forward by the United States to which they objected. This unity in opposition to the United States was not needed in many instances because Latin American members shared common interests with the United States. When Latin American members did oppose a U.S. policy position, however, a number of conditions appeared to facilitate such unity among Latin American members. These factors included a perceived low level of threat to the region and a nonresource-intense policy alternative. When there was not a high level of threat to the region, Latin American members felt less compelled to depend on the United States for protection. This finding was borne out in each case in which the United States did not get its way, including the Falklands/Malvinas War in 1982 between Britain and Argentina, and the U.S. invasion of Panama in 1989. In these two cases, Latin American members disagreed with the U.S. position taken and did not feel greatly threatened by the conflicts. Thus they condemned the U.K. and U.S. actions respectively. Although the causality is certainly more complicated than a simple link between threat level and consensus, over-all, if Latin American members did not feel highly threatened by the dispute in question, then they felt less constrained to agree with U.S. preferences. In addition, if few resources were needed, Latin American members could provide them with or without U.S. support.

Although it is significant to note that Latin American members were able, on occasion, to resist U.S. hegemonic pressures by remaining unified, what is remarkable is that there were few circumstances in which they felt it necessary to try. Chapter 4 examined all 26 cases in which the OAS engaged in pacific settlement (from 1948 to 1989) and in only seven was there a low level of consensus between the United States and Latin American members. The cases discussed in chapter 6 provide examples of the consensus and compromise agreements often reached within the OAS. The cases portray an organization in which members are largely in agreement with each other in decisionmaking, rather than one in which the most powerful member always wields its hegemonic influence.[48]

Post–Cold War Insights
Although the analytical framework was initially developed to explore organizational decisionmaking that was contrary to the preferences of the United States, the four variables also offer some explanations for OAS decisionmaking in the post–Cold War era. The 1990s witnessed an era of remarkable consensus among OAS members supporting the norm of representative democracy. In the five cases when Resolution 1080 or the Democratic Charter were invoked, all members supported the actions taken by the organization to restore democracy in the region. The United States, as well as other members, recognized the strength of unified action based on regional principles. Multilateral actions gave greater legitimacy to the sanctions imposed to restore constitutional order and strengthened the norm of democracy in the region. Because members redefined security interests to include threats to democracy, support for democratic government also helped to promote regional security and stability. Consensus in support for the norm of democracy resulted in swift action because members did not have to negotiate compromises between different positions. In addition, the resolutions adopted in the cases of Peru (1992), Guatemala (1993), Paraguay (1996), and Venezuela (2002) did not require extensive resources, making it easier for states to reach an agreement on the actions to be taken. The one security issue that has not produced such a unified response is narco-trafficking. Disagreements over the best way to reduce this threat have led the United States to respond bilaterally in cooperation with Colombia and other states heavily affected by the drug trade.

Limitations to the Analytical Framework
Just as the analytical framework offers some unique, comparative insights into member interactions within the organization, the application of the framework to the case studies also yields important theoretical feedback about the value of the framework itself. Although each perspective helps

to explain how the United States fails on occasion to dominate the OAS, they do not offer consistent predictions. For example, in all 26 cases of pacific settlement during the Cold War, regional principles were invoked in response to events and in justification of OAS actions. It is evident from the examination of cases over time, however, that different principles gained precedence in different eras. Therefore, recognizing that a U.S. proposal is based on one principle while Latin American members espouse another does not help predict which side will win based on principled arguments alone. In addition, the four perspectives laid out in chapter 2 do not offer much leverage in determining which of the factors has the greatest substantive impact. As is evident from the case studies, consensus, resources, perceived threat level, and regional principles have had an impact on U.S. influence, but not a predictable one. Although patterns can be seen when looking at the cases as a whole, the singular conditions of each case can lead to unique responses by members of the organization. The factors raised in the analytical framework do affect members, but may swing one way or the other depending on the context. This is particularly true for factors assessed to be mid-level. For example, a mid-level threat may or may not be significant enough to give the United States greater influence within the OAS. In the case of the Dominican Republic–Venezuela (1960), the United States had enough influence to force a compromise from Latin American members. In the Nicaraguan case (1978), the United States had no leverage based on the mid-level threat to the region. The framework is useful for highlighting the potential impacts of organizational factors, but offers only limited ability to predict decisionmaking outcomes based on the four factors.

Although the analytical framework has limited predictive power, its unique level of analysis and the emphasis on how the four factors interact is useful not only for studying the OAS, but also for examining other IOs. Neither relative power nor shared interests paint a complete picture of organizational decisionmaking dynamics. The framework highlights that structural, normative, internal relations, and environmental factors have an impact on organizational outcomes, and that these outcomes may be more diverse than many anticipate when a hegemon is involved. Using these four organizational factors to compare the decisions made in other IOs, may shed light on other unexpected outcomes when the most powerful member failed to dominate the organization.

Empirical Findings

In addition to the value of the analytical framework for highlighting previously unexamined aspects of organizational decisionmaking, the examination of 31 cases of conflict resolution by the OAS provides considerable empirical comparisons that are unlikely to be found in any other single volume. A broad comparison of the cases in chapter 4 reveals historical trends and evolutionary changes in the organization's response to security threats. The first decade following the founding of the OAS witnessed a uniquely high level of consensus among members as the Council handled cases of pacific settlement. Threats to the region were mid- to low-level and involved clashes between democracies and dictatorships. The decade of the 1960s saw less consensus among Council members and Foreign Ministers and a more varied level of threats stemming largely from the international spread of communism. The period from 1969 to 1989 was characterized by a relatively low level of consensus among members. Cases tended to be low-level threats to the region and varied in their origins. The most recent post–Cold War era witnessed a renewed level of consensus and cooperation among members in pursuit of strengthening democracy.

A comparison of the 31 cases reveals four different decisionmaking outcomes based on the level of consensus among member states: U.S. dominance, Latin American unity, compromise, and consensus. Despite the presence of the United States as a hegemonic member, less than a third of the cases resulted in U.S. dominance. Surprisingly, Latin American members succeeded in passing their preferred proposals despite U.S. opposition in five cases. Compromises between members with differing views were also seen in a number of cases. Perhaps the most unexpected outcome, however, was that consensus among members on the nature of the threat and the appropriate response to it was the most common outcome. Members of the OAS have long been influenced by the desire to act consensually and multilaterally when possible to address security concerns. This is the foundation of a collective security regime. The actions taken by the organization in each case have been aimed at promoting security and stability in the Western hemisphere according to the Rio Treaty, the OAS Charter, Resolution 1080, and the Democratic Charter.

Future of the OAS

One additional empirical finding that is evident in the comparison of cases across five decades is that the OAS has continued to evolve since its founding. The Council has taken on new tasks; new organs have been established to help with these tasks; the Charter has been revised to include a stronger focus on economic and social development concerns; and regional security concerns have shifted and been redefined over time. The end of the Cold War in 1989 signaled the beginning of yet another new era within the OAS. Anticommunism is no longer a guiding principle to assure regional security. Member states have placed new emphasis on the principle of representative democracy, even at the expense of nonintervention and state sovereignty. This new priority was embodied in the creation of the UPD in 1990, the adoption of Resolution 1080 in 1991, and the Democratic Charter in 2001. The end of the Cold War has allowed the OAS to take up new causes in order to insure regional security, including the promotion of democracy.

The ability of the OAS to shift its focus over time and to respond to changes in the international environment bodes well for its relevance in the future. Although the organization faced a period of decline throughout the 1980s, it has rebounded following the end of the Cold War and addressed the new security concerns of member states. In addition, the organization and its members have displayed a remarkable ability to interact with the regional hegemon in a consensual fashion and yet not become subservient to U.S. interests. This ability to balance the interests of all its member states in order to pursue regional goals has given the organization a strong reputation. The solid reputation of the OAS is evident in the high demand for the organization to monitor elections in member states since the creation of the UPD. This role further reflects the new emphasis on democracy within the organization and the hemisphere.

As the United States restructures its foreign policy in the new millennium, it would be wise to continue to build on the multilateral relationships with Latin American states within the OAS. The common security interests the United States shares with other states in the region and the advantages of acting multilaterally, such as greater international legitimacy, burden sharing, and supporting regional principles, make the OAS a valuable forum for the United States. The 1990s witnessed a high level of consensus within the organization in support of democracy that is likely to continue in the future. Steady efforts are being made to bridge the differences between members on the issue of narco-trafficking to produce a more effective multilateral response. The organization has also rallied in support of the United States following the attacks of September 11, 2001 and has worked through the Inter-American Committee Against Terrorism (CICTE) to strengthen regional cooperation to "prevent, combat and eliminate terrorism." The OAS has proven itself to be a resilient international organization, coming through eras of cooperation, conflict, and consensus to emerge as a relevant actor in international politics today.

Notes

1. Other cases in which the United States was unable to exert its hegemonic influence include: Cuba (1960), Dominican Republic–Venezuela (1960), Panama–United States (1964), Cuba (1975), and Panama–United States (1989). Details in chapter 4.
2. "Institutionalism" has been an approach to IR for over 40 years, extending back to studies by Functionalists and Neo-functionalists such as Ernst B. Haas (1960); David Mitrany (1966) and Donald J. Puchala (1971). As realism has taken a dominant position in the field of IR, scholars such as Robert Axelrod (1984), and Robert Keohane and Joseph Nye (1972) have continued to work to expand our understanding of the role of institutions in IR. Some of the most recent scholars that challenge the realist conception of IR include Robert Keohane and Lisa Martin (1995), Charles Kupchan (1995), and John Gerard Ruggie (1995).
3. Specific studies of the OAS itself provide significant details of the workings of the organization and contribute most to the examination of the case studies in chapters 4–6 rather than to the theoretical foundations of the study discussed in this chapter.
4. See e.g., Charles P. Kindleberger, 1981, "Dominance and Leadership in the International Economy: Exploitation, Public Goods, and Free Rides," *International Studies Quarterly* 25:242–254. Kindleberger, 1986, "Hierarchy Versus Inertial Cooperation," *International Organization* 40:841–847. David A. Lake, 1993, "Leadership, Hegemony, and the International Economy: Naked Emperor or Tattered Monarch with Potential?" *International Studies Quarterly* 37:459–489.
5. Many of the ideas in this approach were first developed in the natural sciences and later adopted by organizational sociology.
6. These documents are discussed in detail in chapter 3.
7. There are several structural variables that are not included in this analysis: the size and composition of the governing body, the hierarchy within it, and the number of authoritative bodies addressing the issue. These variables appear to have little explanatory power because they do not vary across cases with differing outcomes in the OAS. Although one might anticipate that the United States would have more influence if the size of the governing body were limited, the size of the Council and the Meeting of Foreign Ministers does not vary so it is impossible to determine what impact a smaller or larger

body might have. All members are represented and are free to participate in all decisionmaking. Whereas the United States once held an advantage over other members by retaining the chairmanship of the Pan American Union Board, it no longer has this hierarchical advantage. Following the Fifth International Conference of American States in 1923, the position of Council chair became an elected position. The OAS Charter established the chairmanship on a rotating basis among all members. Furthermore, all member states are equal and have one vote in Council. Just as there is not variation in the size of the governing body, similarly there is not significant variation in the number of bodies addressing issues brought before the Organ of Consultation. There are few committees or other bureaucratic departments that handle disputes raised under the Rio Treaty or the OAS Charter. The two types of committees that are seen most often are an investigating committee and an observation committee. There is little evidence to indicate that members are able to exert undue influence within these committees to influence the decisions made by the Organ of Consultation.

8. "Individuals" can be studied at several different levels in this context. This study focuses on the representatives of each state as representatives of the members' interests, not as individual diplomats. Although there is no doubt that the psychological impact of individual leaders and representatives can play a role in the decisions made by the OAS, there are not sufficient data to pursue this particular aspect in this study. Furthermore, it is likely that these individual characteristics are subservient to the state interests that they serve as representatives in the OAS.

9. For example, when the United States sent military forces into Panama in 1989 to seize president and accused drug trafficker, Manuel Noriega, the Twenty-First Meeting of Foreign Ministers condemned the actions of the United States. The ministers passed a resolution that deplored the U.S. invasion, declared the United States to be in violation of international law, called for the immediate cessation of hostilities, and demanded the withdrawal of American forces.

10. The organization did in fact face a decline throughout the 1970s and 1980s due to member dissatisfaction with its handling of security and economic issues.

11. The exclusion of Cuba from participation in the OAS in 1962 is just one example of U.S. pressure to combat communism in the hemisphere.

12. A low-level dispute is one where a single member is involved (i.e, a civil war) and/or there is little risk of escalation or regional instability. A mid-level threat is one in which two more members are involved but with low levels of violence, and in which members believe regional stability is threatened. A high-level threat is rare in the region. It involves considerable violence and/or the risk of affecting all member states (i.e., the Cuban missile crisis). See chapter 4 for a full discussion.

13. The pacific settlement provisions of the Rio Treaty or OAS Charter have been *invoked* in 29 cases. The Council determined that three of these cases did not require an Organ of Consultation to be convoked and were handled through alternative channels. A dispute between the Dominican Republic

and Haiti (1949) was taken up as part of the overall discussion of "Caribbean problems" by the Council in 1950. The border dispute between Ecuador and Peru (1955) was handled by the Guarantor states. A dispute over the Lauca River between Bolivia and Chile was arbitrated by the International Court of Justice. In addition to the remaining 26 cases, Resolution 1080 has been invoked four times since it was established in 1991 by the OAS General Assembly, and the Democratic Charter invoked once as of this writing.

14. First International Conference of American States 1889 (Washington, D.C.), Second Conference 1901 (Mexico City), Third Conference 1906 (Rio de Janeiro), Fourth Conference 1910 (Buenos Aires), Fifth Conference 1923 (Santiago), Sixth Conference 1928 (Havana), Seventh Conference 1933 (Montevideo), Eighth Conference 1938 (Lima).

15. There are a number of ways to characterize these early phases of development. See also Mecham (1961, chapter 2) and Atkins (1997, Introduction).

16. Latin American states were most concerned with Spanish aggression, but also faced occasional threats from France, Great Britain, and the United States.

17. The resolution basically claimed that states owe to foreigners no special rights other than those of their own citizens. The United States did not want to give up any extra protections it might be able to secure for its citizens abroad.

18. Mexico was not represented at this Conference due to disagreements with the United States that resulted in it pulling its ambassador out of Washington.

19. It is important to note that although the provision for Foreign Ministers to handle the consultation meetings did not allow for any organizational autonomy within the bureaucracy of the Inter-American System at this time, the Charter of the OAS and the Rio Treaty both provided for the Council to serve as *provisional* Organ of Consultation, which it did regularly for the first decade of the OAS' existence.

20. The two exceptions were Argentina and Chile. Argentina and Chile did not follow through on their commitments in the Act of Chapultepec and only declared war on Japan and Germany in March 1945. This created some hard feelings on the part of the United States and led to the United States wanting to exclude Argentina from the negotiations of the Rio Treaty (to be discussed later). The United States did not want Argentina to be included in any permanent arrangement after the war. Latin Americans, however, felt that regional unity was too important to leave Argentina out of the negotiations. The United States finally decided that in light of growing tensions with the Soviet Union a treaty that included Argentina was better than no treaty at all (Mecham 1961, 280).

21. It is important to note that the creation of the OAS did not result in the dissolution of the Inter-American System. The OAS is merely one aspect of the Inter-American System, which includes numerous other institutions within the Western hemisphere including the Inter-American Development

Bank and other special agencies and commissions such as the Inter-American Nuclear Energy Commission (IANEC) and the Inter-American Telecommunication Commission (CITEL).

22. Note that references to the numbered articles of the OAS Charter in this section refer to the original charter signed in 1948, not to the revised charters of 1967 or 1993.

23. The secretary general's term was reduced to five years in the 1967 revisions to the Charter.

24. The IAPC was frequently sent to investigate the incident under discussion within the Organ of Consultation. The IAPC had no authority to negotiate agreements. Its purpose was to investigate and to recommend steps conducive for dispute settlement. It was designated as one of the Special Agencies and Commissions by the Council and provided reports to the Council or Foreign Ministers when it was investigating a dispute.

    In 1967 the IAPC became the Inter-American Committee on Peaceful Settlement (IACPS). In 1985, amendments to the Charter eliminated the IACPS, which had become highly controversial.

25. For further discussion of settlement instruments see L. Ronald Scheman, 1988, chapter 3.

26. In table 4.1 consensus is evaluated in two different categories, among Latin American members, and between the United States and Latin American members.

27. Although the record is easiest to trace for those cases in which the Rio Treaty was successfully invoked, I note here one instance in which the Council rejected such a request from a member state. In 1962, Bolivia requested application of the Rio Treaty and a Meeting of Consultation to consider the imminent threat of aggression from Chile against its territorial integrity. Chile's plan to divert Lauca River waters for agricultural purposes without the consent of Bolivia constituted a threat to the peace. The Council met for six sessions and eventually rejected the request, asking both parties to find another means of pacific settlement to reach an agreement. Neither country could agree to a procedure (Chile preferred the International Court of Justice while Bolivia preferred mediation), and the matter remained unresolved.

28. Military resources were used in only the following five cases. Costa Rica–Nicaragua (1955); Panama (1959); Cuba (1962); Dominican Republic (1965); and El Salvador–Honduras (1969).

29. Much of the information in this section and the two that follow is taken from the Annual Reports of the Secretary General, the Applications of the Inter-American Treaty of Reciprocal Assistance, and the Actas (acts and proceedings) of the Council on each case. Later cases include information from the proceedings and Final Acts of the Meetings of Consultation of the Ministers of Foreign Affairs.

30. At this time 13 member states had ratified the Rio Treaty. Costa Rica and Nicaragua were excluded from voting since they were parties to the dispute.

31. It is worth noting in retrospect that these incidents were far narrower in geographic scope than those that followed in the 1960s, provoked for the

most part by the Cuban Revolution. However, members did feel that without an organizational response, these disputes would continue to cause regional instability and thus threaten the security of other member states.

32. The only other case in which Article 11 has been specifically invoked is Cuba (1962) when the Eighth Meeting of Foreign Ministers effectively removed Cuba from participation in the OAS. More on this case is presented in chapter 4.

33. Arbenz's decision to turn to the United Nations was based on the recently issued Declaration of Caracas. This Declaration, issued at the Tenth Inter-American Conference held in March 1954, took a strong anticommunist stance in the hemisphere and was aimed indirectly at regimes such as that of Arbenz in Guatemala. Although Argentina and Mexico strongly sided with Guatemala in opposition to the Declaration because it weakened the principle of nonintervention, most members reluctantly supported it.

34. The first three Meetings of Consultation had been held in the context of World War II, prior to the formation of the OAS in 1948.

35. The Fourth Meeting of Consultation (concerning Korea) had met under the Charter, but this was an extracontinental concern. The Fifth Meeting was the first time the Charter was invoked to address regional tensions.

36. The actual roots of the conflict stemmed from long-standing tensions on issues of immigration. The soccer championship sparked the underlying tensions.

37. The cases that did not involve Cuba and debates about communism included: the Caribbean (1959), Dominican Republic–Venezuela (1960), Dominican Republic–Haiti (1963), Panama–United States (1964), and El Salvador–Honduras (1969). The two cases involving the Dominican Republic closely resemble the types of cases handled in the previous decade. Both are cases of disputes between a dictator and democratic leader that led to tensions between the two countries. The other three cases have already been discussed.

38. From personal correspondence with Dr. Manuel Orozco, Inter-American Dialogue.

39. In 1989, the United Nations and OAS established CIAV (International Commission of Support and Verification) to assist in voluntary demobilization, repatriation, and settlement of the Contras. It also operated in Honduras, El Salvador, and Costa Rica (Atkins 1997, 63).

40. Five additional consensual outcomes were seen following the end of the Cold War and are discussed in chapter 7.

41. One case, Ecuador–United States (1971), has never been resolved so it cannot be categorized by outcome.

42. It is important to note that the high degree of consensus is not equivalent to Latin American subservience to U.S. policy preferences. In many cases the United States did not use its power to force agreement within the organization on issues. Furthermore, the security interests of Latin American countries and the United States were often the same.

43. Cuba was not officially removed as a member state, but has been inactive in the organization since 1962 when the Eighth Meeting of Foreign Ministers

declared that Marxism–Leninism was incompatible with the Inter-American System.

44. It is ironic to note that the United States fully reversed its position on nonintervention a year later when confronted with the Castro regime's attempts to export its revolution.

45. The one exception was Guatemala, which added its own Statement to the Declaration stating that it believed the OAS would have been justified in dealing with Cuba more harshly because its relations with the Soviet Union endangered the peace and security of the hemisphere.

46. Membership has continued to grow over the past several decades as states throughout the Western hemisphere, particularly in the Caribbean basin, have joined the organization's original 21 members. With membership extended to Canada in 1990, all countries in the Western hemisphere participate in the OAS with the exception of Cuba, which has remained inactive since 1962.

47. Peace negotiations resumed in January 1994 with President Jorge de León Carpio, and resulted in both sides signing a Comprehensive Agreement on Human Rights in March 1994. The UN Mission for the Verification of Human Rights (MINUGUA) arrived in November and negotiations on social and economic problems and land reform proceeded throughout 1995. It was not until President Alvaro Arzú took office in January 1996 and replaced hard-line military officers with those willing to compromise with the Guatemalan United Revolutionary Front (URNG) that a final settlement was reached after 36 years of war (Atkins 1997, 200).

48. This level of consensus applies only to the topic of pacific settlement being examined in this study. There may be other issue-areas in which consensus is far less evident. For example, Latin American members have placed a strong emphasis on trade relations as they pertain to economic development for many years. The United States has not always supported the development plans advocated by Latin American members, thus making multilateral trade negotiations difficult.

BIBLIOGRAPHY

Atkins, G. Pope. *Encyclopedia of the Inter-American System*. Westport, CT: Greenwood Press, 1997.

Atkins, G. Pope. *Latin America and the Caribbean in the International System*. 4th ed. Boulder: Westview Press, Inc., 1999.

Axelrod, Robert M. *The Evolution of Cooperation*. New York: Basic Books, 1984.

Axelrod, Robert and Robert O. Keohane. "Achieving Cooperation Under Anarchy: Strategies and Institutions," in *Cooperation Under Anarchy*. Oye, ed. New Jersey: Princeton University Press, 1986.

Bagley, Bruce Michael, ed. *Contadora and the Diplomacy of Peace in Central America*. Boulder: Westview Press, 1989.

Bagley, Bruce M., Robert Alvarez, Katherine J. Hagedorn, eds. *Contadora and the Central American Peace Process: Selected Documents*. Boulder: Westview Press, 1985.

Ball, M. Margaret. *The OAS in Transition*. Durham, NC: Duke University Press, 1969.

Barnett, Michael and Martha Finnemore. "The Politics, Power and Pathologies of International Organizations." *International Organization* 53 (Autumn 1999) 699–732.

Beck, Robert J. *The Grenada Invasion*. Boulder, CO: Westview Press, 1993.

Bennett, Leroy. *International Organizations: Principles and Issues*. Englewood Cliffs, NJ: Prentice-Hall, 1990.

Blasier, Cole. *The Hovering Giant: United States Responses to Revolutionary Changes in Latin America*. Philadelphia: University of Pennsylvania, 1976.

Bloomfield, Richard J. and Gregory F. Treverton, eds. *Alternative to Intervention: A New US Latin American Security Relationship*. Boulder: Lynne Rienner Publishers, 1990.

Boniface, Dexter S. "Is there a democratic norm in the Americas?: An Analysis of the Organization of American States" *Global Governance* 8, 3 (July–Sept. 2002) 365–381.

Council of the Organization of American States. *Actas*. Washington, DC: General Secretariat of the Organization of American States, 1948, 1949,

1954, 1955, 1957, 1959, 1960, 1961, 1962, 1963, 1964, 1965, 1967, 1974, 1978, 1982.

Cyert, Richard M. and James G. March. *A Behavioral Theory of the Firm.* 2nd ed. Cambridge, Mass, USA: Blackwell Business, 1992.

"Declaration of Principles." First Summit of the Americas, 1994.

Dominguez, Jorge I., ed. *International Security and Democracy.* Philadelphia: University of Pittsburgh Press, 1998.

Dreier, John C. *The Organization of American States and the Hemisphere Crisis.* New York: Harper and Row Publishers, 1962.

Eckstein, Harry. *Regarding Politics: Essays on Political Theory, Stability, and Change.* Berkeley: University of California Press, 1992.

Fenwick, Charles G. *The Organization of American States.* Washington, DC: Privately printed, 1963.

Ferguson, Yale H. "Relections on the Inter-American Principle of Non-intervention: A Search for Meaning in Ambiguity." *Journal of Politics* 32 (August 1970).

Finnemore, Martha. *National Interests in International Society.* Ithaca: NY Cornell University Press, 1996.

Finnemore, Martha and Kathryn Sikkink "International Norm Dynamics." *International Organization* 52, 4 (Autumn 1998) 887–917.

Florini, Ann. "The Evolution of International Norms." *International Studies Quarterly* 40 (1996) 363–389.

Franck, Thomas M. *The Power of Legitimacy Among Nations.* New York: Oxford University Press, 1990.

General Assembly of the Organization of American States. "Inter-American Democratic Charter" Lima, Peru, September 11, 2001.

General Assembly of the Organization of American States. "Declaration on Democracy in Venezuela" (AG/Dec 28). Washington, DC, June 4, 2002.

General Secretariat of the Organization of American States, Department of Legal Affairs. *Inter-American Treaty of Reciprocal Assistance: Applications.* Vol. 1, Washington, DC: General Secretariat of the Organizaton of American States, 1948–59.

General Secretariat of the Organization of American States, Department of Legal Affairs. *Inter-American Treaty of Reciprocal Assistance: Applications.* Vol. 2, Washington, DC: General Secretariat of the Organizaton of American States, 1960–72.

General Secretariat of the Organization of American States, Department of Legal Affairs. *Inter-American Treaty of Reciprocal Assistance: Applications.* Vol. 3, Washington, DC: General Secretariat of the Organizaton of American States, 1973–82.

Gilpin, Robert. *War and Change in World Politics.* Cambridge University Press, 1981.

Glinkin, Anatoly. *Inter-American Relations.* Moscow: Progres Publishers, 1990.

Gosselin, Guy and Jean-Phillipe Thérien. "The Organization of American States and Hemispheric Regionalism." Paper presented at AMEI–ISA Joint Conference (December 1997).

Grieco, Joseph M. "Anarchy and the Limits of Cooperation: A Realist Critique of the Newest Liberal Institutionalism." *International Organization* 42 (1988) 485–507.

Haas, Ernst B. *Consensus Formation in the Council of Europe.* Berkeley: University of California Press, 1960.

Haass, Richard. *The Bureaucratic Entrepreneur: How to be Effective in any Unruly Organization.* Washington, D.C.: Brookings Institution Press, 1999.

Hakim, Peter. "Democracy and US Credibility." *The New York Times on the Web.* April 21, 2002.

Halperin, Morton H., Arnold Kanter and Priscilla Clapp. *Bureaucratic Politics and Foreign Policy.* Washington: The Brookings Institution, 1974.

Hasenclever, Andreas, Peter Mayer, and Volker Rittberger. *Theories of International Regimes.* Cambridge: Cambridge University Press, 1997.

Inter-American Commission on Human Rights, Report to the Seventeenth Meeting of Foreign Ministers, October 1978.

Jacobson, Harold K. *Networks of Interdependence: International Organizations and the Global Political System.* New York: Alfred Knopf, 1984.

Kelchner, Warren H. "The Development of the Pan American Union." *Bulletin of the Pan American Union* 54 (April 1930) 15–27.

Keohane, Robert O. and Joseph S. Nye, Jr., eds. *Transnational Relations and World Politics.* Cambridge, Mass: Harvard University Press, 1972.

Keohane, Robert O. and Lisa L. Martin. "The Promise of Institutionalist Theory." *International Security* 20 (Summer 1995) 39–51.

Kindleberger, Charles P. "Dominance and Leadership in the International Economy: Exploitation, Public Goods, and Free Rides." *International Studies Quarterly* 25 (1981) 242–254.

Kindleberger, Charles P. "Hierarchy Versus Inertial Cooperation." *International Organization* 40 (1986) 841–847.

Krasner, Stephen D., ed. *International Regimes.* Ithaca, NY: Cornell University Press, 1983.

Kumar, V. Shiv. *US Interventionism in Latin America: Dominican Crisis and the OAS.* New Delhi: Radiant Publishers, 1987.

Kupchan, Charles A. and Clifford A. "The Promise of Collective Security." *International Security* 20 (Summer 1995) 1, 52.

Lake, Anthony. *Somoza Falling.* Boston: Houghton Mifflin, 1989.

Lake, David A. "Leadership, Hegemony, and the International Economy: Naked Emperor or Tattered Monarch with Potential?" *International Studies Quarterly* 37 (1993) 459–489.

Lowenthal, Abraham. *Dominican Intervention.* Cambridge, MA: Harvard University Press, 1972.

Martin, Lisa L. *Coercive Cooperation*. Princeton, NJ: Princeton University Press, 1992.

Martz, Mary Jeanne Reid. *The Central American Soccer War: Historical Patterns and Internal Dynamics of OAS Settlement Procedures*. Athens: Ohio University Press, 1978.

Mearsheimer, John J. "The False Promise of International Institutions." *International Security* 19 (Winter 1994) 5–49.

Mearsheimer, John J. "A Realist Reply." *International Security* 20 (Summer 1995) 82–93.

Mecham, J. Lloyd. *The United States and Inter-American Security, 1889–1960*. Austin: University of Texas Press, 1961.

Mitrany, David. *A Working Peace System*. Chicago: Quadrangle Books, 1966.

Meeting of Consultation of Ministers of Foreign Affairs, Fifth. *Final Act*. Washington, DC: General Secretariat of the Organization of American States, 1960.

Meeting of Consultation of Ministers of Foreign Affairs, Seventh. *Documents*. Washington, DC: General Secretariat of the Organization of American States, August 25, 1960.

Meeting of Consultation of Ministers of Foreign Affairs, Seventh. *Final Act*. Washington, DC: General Secretariat of the Organization of American States, 1960.

Meeting of Consultation of Ministers of Foreign Affairs, Tenth. *Final Act*. Washington, DC: General Secretariat of the Organization of American States, 1965.

Meeting of Consultation of Ministers of Foreign Affairs, Twelfth. *Actas*. Washington, DC: General Secretariat of the Organization of American States, 1967–68.

Meeting of Consultation of Ministers of Foreign Affairs, Twelfth. *Final Act*. Washington, DC: General Secretariat of the Organization of American States, 1968.

Meeting of Consultation of Ministers of Foreign Affairs, Eleventh. *Proceedings and Documents*. Washington, DC: General Secretariat of the Organization of American States, 1971.

Meeting of Consultation of Ministers of Foreign Affairs, Fourteenth. *Actas*. Washington, DC: General Secretariat of the Organization of American States, 1971.

Meeting of Consultation of Ministers of Foreign Affairs, Fifteenth. *Actas*. Washington, DC: General Secretariat of the Organization of American States, 1974.

Meeting of Consultation of Ministers of Foreign Affairs, Sixteenth. *Actas*. Washington, DC: General Secretariat of the Organization of American States, 1978–79.

Meeting of Consultation of Ministers of Foreign Affairs, Seventeenth. *Actas.* Washington, DC: General Secretariat of the Organization of American States, 1978–79.

Meeting of Consultation of Ministers of Foreign Affairs, Thirteenth. *Actas.* Washington, DC: General Secretariat of the Organization of American States, 1984.

Meeting of Consultation of Ministers of Foreign Affairs, Thirteenth. *Final Act.* Washington, DC: General Secretariat of the Organization of American States, 1984.

Meeting of Consultation of Ministers of Foreign Affairs, Nineteenth. *Actas.* Washington, DC: General Secretariat of the Organization of American States, 1984.

Meeting of Consultation of Ministers of Foreign Affairs, Nineteenth. *Final Act.* Washington, DC: General Secretariat of the Organization of American States, 1984.

Meeting of Consultation of Ministers of Foreign Affairs, Twentieth. *Final Act.* Washington, DC: General Secretariat of the Organization of American States, 1986.

Morgenthau, Hans, *Politics Among Nations.* New York: A.A. Knopf, 1948.

Morley, Morris H. *Washington, Somoza, and the Sandinistas.* Cambridge University Press, 1994.

Nye, Joseph S. *Peace in Parts: Integration and Conflict in Regional Organizations.* Boston: Little, Brown, 1971.

Olson, Mancur. *The Logic of Collective Action: Public Goods and the Theory of Groups.* Cambridge, MA: Harvard University Press, 1965.

Organization of American States Annual Report of the Secretary General. Washington, DC: General Secretariat of the Organization of American States, Fiscal Year 1955–56; 1960–61; 1963–64; 1966–67; 1967–68; 1969–70; 1970–71; 1973–74; 1974–75; 1980–81; 1994–95.

Orozco, Manuel. *Inter-American Dialogue.* Correspondence with author, April 26, 2000.

Palmer, General Bruce, Jr. *Intervention in the Caribbean: The Dominican Crisis of 1965.* Lexington, KY: The University Press of Kentucky, 1989.

Pastor, Robert *Whirlpool: US Foreign Policy Toward Latin America and the Caribbean.* Princeton, NJ: Princeton University Press, 1992.

Permanent Council of the Organization of American States. "Situation in Venezuela" (CP/Res 811). Washington, DC, April 13, 2002.

Permanent Council of the Organization of American States. "Support for the Democratic Institutional Structure in Venezuela and the Facilitation Efforts of the OAS Secretary General" (CP/Res 833). Washington, DC, December 16, 2002.

Perrow, Charles. *Complex Organizations: A Critical Essay.* 2nd ed. Glenview, Ill: Scott, Foresman, 1979.

Powell, Robert. "Anarchy in International Relations Theory: The Neorealist-Neoliberal Debate." *International Organization* 48 (Spring 1994) 313–344.

Przeworski, Adam and Henry Teune. *The Logic of Comparative Social Inquiry.* New York: Wiley-Interscience, 1970.

Puchala, Donald James. *International Politics Today.* New York: Dodd, Mead, 1971.

Report of the Inter-American Peace Committee to the Seventh Meeting of Consultation of Ministers of Foreign Affairs. August 5, 1960.

Robinson, Linda, Gordon Witkin and Richard J. Newman. "Is Colombia Lost to Rebels?" *U.S. News and World Report* (May 11, 1998).

Ruggie, John Gerard "The False Premise of Realism." *International Security* 20 (Summer 1995) 1, 62.

Scheman, L. Ronald. *The Inter-American Dilemma.* New York, NY: Praeger, 1988.

Scott, W. Richard. *Organization: Rational, Natural, and Open Systems.* 4th ed. New Jersey: Prentice-Hall, 1998.

Snidal, Duncan. "The Limits of Hegemonic Stability Theory." *International Organization* 39 (1985) 579–614.

Snidal, Duncan. "Relative Gains and the Pattern of International Cooperation." *American Political Science Review* 85 (September 1991) 701–726.

Solis, Luis G. "Collective Mediations in the Caribbean Basin," in *Collective Responses to Regional Problems: The Case of Latin America and the Caribbean.* Carl Kaysen, Robert A. Pastor, and Laura W. Reed, eds. Cambridge, MA: Committee on International Security Studies, 1994.

Sterling-Folker, Jennifer. "Competing Paradigms or Birds of a Feather? Constructivism and Neoliberal Institutionalism Compared." *International Studies Quarterly* 44 (March 2000) 97–120.

Stein, Arthur A. "Coordination and Collaboration: Regimes in an Anarchic World," in *International Regimes.* Stephen D. Krasner, ed. Ithaca, NY: Cornell University Press, 1983.

Stoetzer, O. Carlos. *The Organization of American States.* 2nd ed. Westport, CT: Praeger, 1993.

"Strengthening Cooperation Against Drugs." 1999. *OAS News.* Washington, DC, March–April.

Tascan, Joaquin. "Searching for OAS/UN Task-Sharing Opportunities in Central America and Haiti," in *Beyond Subcontracting.* Thomas G. Weiss, ed. New York: St. Martin's Press, Inc., 1998.

Tomasek, Robert. "The Haiti- DR Controversy of 1963 and the OAS." *Orbis* 12.1 (Spring 1968) 294–313.

Tomasek, Robert. "The Organization of American States and Dispute Settlement from 1948 to 1981—An Assessment." *Interamerican Review of Bibliography* 39.4 (1989) 461–476.

Thompson, James D. *Organizations in Action: Social Science Bases of Administrative Theory.* New York: McGraw-Hill, 1967.

Vaky, Viron P. and Heraldo Muñoz. *The Future of the Organization of American States*. New York, NY: Twentieth Century Fund Press, 1993.

Villagran de Leon, Francisco. *The OAS and Democratic Development*. Washington, DC: United States Institute of Peace, 1992a.

Villagran de Leon, Francisco. *The OAS and Regional Security*. Washington, DC: United States Institute of Peace, 1992b.

Waltz, Kenneth. *Theory of International Politics*. New York, NY: Random House, 1979.

Walker, Thomas W., ed. *Nicaragua in Revolution*. New York, NY: Praeger Press, 1982.

Wendt, Alexander. "Anarchy is What States Make of it: The Social Construction of Power Politics." *International Studies* 46 (1992a) 391–425.

Wendt, Alexander. "Levels of Analysis vs. Agents and Structures: Part III." *Review of International Studies* 18 (1992b) 181–185.

www.state.gov, U.S. State Department website.

www.oas.org, Organization of American States website.

www.upd.oas.org, Unit for the Promotion of Democracy website.

http://news.bbc.co.uk, Brittish Broadcast Company website.

www.nytimes.com, New York Times website.

Whitaker, Arthur P. *The Western Hemisphere Idea: Its Rise and Decline*. Ithaca, NY: Cornell University Press, 1954.

Wiarda, Howard J. "After Miami: The Summit, the Peso Crisis, and the Future of US–Latin American Relations." *Journal of Interamerican Studies and World Affairs* 37 (Spring 1995) 43–69.

Wilson, Larman C. "The Concept of 'Collective Economic Security for Development' and Contemporary Latin American, U.S. Relations." *Towson State Journal of International Affairs* 12 (Fall 1977) 7–42.

INDEX

Italics indicate table

Ad Hoc committees, 104, 106, 125, 142
American Convention on Human Rights, 168
anarchy, 5–7, 17–18, 21–22
anticommunists, 83, 103, 112–113, 116, 191
antiterrorist campaigns, 2, 159
Arbenz, Jacabo, *72*, 75, 79, 99, 102, 191
arbitration, 33, 41–42, 44, 46, 49, 51, 53, 56–57
Argentina, 20–21, 36, 43, 68, 74, 76, 87–88, 91, 98, 106, 108, 124, 152, 161, 168, 182, 189, 191
Aristide, Jean Bertrand, *97*, 152, 155, 160–162
Atkins, G. Pope, 39, 45, 54, 60, 62, 81–82, 86, 103, 145, 161–163, 166, 189, 191–192
Axelrod, Robert M., 21, 187

Balaguer, Joaquin, 104
Betancourt, Rómulo, *73*, 85, *99*, 117–118
bilateral issues, 143, 145
Bolívar, Simón, 43
border disputes, 1, 81, 88, 189
Bosch, Juan, 85, 103–104
Brazil, 67, 79, 88, 105–106, 119
Britain, 20–21, 37, 182, 189

Caribbean, 11, 13, 39, 50, 53, 65, 68, *72–73*, 75–78, 80–83, 98, 116, 119, 133–134, 136–138, 140–142, 146, 148–149, 189, 191–192
Carter, Jimmy, 124–125, 128, 168
Castro, Fidel, 1, 4, 11, 37, 80, 84–85, 89, 112, 115, 118, 127, 135, 141, 145, 192
Cedras, Raoul, 152, 155, 161–162
Chavez, Hugo, *97*, 156, 159, 167–171
Chile, 3, 43, 68, 81, 88, 91, 104, 106, 108, 111–115, 155, 189–190
Clinton, Bill, 2, 157, 172
Cold War era, 3, 13, 35, 59, 63, 80, 151–152, 156–157, 173, 184, 186
post-Cold War era, 62, 153, 173–175, 183, 185
collective action, 1, 18, 22, 117
collective security, 1–2, 6, 12, 15, 17–18, 29, 34, 42, 54, 56–57, 59, 175
Colombia, 3, 13, 43–44, 79, 85, 106, 159–160, 171–174, 183
Commercial Bureau for the International Union of American Republics, 46
common interests, 5–7, 9, 18, 20–21, 27, 37–38, 70, 81–83, 87, 178